THE EMOTIONAL ORGANIZATION

Praise for *The Emotional Organization*

"This fresh, innovative collection of essays offers the reader a wondrous range of voices -- among them an assistant director for hospitality on a cruise ship, an intake worker at a rape crisis center, a call center trainer coaching trainees to 'sound right,' and a job center employee managing the frustration of despairing job seekers. All these and more provide take-off points for some of the most exciting forays into basic theory of emotion I've seen in a long while. This is a great collection."

Arlie Russell Hochschild, author of The Managed Heart *and*
The Commercialization of Intimate Life

"Finally, a book that brings together emotion, power, and identity: Steve Fineman has gathered a fine group of researchers and some fascinating studies to provide us with invaluable new insights about what it means to work in the emotional organization."

Cynthia Hardy, University of Melbourne

"The study of emotion work has become a fertile area of theory and research concerning work and identity in modern society. This important volume adds significantly to this field by providing new theoretical and empirical insights that will add greatly to this already lively field. It will be essential reading for social scientists with an interest in the nature of the contemporary workplace."

Alan Bryman, University of Leicester

THE EMOTIONAL ORGANIZATION

Passions and Power

Edited by Stephen Fineman

Blackwell
Publishing

BLACKWELL PUBLISHING
350 Main Street, Malden, MA 02148-5020, USA
9600 Garsington Road, Oxford OX4 2DQ, UK
550 Swanston Street, Carlton, Victoria 3053, Australia

The right of Stephen Fineman to be identified as the author of the editorial material in this work has been asserted in accordance with the UK Copyright, Designs, and Patents Act 1988.

Designations used by companies to distinguish their products are often claimed as trademarks. All brand names and product names used in this book are trade names, service marks, trademarks, or registered trademarks of their respective owners. The publisher is not associated with any product or vendor mentioned in this book.

This publication is designed to provide accurate and authoritative information in regard to the subject matter covered. It is sold on the understanding that the publisher is not engaged in rendering professional services. If professional advice or other expert assistance is required, the services of a competent professional should be sought.

First published 2008 by Blackwell Publishing Ltd

1   2008

Library of Congress Cataloging-in-Publication Data

The emotional organization : passions and power / edited by Stephen Fineman.
     p. cm.
  ISBN 978-1-4051-6030-8 (pbk. : alk. paper)
1. Organizational behavior.   2. Social institutions—Psychological aspects.   3. Emotions.   4. Social norms.   5. Identity (Psychology)—Social aspects.   6. Power (Social sciences)—Psychological aspects.   I. Fineman, Stephen.

  HD58.7.E4375 2008
  302.3′5—dc22

                    2007010744

A catalogue record for this title is available from the British Library.

Set in 10.5 on 13 pt Minion
by SNP Best-set Typesetter Ltd, Hong Kong
Printed and bound in Singapore
by Utopia Press Pte Ltd

The publisher's policy is to use permanent paper from mills that operate a sustainable forestry policy, and which has been manufactured from pulp processed using acid-free and elementary chlorine-free practices. Furthermore, the publisher ensures that the text paper and cover board used have met acceptable environmental accreditation standards.

For further information on
Blackwell Publishing, visit our website at
www.blackwellpublishing.com

Contents

List of Contributors

Stephen Fineman, School of Management, University of Bath, UK

Victoria Bishop, Manchester Business School, The University of Manchester, UK

Sharon C. Bolton, University of Strathclyde Business School, UK

Timothy Clark, Durham Business School, Durham University, UK

Robin Fincham, Department of Management and Organization, Stirling University, UK

Mary Haman, Department of Communication Arts and Sciences, Pennsylvania State University, USA

Philip Hancock, Warwick Business School, The University of Warwick, UK

Karen Handley, Department of Learning and Teaching, Oxford Brookes University, UK

Caroline Hatcher, Brisbane Graduate School of Business, Queensland University of Technology, Australia

Jeff Hearn, Swedish School of Economics and Business Administration, Helsinki, Finland

Nicole L. Kangas, Department of Sociology, Stanford University, USA

Marek Korczynski, The Business School, Loughborough University, UK

Margaret Leaf, Department of Sociology, Florida State University, USA

Katy Marsh, Newcastle University Business School, Newcastle, UK

Patricia Yancey Martin, Department of Sociology, Florida State University, USA

Debra E. Meyerson, School of Education, Stanford University, USA

Kiran Mirchandani, Department of Adult Education, University of Toronto, Canada

Gill Musson, The Management School, Sheffield University, UK

Linda L. Putnam, Department of Communication, University of California – Santa Barbara, USA

Douglas Schrock, Department of Sociology, Florida State University, USA

Stephanie A. Shields, Department of Psychology, Pennsylvania State University, USA

Andrew Sturdy, Warwick Business School, The University of Warwick, UK.

Sarah J. Tracy, Hugh Downs School of Human Communication, Arizona State University, USA

Melissa Tyler, The Business School, Loughborough University, UK

Carmen Von Rohr, Department of Sociology, Florida State University, USA

Leah R. Warner, Department of Psychology, Pennsylvania State University, USA

CHAPTER 1

Introducing the Emotional Organization

Stephen Fineman

This book is about emotion; emotion embedded in the political agendas of organizational life. It advocates a frame-shift in our understanding of emotion – from an ideologically neutral, within-the-individual, experience to one that is firmly shaped by social structures and the norms and values of the organization.

From this angle, emotions such as love, fear, anger, fury, resentment, embarrassment, happiness, joy, envy, and sadness appear as tradable social resources or commodities; something that can be negotiated, manipulated or pushed aside; engineered by cultural patterning or managerial prerogative; subtly steered or perverted in social encounters; bought and sold. Accordingly, they are a vital medium through which to understand the minutiae of interpersonal encounters, as well as broader patterns of voice in the workplace, especially inequality and oppression. They raise questions of power: whose interests are really being served when management targets employee feelings, such as their emotional intelligence, stress, fun, happiness, or well-being? They provide special leverage on the character and dilemmas of our emotional and aesthetic identities as the pace and place of work change, such as from the confines of the urban office to any space that can accommodate a computer and connection to the World Wide Web. Who am I, who are "they," what do I feel when my work colleagues or customers are mainly phantoms in a global virtual world?

The contributors to this book all share this standpoint; in short, a critical perspective on what emotion is and does. Criticality here is beyond the usual sense of being circumspect in one's evaluation and judgment. It reflects a particular outlook on emotions in organizations – that they are produced through interpersonal work that is conditioned by cultural imperatives: the social rules that sanction what is appropriate to feel and express.

Emotions, therefore, are remarkable social products that "make" all forms of human communication. However, of particular interest to critical scholars are the social contours or biases that act like invisible hands on emotion – to privilege some forms of expressiveness over others; to silence or oppress some voices but not others.[1-5] We see this, for instance, in the gendering of emotion – the kinds of feelings that men or women "should" express in particular situations – and in the stigma attached to deviants. Emotion, thus, is also a medium of valuation and power where the objects of joy, celebration, revulsion, or distaste are societally prefigured. There are, for example, the prevalent feelings towards minority groups, asylum seekers, city "fat cats," royalty, or celebrities. The social valuation produces an *emotionology* – society's "take" on the way certain emotions are to be directed and expressed. In sum, while emotions have biological roots, they are soon overwritten by social and moral discourses; we are born into a world where emotionologies take a grip on our experiences and behaviors.

Emotionologies

Emotionologies are produced and reproduced through all manner of discursive and institutional practices, some more potent and enduring than others.[6] They include the family, television programs, films, schools, the internet, religious authorities, and governments. Each source will vary somewhat in authority and form, but they are linked by the dominant ideologies of their resident culture. So we inherit emotionologies that soon appear natural and typically go unchallenged. They will inform how we should feel, and express our feelings, about ourselves ("happy," "positive," "fine") as well as how to feel about others – such as a love of winners, disgust for muggers, cynicism about politicians, and ambivalence towards teenagers. They shape and underpin the deference patterns of particular social encounters – what to feel or reveal at weddings, funerals, dinner parties, places of worship, or before a judge.

   Emotionologies reflect their social times. For instance, early nineteenth century European and American cultures were preoccupied with melancholy. People paraded their nostalgia and sentimentalism; sadness became a "badge of a way of life."[7] This contrasts with contemporary American cheerfulness – a later modern invention born of tough economic times. Good cheer came to represent "an active personality, capable of solving its own problem . . . by keeping in good spirits at all times."[8] Expressed in the ubiquitous smile, and deeply embedded in American etiquette, good cheer has become a potent symbol of consumerist well-being, reproduced in all manner of product advertisements and customer services. It has even spawned activist groups devoted to its protection, such as "The Great American Grump Out" – fighting cantankerousness "with fun." Their website organizes action days where "America is asked to go for 24 hours without being crabby or rude." Activists are instructed to "wear a smile on a T-shirt, a cap, a button, or on your face."[9] We may contrast such displays with British reserve: the norm to tolerate, even celebrate, grumpiness, as epitomized in prime-time television programs such as *Grumpy Old Men* and *Grumpy Old Women*. In each, a selection of eloquent, "grumpy" media celebrities sardonically expose the absurdities of a wide range of everyday social practices.

   In the workplace, emotionologies are embedded in, and shaped by, different organizational routines, from employee appraisals and interviews to team meetings and negotiations with customers. In such settings, emotionologies underpin – with varying degrees of consistency – what we "do" with our frustration, boredom, anger, envy, sadness, embarrassment, lust, hope, or happiness to make and sustain the routine and power balance. In these terms, emotionologies are the building blocks of "organization" and its emotion culture, infusing interactions with predictability, order, and meaning. This extends to rivalry and conflict. For instance, deriding an enemy's political, economic, or religious system, while feeling commitment or pride for one's own, has long reinforced "the reason" for a conflict. The corporate world has institutionalized such sentiments in its philosophy of marketplace wars and battles, so much so that one management consultant advocates "a battle cry drilled into the skull of every employee, from top to bottom."[10] In casting competitors as enemies, it follows that they can be derided and "crushed," and their defeat celebrated. Conversely, losing a battle is to be attended by feelings of humiliation and resentment – and then aggression to fuel a further round in the competitive "war."

Critical Roots

Through a critical lens, emotionologies are fundamental to the political texturing and social construction of emotion. Yet the intellectual roots of critical thought on organizations are mixed. Some attest to Marxism and related theories of the labor process.[11,12] Here key organizational structures are seen to be fixed, favoring the owners and managers of capital, dividing power and privilege such that tension, disputation, and resistance are never far from the surface. The emotional order is, therefore, always under strain as individuals and coalitions vie for position or dominance, but against a background where executives and managers control the key resources. When such power differences are abused, oppressive practices are not far behind, such as corruption, harassment, bullying, racism, or homophobia.

Other critical approaches testify to postmodern, or poststructural, variants of social constructionism and discourse theory.[13,14] Power is said to reside in the way existing narratives of value and feeling are impressed on people, often in unnoticed ways.[15,16] Some renditions argue that this is all pervasive within a culture or subculture and difficult to resist. For instance, the history of African-American integration into white mainstream culture has been marked by periods when the white construction of their emotionality as "inferior" has acted as a distinct barrier to their entry to particular organizations.[17] And we can see similar patterns as different minority groups, by virtue of their nationality, ethnicity, religion, gender, age, or psychological/physical health, are pathologized and excluded because of their "inappropriate" or "odd" emotions.[18,19]

The hold of dominant emotionalities, then, can be significant. But the full extent of their influence is debatable. Some critical approaches are less totalizing than others, giving more credence to individual actors as active agents in shaping the repertoires and norms of emotion.[20,21] Still others, though, suggest, pessimistically, that we have now reached a "postemotional" phase in cultural and economic development, where emotionologies no longer serve deeply rooted social mores or moral concerns. They are ephemeral phenomena, packaged by media and marketing experts, and transmitted in superficial virtual and interpersonal exchanges. In a world of shifting and unstable meanings, our emotions owe more to soap operas, scripted "nice day" encounters, celebrity lifestyles, sound bite advertisements telling us what makes us "feel right," and manufactured "fun experiences." Together they create a hollow shell of emotion, which, beyond a fleeting exchange-value, is void of feeling and moral consequence.[22] Meštrović[23] regards this as the "mechanization" of emotion, while Baudrillard[24] is more forceful in his imagery – he speaks of "cryogenized," or half-dead, emotions.

While there are differences between critical approaches, they do have a common denominator: they worry away at the surface appearances of emotion to expose the systemic biases that shape our subjectivities – our sense about who we are and what we feel. For example, in recent years, control in many organizations has shifted from being overtly coercive to diffuse. It now aims to engage employees' energy and commitment through empowerment – flattening organizational hierarchies and pushing responsibility downwards. Significantly, it promises a happier employee. At first blush this appears appealing and liberating. Who would not want to be empowered, especially when it is presented as a way of increasing one's pleasure at work? Critical researchers, though, are skeptical. They point to the paradox of management using its own power to "empower" others – but usually on management's terms. Beneath empowerment's humanistic trappings, one can see a subtle form of control aimed at getting more performance from workers, often for relatively less reward, leading one writer to describe empowerment as a "therapeutic fiction."[25] And, indeed, against the success stories of empowerment reported in the popular management literature, there is a growing body of evidence on failures. Far from raising employee happiness, this research reveals increasing levels of cynicism and resistance.[26–28]

Critical research does a stalwart job in exposing the structural oppressions of organizational life, but it would be wrong to assume that its quest ends there. A critical lens also brings into focus the micro-politics and power-flows of different emotions crucial to workaday feelings and meanings. Elsewhere, I have suggested that these processes are best understood as *emotional arenas*,[29,30] a dramaturgical metaphor that headlines the first section of this book. In such arenas, emotion is "performed" in a particular context for a particular audience (bosses, colleagues, customers, clients, patients, competitors) – people to be influenced or impressed, placated or befriended, repelled or shamed. Emotion, far from being an out-of-control impulse, is acted-out through vocal and bodily postures aligned to the micro-structure of the situation. In this manner, emotion is an important strategic resource. The expression of anger, affection, nostalgia, love, fear, boredom, frustration, embarrassment, remorse, pity, or hope are, then, skillful accomplishments that help sustain, augment, or destabilize micro-social orders.

Each emotional arena will have its political and regulatory peculiarities. Compare, for instance, Disney World with a hospital, a doctor's surgery with a McDonald's outlet, or a solicitor's office with a travel agent. The emotions that define and maintain "proper" professional conduct in these settings vary in their profile of appropriate smiles/compassion/seriousness. Moreover, each arena will comprise zones where different, tacit, emotion rules apply – back stage or front stage, corridor or car park, water cooler or rest room. To an extent, then, our emotional life, like other aspects of life, is always hedged in – but, arguably, not entirely caged. We are also agents of our emotional destinies as we test the boundaries of our arenas. Where there are tensions, ambiguities, uncertainties, or spaces, we may feel impelled to "do something different" – a burst of anger, a joke, a pained expression, a loud sigh, a broad smile, and so forth.

Such spontaneous interventions are rarely without social precedence or model, but that does not obviate risk; their acceptability within a given social order cannot be taken for granted. Moreover, the playing field for impulsivity or deviation is rarely an even one; some people will have more confidence, power, or status than others to experiment with an emotion order. There are, for instance, the "tempered radicals"[31] – ordinary organizational members who are committed to their organization but also frustrated by its dominant culture (e.g. it deprecates women, it jokes about minorities, it humiliates novices). They are prepared to challenge the guardians of the culture, hoping for small wins. Bigger "wins" are possible (although far from guaranteed) when the experiment is hierarchically driven, from the top. Here, for instance, we have grand designs to change the valuation or tone of emotion in an organization, such as attempts to make it more aggressive, fun, compassionate, or positive.[32,33] Typically, such corporate emotionologies are set in the executive boardroom and cascaded throughout the organization.

Identity Matters

From what has been said so far, it should be apparent that a critical view of emotion has implications for social identity – the focus of the second part of this book. The traditional, modernist, view is that identity in organizations is a stable phenomenon concerning the social or occupational groups to which we see ourselves belonging (e.g. managers, students, the sick, black, the stressed, women, gays, secretaries, porters, cleaners) contrasted with those to which we do not relate. In postmodern thinking, however, identity is more than a static, self-classificatory, niche. It is a process of holding and resolving different social-emotional narratives about who we are, who we were, and who we wish to be.[34–36] This implicates, initially, an affective pecking order of jobs: those that society prizes, is ambivalent about, or scorns. We see this, for instance, in the high esteem that Americans currently attribute to those working as firefighters, doctors, nurses, military officers, teachers, or police officers. In comparison, there is a distinct lack of affection – "hardly any prestige" – for real estate brokers, stockbrokers, actors, bankers, and journalists.[37] But such a snapshot disguises the shifting sands that underpin some occupations. Over the past quarter century, US polls tell us, lawyers, scientists, and business executives have suffered progressively less esteem in the public eye while, recently, firefighters, nurses, and teachers have enjoyed a sharp elevation in respect.[37]

We may contemplate some of the possible reasons behind these shifts, such as firefighters' heroic roles in the aftermath of the attack of September 11, 2001 and the corporate scandals at Enron and WorldCom. They are reminders that occupational esteem is a product of particular cultural, ideological, and market conditions. Importantly, though, such valuations will comprise first-line identity messages that members of an occupation have to confront. They are the backdrop to more localized emotionologies about, for instance, one's specific organizational role (appreciated or deprecated), one's physical appearance ("being attractive"), and reactions to one's accent, gender, religion, or age. In this context, identity narratives are, as postmodern theorists suggest, in flux, a flux to be addressed through *identity work.*

As a concept, identity work draws attention to the feelings and meanings that are ongoing as actors "work" on their identities – individually and socially.[38,39] Identity work is invariably emotional, implicating pride, pleasure, fear, anxiety, or despair. Identity work is likely to be particularly burdensome when imputed attributes are received as disruptive, discordant, or, in the extreme, denigrating. Some features of identity, especially those emanating from wider occupational emotionologies, may feel comfortable; others less so. Still others will be fragile and contingent. For instance, in the UK the social worker is often viewed with some suspicion, a perception to be "held" (internalized, defended, rationalized) by the resource-starved incumbent as she faces challenging clients – some of whom do not welcome her intervention. Identity work, especially with colleagues, aims to add some stability of meaning to these various tensions.

In a fragmented, postmodern, landscape, some of the means to achieve stability are, ironically, also provided by postmodernism – in the form of different narratives of self to explore and appropriate.[40] We are offered heroic images of "emotional intelligent," "solutions oriented," "flexible," "reflective," "unconditional positive regard" practitioners. Other accounts tell of the wounded self, such as from the "traumas" of job loss or downsizing, being a "toxin handler," or "suffering" discrimination or stress in the workplace. These comprise an identity tool kit for adjusting social-emotional scripts, tightening storylines and plots, and designing alternative self-descriptions for different audiences – including oneself. Identity work derives much of its edge from the history and positioning of relationships between individuals and those who have an apparent stake in their identity. Who, of these stakeholders, has one felt appreciated by, admired, disliked, or feared? Who has to be pleased or appeased? To whom should one not reveal weakness or displeasure? Where is it appropriate to express warmth and appreciation and when should these feelings be disguised? Identity work leads to the conclusion that identity, rather than being a fixed "thing," is a continuous socio-emotional process of becoming.

The contributors to this book reflect the themes I have outlined. In their different ways, they demonstrate how emotion is produced and reproduced by structural and social conditions and powerful "reality senders." Within these settings, some organizational actors are trapped and struggling, others are well-conditioned to what "is," and still others are able to carve significant emotional spaces for themselves.

The Book's Contents

Part I: Emotional arenas

In part I, nine different emotional arenas are explored. It begins with the ward of a hospital (chapter 2). Sharon Bolton observes the interactional rituals between nurses and patients from the vantage point of a hospital patient – herself. Through her revealing, often intimate, ethnography, she reveals the fine texture of the moral order and emotional politics of the ward, and the nurse–patient interaction. She challenges post-modernists who regard emotion as a cynical performance, devoid of "real" passion or compassion.

In chapter 3, Sarah Tracy takes us into the closed and murky world of prisons. Her interest, as a critical ethnographer, is to expose the structural mechanisms of power and control that bear down on front-line prison officers. She describes a complex web of structural tensions, status challenges, and double-binds that rob officers of power to enact some of the most basic functions of their role. Their prevalent burnout, she argues, is deeply rooted in these identity-eroding discourses and processes.

Chapter 4 unpacks what is arguably one of the most emotive work settings – crisis work with rape victims. Patricia Martin, Douglas Schrock, Margaret Leaf, and Carmen Von Rohr show how rape victims are subject to a range of different professional helpers and agents of the state who are themselves captured by the emotion cultures in which they work. This complicates, if not negates, emotional supportiveness for the victim. The roots of the difficulties, according to the authors, lie in the emotionologies of institutions, such as medicine and criminal justice, which define both "rape" and "victim." They powerfully determine the relative worth of working with rape victims, as well as the degree of respect, concern, or empathy that they deserve.

In chapter 5, Mary Haman and Linda Putnam take a sideways look at the "bright, fun" demeanor of service workers in the USA. They focus on trainers and related staff in a sports and recreation center where good cheer is part of the job description, and emotional labor is de rigueur. They show that, unusually, most of the control and surveillance comes, not from management, but from peers, determined to impose the "right" form of emotional labor on their co-workers. This has the insidious effect of demonizing and marginalizing those colleagues who are seen to be "just acting," even though their acts might be convincing. It is a subtle, but powerful, emotion order that eventually undermines confidence and impels some to leave.

Chapter 6 concerns jobs centers, a public service in the UK that aims to support the unemployed. Marek Korczynski and Victoria Bishop look closely at the high incidence of violence by customers against staff in these centers and seek explanations, drawing upon a qualitative study of the sector. They pin the blame on the ethic of customer sovereignty – "the customer is always right" – imported from the private sector. Violence, they suggest, is less a breakdown in societal norms, but a consequence of them. Job center staff are drilled to take personal responsibility for causing, containing, or assuaging customer anger and violence, on which they are judged by their managers. Many of them internalize this unquestioningly, akin to the "self-disciplining" described by some postmodern discourse theorists. Abuse becomes normalized, accepted. This, the authors argue, traps them in an ideological cage, which limits the feelings that they are able publicly to express, while also routinely exposing them to customer frustration and abuse, often for reasons beyond workers' control. They suggest that such violence be de-legitimized by relabeling it "customer bullying."

Chapter 7, by Kiran Mirchandani, casts a critical eye over the trend among major corporations to outsource their call center operations to countries where labor is cheap. She reports on an Indian-based call center where indigenous operators regularly have to deal with customer racism and abuse and, akin to job center staff, have to take it all in their stride. They work under close managerial surveillance and scripted inter-actions, yet the job is presented to them as being professional and exclusively graduate. Mirchandani concludes that globalized work creates special tensions for emotional and aesthetic labor, conditioned by colonial legacies of superiority and deference. This means workers have to acquiesce to the power of a distant client down the line, while also finding ways of preserving their own dignity.

In chapter 8, Nicole Kangas and Debra Meyerson take us into website work. Their field setting is an internet publishing company, I.com, offering entertain-ment, games, and related news through the web to a young audience. The authors reveal how employees' politicized and gendered identities influence their experience of their work, their feelings of "flow," and how time speeds by or drags. In what is close to a natural experiment, they compare two work groups doing very similar work in the same timescale – one comprising women producing a publication for girls, the other consisting of men working on a boys' publication. Kangas and Meyerson found that the men were engrossed in their work and full of energy. They were feted as corporate heroes, at one with the masculinity, violence, and sex preferences of their audience. In contrast, the women felt disempowered and disaffected. Their progressive beliefs about gender and womanhood were not legitimized by I.com executives or advertisers, leading to much fretting, ambivalence, and angst within the group.

The gendered order of society is also the concern of Gill Musson and Katy Marsh in their chapter on home-based telework (chapter 9). They focus on how men and women deal with culturally gendered narratives of role and feeling when they are dis-rupted by the very conditions and mechanisms of work – being at home and working virtually. Their case study illuminates the struggles and contradictions of those who go against the cultural stereotype of working parents, and how they marshal the dis-courses available to them in order to cope.

Chapter 10, the last chapter in this part of the book, delves into the emo-tional dynamics of management consultancy. Andrew Sturdy, Timothy Clark, Robin Fincham, and Karen Handley expose important emotion subtexts, expressed as humor, in what otherwise seem to be emotionless exchanges between clients and consultants. The humor emerges as a response to the asymmetrical power and status relations of the encounter. They illustrate how humor both obfuscates and attenuates tensions and anxieties, especially in "put downs" from clients feeling threatened, and how jokes – from either party – place the consultant at a safer operational distance.

Part 2: Shifting identities

The second part of the book is a critical examination of the wider trends in the emo-tionalization of identity, in and around organizations.

Caroline Hatcher (chapter 11) opens the section with a critical discussion of the historical discourses that have defined the identity of the ideal "corporate character," and "his" emotional makeup. She argues that the discourse of emotional intelligence marks a watershed, creating the impression that there is now a new and legitimate space for women as "emotionally intelligent" in the upper echelons of organizations. But in deconstructing the rhetoric and key texts on emotional intelligence, alongside related discourses on identity, emotion, aesthetics, and sexuality, Hatcher is led to a very different conclusion: that women are judged as having the wrong sort of emotionality to earn their place as superior performers, which remain the preserve of men. *Plus ça change.*

Chapter 12, by Stephanie Shields and Leah Warner, can read as an excellent companion to Hatcher's in that they reach a similar conclusion, but in a different way. They explore the political and cultural conditions that have favored the emergence of emotional intelligence, especially the recent valuation of skillfully regulated expressiveness in US public life. From their detailed examination of emotional intelligence, they detect a distinct gender bias, leading to the "disappearing" of women's emotional competencies. The vanishing act is achieved, in part, by circularity in defining those (men) who are already in positions of power as already possessors of emotional intelligence. People who do not fit the dominant emotionology remain outsiders. Shields and Warner grasp the "change" nettle to discuss different ways that a gender-fair emotional intelligence might be made possible – not least by focusing more on emotion structures than on emotion traits.

In chapter 13, Jeff Hearn brings the emotionalities of identity into a global milieu. The institutions and organizations that shape and define our selves and emotions are, he argues, becoming progressively transnational. He outlines the political, economic, and technological changes that have affected the movement of information, religion, goods, and services and have permeated organizations. They have created a medley, if not confusion, of emotionologies as people shift across, or live between, different national boundaries. These fragment or recast emotion expectations, gender positioning, emotion language, and feeling rules. Hearn illustrates his thesis through scenarios in academia, migration, transnational corporations, the military, and virtual communications.

Chapter 14 is by Philip Hancock and Melissa Tyler. They argue for a blending of the aesthetic and the emotional in our critical understanding of emotions in organizations – concepts that have traditionally traveled separate trajectories in organizational theory. They suggest that aesthetic manipulations of an organization's physical space and objects – their design, shape, colour, and texture – not only evoke particular "designer" feelings and emotional attachments, but also exert control over those who work in, or are consumers of, that space. Such emotive-aesthetic managing extends to "branded bodies," where employees are required to possess the body shape, appearance, or dress that "sells"; they must express the "correct" marketing image and its artistry. Those who do not match up, or cannot perform the appropriate aesthetic labor, are stigmatized or excluded. This, the authors suggest, is a manifestation of "staging value" in an "aesthetic economy" where seducing the senses is a mechanism of organizational power and control. It helps align the organization's political ambitions with the desires of the consumer and, at times, the employee.

In the epilogue, I reflect on the overarching themes of the book and on some of the prospects for critical approaches to emotion.

References

1. Lewis, P. and Simpson, R. (2007) *Gendering Emotions in Organizations*. Houndsmills, Basingstoke: Palgrave Macmillan.
2. Hancock, P. and Tyler, M. (2001) *Work, Postmodernism and Organization: A Critical Introduction*. London: Sage.
3. Hochschild, A. (1983) *The Managed Heart*. Berkeley: University of California.
4. Bendelow, G. and Williams, S. J. (1998) *Emotions in Social Life*. London: Routledge.
5. Kemper, T. (1991) An introduction to the sociology of emotions. In Strongman, D. (ed.) *International Review of Studies in Emotion*. Chichester: Wiley, 301–49.
6. Stearns, P. N. and Stearns, C. Z. (1985) Emotionology: clarifying the history of emotions, *American Historical Review*, XC, 813–36.
7. Amend, A. (2001) Melancholy. In Delon, M. (ed.) *Encyclopedia of the Enlightenment*. Chicago: Fitzroy Dearborn, 822–6.
8. Kotchemidova, C. (2005) From good cheer to "drive-by smiling": A social history of cheerfulness, *Journal of Social History*, 39, 5–37.
9. "The Great American Grump Out," http://smilemania.com/wst_page6.html
10. Emmerling Communications, www.emmerling.com/v2/column-battle-cry-cbs.html
11. Edwards, R. (1979) *Contested Terrain*. New York: Basic Books.
12. Salaman, G. (1981) *Class and Corporation*. London: Fontana.
13. Deetz, S. and Mumby, D. (1990) Power, discourse and the workplace: reclaiming the critical tradition in communication studies in organizations. In Anderson, J. (ed.) *Communication Yearbook 13*. Newbury Park, CA: Sage, 18–47.
14. Weedon, C. (1997) *Feminist Practice and Poststructualist Theory* (2nd edn). Oxford: Blackwell.
15. Clegg, S. and Hardy, C. (2006) Some dare call it power. In Clegg, S., Hardy, C., Lawrence, T. B., and Nord, W. R. (eds) *Handbook of Organization Studies* (2nd edn). London: Sage, 754–5.
16. Foucault, M. (1977) *Discipline and Punish*. London: Allen and Unwin.
17. Corrigan, J. (2002) *Business of the Heart: Religion and Emotion in the Nineteenth Century*. Berkeley: University of California Press.
18. Leyens, J.-P., Paladino, P. M., Rodriguez-Torre, R., Vaes, J., Demoulin, S., Rodriguez-Perez, A., and Gaunt, R. (2000) The emotional side of prejudice: The attribution of secondary emotions to ingroups and outgroups, *Personality and Social Psychology Review*, 4, 186–97.
19. Shields, S. A. (2002) *Speaking From the Heart: Gender and the Social Meaning of Emotion*. Cambridge: Cambridge University Press.
20. Fitzghughj, M. L. and Leckie, W. H. (2001) Agency, postmodernism, and the causes of change, *History and Theory*, 58–81.
21. Gubrium, F. and Holstein, J. (1995) Individual agency, the ordinary, and postmodern life, *The Sociological Quarterly*, 36, 555–70.
22. Bryman, A. (1999) The Disneyization of society, *The Sociological Review*, 47, 25–47.
23. Meštrović, S. G. (1997) *Postemotional Society*. London: Sage.
24. Baudrillard, J. (1988) *Selected Writings*. Cambridge: Polity Press.
25. Ciulla, J. B. (2000) *The Working Life*. New York: Three Rivers Press.
26. Doughty, H. A. (2004) Employee empowerment: Democracy or delusion? *The Innovation Journal*, 9, 1–24.
27. Belanger, J., Giles, A., and Murray, G. (2002) Towards a new production model: Potentialities, tensions and contradictions. In Murray, G., Belanger, J., Giles, A., and Lapointe, P. A. (eds) *Work and Employment in the High-Performance Workplace*. London: Continuum, 15–71.
28. Danford, A., Richardson, M., Stewart, P., Tailby, S., and Upchurch, M. (2004) High performance work systems and workplace partnership: A case study of aerospace workers. *New Technology, Work and Employment*, 19, 14–29.
29. Fineman, S. (1993) *Emotion in Organizations*. London: Sage.

30. Fineman, S. (2000) Emotional arenas revisited. In Fineman, S. (ed.) *Emotion in Organizations* (2nd edn). London: Sage, 1–24.
31. Meyerson, D. and Scully, M. (1995) Tempered radicalism and the politics of ambivalence and change, *Organizational Science*, 6, 585–600.
32. Callaghan, G. and Thomson, P. (2002) "We recruit attitude": The selection and shaping of routine call centre labour, *Journal of Management Studies*, 39, 233–54.
33. Fineman, S. (2006) On being positive: Concerns and counterpoints, *Academy of Management Review*, 31, 270–91.
34. Harré, R. (1989) Language games and the texts of identity. In Shotter, J. and Gergen, K. (eds) *Texts of Identity*. London: Sage.
35. Shotter, J. and Gergen, K. (1989) *Texts of Identity*. Newbury Park: Sage.
36. Gubrium, J. and Holstein, J. (2001) Introduction: Trying times, troubled selves. In Gubrium, J. and Holstein, J. (eds) *Institutional Selves*. Oxford: Oxford University Press, 1–22.
37. The Harris Poll, No. 58, July 26, 2006, www.harrisinteractive.com
38. Karreman, D. and Alvesson, M. (2001) Making newsmakers: Conversational identity at work, *Organizational Studies*, 22, 59–61.
39. Tracy, K. and Naughton, J. (1994). The identity work of questioning in intellectual discussion, *Communication Monographs*, 61, 281–302.
40. Frank, A. W. (1995) *The Wounded Storyteller*. Chicago: The University of Chicago Press.

PART I

EMOTIONAL ARENAS

CHAPTER 2

THE HOSPITAL

Me, Morphine, and Humanity: Experiencing the Emotional Community on Ward 8

Sharon C. Bolton

This chapter tells a personal story. It is not in the conventional form of academic critique; nevertheless it does offer some relevant and pressing comments on the received orthodoxy around emotion and work. At the heart of the story are my own observations during a nine-day stay in an NHS hospital ward, which prompted a review and refutation of assertions made by a body of thought that describes the current status of society as "postemotional," social actors and their interactions with each other as simulations, and service workers as simulacrums. The chapter's aim is to reintroduce the notion of humanity into the analysis of social interaction, to endorse the strength and interconnectedness of social ties, and, particularly, to make a renewed case for the role of agency in the study of emotional communities at work. While the origins and presentation of the chapter may be in part unconventional, academic convention is followed in its contribution, which includes: a brief review of the literature concerning the "death of the social," an alternative conceptual framework in the shape of Goffman's work on the interaction order, and a body of empirical data, albeit collected in an irregular way. Finally, I would like to believe that the argument presented in this chapter proffers a passionate conviction that we need not be drowned in the nihilistic premonitions concerning the death of the social.

The Public and the Private Worlds of Emotion

There are competing accounts concerning developments in how emotion might be viewed. Borrowing extensively from Elias,[1] Wouters[2,3] suggests that the boundary between the public and the private spheres is being redrawn as the result of a general "informalization of feeling":

> There is enough empirical data to show that during approximately the last hundred years the models of emotion exchange have become more varied, more escapable and more open for idiosyncratic nuances, thus less rigid and coercive.[2:105]

Wouters takes evidence of the breaking down of social barriers in modern society to show how social actors are all now much more familiar with cultures different than their own. They have developed the ability to switch and swap faces according to the demands of many different situations.[2,3] Nevertheless, the informalization of emotion has not led to a breaking down of the order of social interaction. On the contrary, the wider variances available to social actors in the presentation of self has led to the need for a greater awareness of rituals of deference and demeanor, and, as a result, men and women "have become more strongly integrated into tighter knit networks of interdependencies in which the level of mutually expected self-restraint has risen."[3:449]

For others, the focus of their analysis is on the very opposite of "interdependencies." The pressures of modern life have led to a move toward the routinization of emotion, leading to claims of a postemotional,[4] sentimentalized,[5] Disneyized[6] or, even, "post-ironic"[7] society. This does not mean that society is emotionless but that the emotions presented are manufactured states devoid of human feeling. In other words, it is often claimed that what we are on the outside and the person we present to others has become disconnected from feelings and motivations that were once prompted by a sense of belonging to a "moral order," which, in turn, relied on reciprocity and mutual obligation to create and sustain social relationships. Instead, emotions are now rooted in a society dominated by consumption where we become attached to new media-created images of artificial humanity.

From this standpoint, it is argued that, in the unreliable, fragmented conditions of consumer capitalism, consumption and production are inextricably linked and the boundaries between the public and private blurred. Hence, people search for a sense of coherence and meaning and, in this context, the world of production offers a stable platform where identities can be confirmed and people can take their rightful place in the world of consumption.[8] Thus, the new source of control is the imperative of the free market and the related culture industry, as both producers and consumers willingly collaborate in their own exploitation and "personalities" are saturated with the "culture of enterprise."[7,9] So vacuous – or "smooth," depending on one's focus of analysis – is the process that there is no longer any space for the outward expression of "real" feelings – especially those involving so-called negative emotions – as every emotional energy must be targeted towards a marketing of the self.[7] In the postemotional society then, it would seem that people are incapable of acting socially. Emotional communities in and out of work, and our moral commitments to them, have been deracinated, and replaced with universal cynicism, superficial niceties in the form of neutralized and buffered emotions, and entirely autonomous social actors who only pursue the satisfaction of their own desires.[4,8,10,11] Meštrović summarizes this process, in what he describes as the collapse of the sacred into the profane:

> . . . the category of the sacred really pertains to the emotional side of humanity, while the profane is the languishing, dull, non-emotional side. But the sacred canopy has collapsed, nothing is sacred anymore, and that which was formerly sacred and emotional has become public, pedestrian, accessible to all – in a word, it has been profaned.[4:xii]

It would appear to me that, in its articulation of the death of the social, the postemotional thesis produces an unrecognizable image of emotionally anorexic social actors who are entirely disconnected from society. This, I suggest, actually represents a growing confusion over the mechanization of work and the mechanization of the self – presuming, as it does, they can be classified and analyzed as one and the same thing. In effect, by overestimating the power and reach of the discourse of enterprise and its nihilistic effects on the fabric of social life, there has been a dangerous dislocation in the sacred and the profane: both consumers and producers have been moved from the "fat and the living to the thin and the dead."[12:152] This "vulgar tendency," as Goffman usefully describes it, portrays a lifeless, if not dismal, picture of organizational life, devoid of humanity. For those of us who work and live within the boundaries of various organizations, this is surely not a portrayal that is readily recognized. Yes, there is little doubt that many of our everyday interactions are routinized and predictable, especially those between customer and service-provider, but that does not mean they consist of an off-the-shelf package of artificial humanity.[13] Emotion is a lived, interactional experience with traffic rules of interaction framing how it is expressed and shared. To experience the presentation of "carefully crafted emotion" is not to be subjected to a simulation but to be part of the ongoing "civilization process" and to continually create and maintain a moral order upon which social interaction depends.

Goffman, the Interaction Order, and the Management of Emotion

For the analysis presented in this chapter, it is the processes of interaction that are of interest to an understanding of emotion, the minutiae of everyday life, and the norms that inform its conduct.[14–16] It is through his study of the intricacies of social interaction that Goffman is able to present social actors who are capable of moral commitment, who are involved with society, *and* whose activities take place within multiple and layered frameworks of action. Going "public" with emotion – what Goffman[15] would describe as presenting a "face" – shows how it is interwoven with social life and, unlike the majority of interactionists with whom he is associated, Goffman offers layers of reality by taking us through various "frameworks" of activity and the other differentials involved, frameworks that are not static, cultural entities but are subject to continuous change and variable influence. He talks of the structural relations of society, the inequalities inherent in many social situations, the creation of certain "moral orders," and the traffic rules of interaction that influence how interactions are played out. In offering detailed insights into routine social interactions, Goffman is all too aware of the shaping forces of the social, political, and economic; as he states when he talks of the need for establishing frames of analysis to understand micro-worlds of interaction: "social life is dubious enough and ludicrous enough without having to wish it further into unreality."[17:2] Drawing on this approach it becomes possible to see quite clearly how emotions are social things, derived from a "natural" substrata but mediated by active, reflective agents through the situations (that both constrain and enable) they confront.[13]

For Goffman, human interaction can never be a mere simulation. His argument rests on the assumption that social actors define their identity as individuals in terms of their capacity to manage their emotions in particular ways, depending on the levels of commitment to, and position within, various "moral orders."[15] For example, the interaction order depends on mutual responsibilities of communication, where actors constantly monitor each other's conduct, thus sustaining the predictability of much of day-to-day social life. Even though much of the action is routinized, this does not mean that it is habitually enacted unconsciously. Many routines are tactfully carried out as a means of saving the actor's own "face" or that of another, and agents reflexively adjust their performances accordingly. Without this, social actors would appear to exist in a cynical world of self-concerned agents, when in fact "face," and the corresponding sense of self, is a sacred thing and much of social interaction is centered around not only saving actors' own "faces" but also those around them.

Goffman usefully situates the minor courtesies of social interaction into a larger setting, showing how the conditions in which it takes place must be conducive to producing the necessary reciprocity:

> It is therefore important to see that the self is in part a ceremonial thing, a sacred object which must be treated with proper ritual care and in turn must be presented in a proper light to others. As a means through which this self is established, the individual acts with proper demeanor while in contact with others and is treated by others with deference.[15:91]

The continuous monitoring and treatment of fellow interactants with "ritual care" produces and reproduces a moral order: the aim may be to save face but the effect is to save the situation and the "ritual structure of the self."[15:39] This brings into play ritualized acts of deference and demeanor that can be found in everyday social encounters.

Despite, or because of, shifting social boundaries social interaction can be viewed as "a little social system with its own boundary maintaining tendencies; it is a little patch of commitment and loyalty with its own heroes and its own villains."[15:114] Yet, if the heroes are those who consistently engage in face-saving activity, what of the villains? Goffman recognizes that in all arenas of social life there will be those who aggressively manipulate the rules of social exchange for personal gain or fail to invest the required level of mutual face-work or where the need for deference and demeanor is differently distributed.[15] In these instances, the encounter becomes "less a scene of mutual considerateness than an arena in which a contest or match is held."[15:24] Interaction becomes strategic; interactants do not fulfill the reciprocal obligations of the interaction order and can be viewed as performers who appear to present "themselves to others in a false or manipulative fashion."[18:112] The strength of Goffman's analysis resides in the way in which he recognizes that social actors are both heroes and villains – sometimes at the very same time – as feeling rules are continually interpreted and adjusted according to the demands and power differentials involved in particular situations.[19]

The understanding of humanity that is derived from Goffman's work talks about our relations with the world; it links the parts and the people, the inside and the outside, the self and society, but without assuming their inseparability. In fact Goffman, in contrast to Meštrović's shifting of the sacred to the profane, warns of the dangers of using any such divisions when discussing human conduct:

> There is a vulgar tendency in social thought to divide the conduct of the individual into a profane and sacred part, . . . The profane part is attributed to the obligatory world of social roles; it is formal, stiff, and dead; it is exacted by society. The sacred part has to do with "personal" matters and "personal" relationships – with what an individual is "really" like underneath it all when he relaxes and breaks through to those in his presence. It is here, in this personal capacity, that an individual can be warm, spontaneous, and touched by humor. . . . And so it is, that in showing that a given piece of conduct is part of the obligations and trappings of a role, one shifts it from the sacred category to the profane, from the fat and living to the thin and dead."[12:52]

Goffman's emotion workers belong neither to the sacred nor the profane but continually cross boundaries – sometimes cynical, sometimes sincere, sometimes the hero, sometimes the villain, but all always present to some degree.[13] They are image-makers rather than mere images and their emotions are agential experiences not cultural artifacts.

Methodology and Background

Data presented in this paper were collected during a recent stay on a British National Health Service orthopaedic ward. While waiting for major surgery to piece back together a broken ankle, I read Meštrović's[4] account of the "postemotional society" and became increasingly agitated over an analysis of social life that did not seem to bear any relation to that which existed around me and in which I myself participated. The role of patient and social researcher blended together as previously relatively unfocused observations concerning the activity and associated emotional community of Ward 8 came very sharply into focus in their contradiction of Meštrović's thesis.

In attempting to "know the unknowable"[20] and capture the processes of the interaction order within particular emotional communities, complete immersion within one particular world would appear to be a most pertinent methodological option. This, however, brings its own dangers, particularly the inability to see outside of that world and to bring alternative interpretations to the data collected. In this case, being both patient and social researcher will have undoubtedly had an impact on the way I engaged with the world around me and deeply affected my own sensemaking concerning the activities on Ward 8. My immersion in the world of Ward 8 was relatively short – nine days in total – but for all of that was an intense experience. It was also a different experience to previous ethnographic research carried out within close nursing communities.[21–23] Nevertheless, the time spent on Ward 8 was enough to seize a snapshot of that world at a particular moment in time, enough to capture some of the routines and flavors of life for regular participants in that world, and enough to offer a very clear picture of a world that expresses its humanity in myriad ways but that essentially affirms the fundamentals of the interaction order.

Data collected are based entirely on participant observation and casual conversations. Nurses[i] feature largely: whispered conversations during long, sleepless nights; observances of their impatience, frustration, and joy for the work that they do; and their conduct with each other. It was with a great deal of humor that nurses recognized my dual position as patient and researcher, and constant comments were made querying the effects of morphine on the research process. Nurses were well aware of themselves as research subjects but for two central reasons were not uncomfortable in that position. First, my presence as a patient made me almost invisible as an opportunistic researcher. Second, even when obviously scribbling notes and asking questions, my vulnerable, bed-ridden condition altered the usual power differentials in the researcher–researched relationship. As a result, nurses were open and interested and would go out of their way to explain the background to situations that occurred and to help me make "sense" of activity on the ward.[ii]

Patients and their visitors also contributed largely to the emotional community of Ward 8. Nevertheless, it will come as no surprise that many of the interactions observed between patients and nurses form the core of the analysis in this paper. As with the nurses, the patients covered a large variance in age group and social status, though all staff and patients were female. The gendered aspects of these interactions are not analyzed in any sort of depth in this chapter – though, based on other studies of gendered "spaces," this could be a fruitful line of analysis.

The research process and findings presented in this chapter may be unconventional and open to questions of subjective bias: however, it has long been recognized that the study of emotion requires "methodological ingenuity."[24] The analysis presented here is based on captured moments and lies more with the tradition of storytelling than the presentation of data and this in itself counters the grim portrayal of the postemotional society. The data/stories presented here are not empty of feeling and they are not simulations but represent a personal mode of engagement in the intense emotional community of Ward 8.

Ward 8 and a Moral Order

Each professional discipline has its own set of "implicit feeling rules" that represent what they claim to be their unique mission. Nursing is a clear representation of this. Nurses willingly internalize the norms of a professional code of conduct in order to meet the expectations of their colleagues and the public concerning the "right" image of a caring professional. Though many nurses on Ward 8 talked about their training and a professional code of conduct, it is less a matter of concrete rules and more a basis of shared understandings that provide stable prompters of action. The norms of the profession, however implicit, provide a set of symbols that nurses draw upon in a sensemaking process. On Ward 8, there are norms and symbolic clues that differ from other healthcare settings. This has to be the case to cater for the varying protocols and patients' needs associated with each medical specialty. There is also an element of local knowledge brought by each regular participant in the micro-world of Ward 8. As one nurse proudly stated: "We're all northern lasses on here. You won't get any flannel from us. We tell it like it is and get things done without any faffing about." A combination of all of these elements continually creates and re-creates what can be clearly recognized as a particular framework of action and moral order that is maintained moment-by-moment through the interactions of the staff – with each other, with patients, with doctors, with visitors. The moral order provides the "interactional clues" that guide action and reaction on the ward, establishing norms of conduct that crosscut many "activity systems."[17]

Many of these "interactional clues" are centered on how the nurse presents herself to, and is seen by, others. All the nurses on Ward 8 appeared to have established ideas concerning the presentation of self and there was a clear consensus that maintaining a certain demeanor is an essential part of being a professional. A nurse described how she sees herself as a caring professional:

> I think nurses need to be professional at all times. By that I mean to be calm, even if things are hectic, to care for patients but not to get involved and to keep up-to-date with new drugs and technology so that we can explain things to patients and do our best for them.

It is not surprising to note that many nurses described maintaining a professional demeanor as a "mask" that must not slip lest the image of the profession would be damaged. In fact, the presentation of self is a widely recognized and admired trait among the staff on Ward 8. In the aftermath of a particularly stunning performance in which the Nurse Manager firmly put a junior doctor in his place without disturbing the "ceremonial order"[15] of interaction, another nurse remarked admiringly: "Eeeh, she's great, isn't she? Got more front than Blackpool!" However, the maintenance of the professional façade is often described as hard work and would seem to be an unbearable burden for the nurses involved. Various accounts, though, tell us that this is not so, for two central reasons. First, professional norms of conduct have the capacity to act as a shielding mechanism – the mask is a protective veneer that protects the self from the emotional demands of the job. Second, the nurse is so sincerely attached to the image of the professional (and its associated social status) that the extraordinary effort involved in maintaining this image is hardly seen as hard work at all, but rather an integral, and mostly invisible, part of the job.

Observations on Ward 8 confirmed this. Ethel, an elderly patient who reportedly weighed 350 pounds, sorely tried the patience of nurses involved in her care. Ethel required intensive physical nursing and was also very demanding of nurses' attention to her emotional needs. Due to the heavy lifting involved in caring for Ethel, she did not have a "named nurse" as staff on each shift took turns to cater to Ethel's needs. Often, Ethel's carers were perfunctory in their manner when caring for Ethel, displaying some of their frustrations with the difficulties involved in the job but never being obviously unkind or uncaring. Yet, when Ethel was experiencing a "low moment," nurses showed extraordinary kindness and cajoled and teased her into a brighter mood. Only when talking intimately to the nurses was the extent of their concern in caring for Ethel revealed. They were concerned over the health and safety aspects of the heavy lifting and they were concerned that they couldn't actually do much for her. From the interactions between staff and Ethel that were observed, the professional demeanor appeared to remain intact; so much so, that when a new member of staff threatened to disrupt this moral order by addressing Ethel very sharply and instructing her to "shape up, woman," she was turned on immediately by other staff present, and sent away from the scene. Soothing comments were then made to Ethel: "There, there, luvvie; she's a new girl and doesn't know how things are done yet."

Everyday Incivility

When social life is examined, a constant reminder is found that daily interactions between actors are not based on a mute consensus. And this is the case even in an organizational setting where rules and norms may be more obviously applied. Different emotional communities offer generalized modes of conduct that guide participants' actions. However, each actor interprets situations differently and reacts in a variety of ways. The reinterpretation of rules by individuals inevitably leads to differences in how they are enacted. The possibility of leakage from existing boundaries of norms arises and new boundaries may be created. What Goffman describes as "civil inattention" is just as vital a part of the interaction order as the notion of deference and demeanor.

Interestingly, everyday incivility is as ordered as everyday reciprocity and may even be a stable and accepted part of the moral order. This was certainly the case on Ward 8. A middle-aged patient called Maisie tested the notion of the presentation of the professional self to its limits. She was incessantly demanding, did not comply with any of the routines of hospital life on a ward, and would loudly insult anyone who happened to pass: staff, patients, visitors – Maisie didn't discriminate. Yet, it became obvious that staff had adjusted to Maisie's interactional style and would, as if by courtesy, reciprocate in kind. For instance, in reply to a stream of verbal abuse from Maisie, a nurse quietly stated: "Maisie, we all know you're a bitch so why do you have to keep proving it. Just behave yourself for once." Masie's quick, and consistent, reply was as always "F*** you!" As the days went on, nurses began to retort "F*** you back, Maisie!" and this would be greeted with laughter from both the nurses and Maisie. The ritual was complete and the order of interaction surprisingly maintained. Nurses were asked if they felt offended by Maisie. Why did they not refuse to care for her given her recalcitrant attitudes to simple things like washing and dressing and her stubborn refusal to abide by hospital rules, such as "no smoking." Nurses replied: "That's Maisie, that's how she is." The incivilities shared between the nurses and Maisie were an integral part of the emotional community on Ward 8. This was so to such a degree that when one morning Maisie appeared relatively docile and compliant, the nurses did not see this as a cause for celebration but as a very real concern for her health and overall well-being. Doctors were called, trips off the ward arranged, and special food ordered until Maisie's loud expletives could be heard once again and the nurses felt relieved that all was "back to normal."

Humanity Shared

An essential element of the interaction order is in the rituals of deference and demeanor offered to fellow participants. As Goffman consistently points out, social interaction involves much face-saving activity – of one's own face and that of a fellow interactant. The major weakness of the postemotional society thesis is the assumption that the sacred has collapsed into the profane; that any chance of creating "collective efferves-cence" is gone.[4] The assumption that social interaction is now empty of "human values and virtues"[25:266] and as such involves only "dead, abstracted emotion"[4:26] tears the heart from the foundations of an understanding of the interaction order. Such an analysis entirely neglects the various motivations and feelings of social connectedness that people bring to the process of social interaction.

Initial observances on Ward 8 focused on episodes of very human interaction, not because they were unusual occurrences that disrupted the moral order but because at a time of vulnerability and entering into a new emotional community these are the episodes that confirm our interconnectedness with others and restore a sense of the sacred. This is done in small ways – a kindness shown by a nurse; a shared "story" from another patient; a communal whine about the food, the noisy neighbors, the abrupt doctors – or small incidents that continually affirm that the interaction order is a collective achievement. As Goffman so eloquently states, it is these small moments that express our humanity: "Our status is backed by the solid buildings of the world, while our sense of identity often resides in the cracks."[26:280]

There were many small gestures observed during the nine-day stay on Ward 8, gestures that eventually led to the critique of the postemotional society presented in this chapter: the long-term patient who flung her arms around her favourite nurse on her returning from three days' leave; the overplayed rituals of deference and demeanor for the benefit of a genteel elderly lady who had broken her hip and who was very fearful of her new surroundings; the frustrated nurse who stamped her foot in the middle of the ward and shouted "if I have to clean up any more 'p***' and 's***' today I'm going to shoot myself"; and the ridiculous giggles involved in the simple act of making a bed. These are not empty performances that signify the end of the social but very human acts that signify the joys, in addition to the stresses, strains, and sorrows, involved in one particular emotional community. An experienced nurse summarizes the need for these expressions of humanity:

> I've worked on here a long time. Some days I could quite happily leave the job; I'm not far off retirement. Then I realize what I'd miss: the people – the good and the bad. And boy oh boy, do we get some bad! But it's the human contact in this job that makes it worth while. It means every day is different but there's a sort of pattern too. Yes, it's the people and their funny ways I'll miss the most.

Conclusion

Utilizing insights into the "interaction order," it seems that the ritual of everyday social interaction is something of a feat. It is a social process that relies on participants monitoring and regulating their own and others' conduct in order to achieve the "socialized trance"[15:113] of involvement. Though the order of interaction has "solid foundations,"[16] its creation, maintenance, and re-creation is a dynamic process that entails both conformity and rebellion. There is much emotion work involved in achieving the order of interaction and we all invest heavily in this social process in order to achieve the desired "ontological security."[27] It is something of a fragile achievement because so many diverse interpretations of interactional clues take place at any one moment and various frameworks for action offer different foundations for action. This is why the interaction order is such a collective triumph – a triumph of interconnectedness that signifies why there can never be just one unrivalled dialogue as suggested by the "discourse of enterprise."

The moral order achieved on Ward 8 represents this very clearly. The professional norms of conduct exert powerful external and normative controls and yet the dynamics of human interaction alter how they are enacted – take the unceremonial exchanges between the nurses and Maisie, for instance, or the nurse stamping her foot in rage, clearly rebelling against the "dirty work" involved in her job but also defying the norms of conduct that tell her she must not show her distress. The emotional culture on Ward 8 does not only rely on "nice guy theories" of social interaction but also requires an understanding of everyday incivility. In the setting of a hospital ward, we see the best and the worst of human conduct – perhaps the closest we can get to the image of the "noble savage" so celebrated by the postemotional society advocates. However, it is also surprisingly ordered and even the "failed" interactions[10] follow certain traffic rules and the more "savage" elements of life on an orthopedic ward are rendered "noble" through the process of shared interaction.

In conforming to interactional rules, social life consists of both cynical and sincere performances. However, though the nurses' feelings may not match the presented face, this does not mean their performances are emotionally vacuous. The masks displayed by these nurses are not "invasive intimacy without care, neglect dressed up as concern, a hideous and thrusting theatrical mask."[25:266] They are not exhibiting a "displaced, viscerated compassion."[4:26] Nurses are able to present a professional demeanor that distances them from distressing or over-demanding elements of their caring work, but at the same time they are emotionally present and fully engaged in the interaction order.

Of course, the nature of professionals' work is widely acknowledged to be more emotionally complex than that of the "emotional proletariat" involved in routine front-line service work and is supported by entirely different motivations. It is commonly recognized that caring professionals will work hard on the presentation of self, particularly with clients, in order to create a stable emotional climate and maintain poise for the carrying out of "dirty work" such as body care, disturbing behaviour, or imparting bad news. As such, it could be claimed that stories from Ward 8 cannot be used to make generalized claims concerning emotional activity in organizations or in social life in general. Fortunately, Ward 8 is not alone in its "collective effervescence." Ample evidence exists that affirms the stability of the interaction order and the emotion work on which it is founded – for instance, customer service agents offering kindnesses to customers,[28,29] air-cabin crew supporting each other in times of crisis,[30] and telesales agents creating "communities of coping."[31]

The observation and analysis presented here demonstrate that social life is far from a lifeless landscape; rather, it displays the emotional life of a particular organizational world with all of its pains and pleasures. I would, therefore, suggest that the emotional in the postemotional thesis would be better understood if we recognize that emotions are social things and that humanity is expressed, shared, and supported in myriad ways as part of the "interaction order." Rather than be overwhelmed by the "discourses of despair"[32] that divide the emotional life of the workplace into the prescribed and the liberated, we should recognize that expressions of humanity continually cross boundaries – from the profane to the sacred. In other words, the apparent mechanization of both consumption and production, via processes of McDonaldization, Disneyization, and sentimentalization, should not be confused with a mechanization of the self.

Acknowledgments

Thanks go to Maeve Houlihan, UCD, for comments on an early draft of this chapter, to Paul Thompson and Phil Taylor for inspiration on the title, and to participants at the 22nd International Labour Process Conference for valuable feedback.

Notes

i.   The description of nurse relates to all grades within the nursing hierarchy, including healthcare assistants, who were involved in the day-to-day caring activities on Ward 8.
ii. Nurses were always careful to protect patient confidentiality and never discussed other patients' details, and I never asked for them. This information would not have contributed anything to the understanding of the emotional culture on Ward 8.

References

1. Elias, N. (1994) *The Civilizing Process*. Oxford: Blackwell.
2. Wouters, C. (1989a) The sociology of emotions and flight attendants: Hochschild's Managed Heart, *Theory, Culture and Society*, 6, 95–123.
3. Wouters, C. (1989b) Response to Hochschild's reply, *Theory, Culture and Society*, 6, 447–50.
4. Meštrović, S. G. (1997) *Postemotional Society*. London: Sage.
5. Anderson, D. and Mullen, P. (1998) *Faking It: The Sentimentalisation of Modern Society*. London: The Social Affairs Unit.
6. Bryman, A. (1999) The Disneyization of society, *Sociological Review*, 47 (1), 26–47.
7. Cremin, C. S. (2003) Self-starters, can-doers and mobile phoneys: situations vacant column and the personality culture in employment, *Sociological Review*, 51 (1), 109–28.
8. Rose, N. (1999) *Governing the Soul: The Shaping of the Private Self*. London: Free Association Books.
9. du Gay, P. (1996) *Consumption and Identity at Work*. London: Sage.
10. Baudrillard, J. (1983) *In the Shadow of the Silent Majorities . . . or the End of the Social and Other Essays*. New York: Semiotext.

11. Ritzer, G. (1999) *Enchanting a Disenchanted World*. Thousand Oaks, CA: Pine Forge Press.
12. Goffman, E. (1961a) *Encounters*. New York: The Bobbs-Merrill Company Ltd.
13. Archer, M. (2000) *Being Human: The Problem of Agency*. Cambridge: Cambridge University Press.
14. Goffman, E. (1959) *The Presentation of Self in Everyday Life*. London: Penguin Books.
15. Goffman, E. (1967) *Interaction Ritual: Essays in Face-To-Face Behavior*. Chicago: Aldine Publishing Company.
16. Goffman, E. (1991) The interaction order: American Sociological Association, 1982 Presidential Address. In Plummer, K. (ed.) *Symbolic Interactionism: Contemporary Issues*. London: Edward Elgar Ltd.
17. Goffman, E. (1974) *Frame Analysis*. Boston: Northeastern University Press.
18. Giddens, A. (1987) *Social Theory and Modern Sociology*. Cambridge: Polity Press.
19. Bolton, S. (2005) *Emotion Management in the Workplace*. London: Palgrave.
20. Sturdy, A. (2003) Knowing the unknowable? A discussion of methodological and theoretical issues in emotion research and organizational studies, *Organization*, 10 (1), 81–105.
21. Bolton, S. (2000) Who cares? Offering emotion work as a "gift" in the nursing labour process, *Journal of Advanced Nursing*, 32 (3), 580–6.
22. Bolton, S. (2001) Changing faces: Nurses as emotional jugglers, *Sociology of Health and Illness*, 23 (1), 85–100.
23. Bolton, S. (2004) A simple matter of control? NHS hospital nurses and new management, *Journal of Management Studies*, 41 (6), 317–33.
24. Fineman, S. (1993) *Emotion in Organizations*. London: Sage.
25. Hopfl, H. (2002) Playing the part: Reflections of aspects of mere performance in the customer–client relationship, *Journal of Management Studies*, 39 (2), 255–67.
26. Goffman, E. (1961b) *Asylums*. London: Penguin Books.
27. Giddens, A. (1984) *The Constitution of Society*. Cambridge: Polity Press.
28. Callaghan, G. and Thompson, P. (2002) We recruit attitude: The selection and shaping of routine call centre labour, *Journal of Management Studies*, 39 (2), 233–53.
29. Wray-Bliss, E. (2001) Representing customer service: Telephones and texts. In Sturdy, A., Grugulis, I., and Willmott, H. (eds) *Customer Service*. London: Palgrave.
30. Bolton, S. and Boyd, C. (2003) Trolley dolly or skilled emotion manager? *Work, Employment and Society*, 17 (2), 289–308.
31. Korczynski, M. (2003) Communities of coping: Collective emotional labour in service work, *Organization*, 10 (1), 55–79.
32. Thompson, P. and Smith, C. (2001) Follow the redbrick road: Reflections on pathways in and out of the labour process debate, *International Studies of Management and Organization*, 30 (4), 40–67.

CHAPTER 3

THE PRISON

Power, Paradox, Social Support, and Prestige: A Critical Approach to Addressing Correctional Officer Burnout

Sarah J. Tracy

Many critical ethnographers choose their research foci based on a fundamental belief that issues of power and struggle underlie most social behavior. Whether or not you are convinced by this tenet, however, I think the critical approach is an excellent way to make sense of everyday problems and injustices. Simply, critical theory provides a deep and plentiful toolbox for helping understand and undermine situations that are "not nice."[1] In particular, I have used a critical poststructuralist approach to explicate and make sense of everyday dilemmas employees experience with emotion labor and organizational burnout. As such, my aim has been not only to ask "what is?" but also "what could be?" – to study organizational cultures not only for reasons of description, but also for the opportunity to provide a window of transformation.

This chapter uses a critical poststructuralist viewpoint to unpack problems experienced by correctional officers (also known as prison officers) as they deal with emotion labor and organizational burnout. In the course of officers' formal duties of watching over inmates and enforcing jail and prison rules and regulations, they also must engage in a range of emotional fronts and confront high levels of emotional exhaustion. Before I begin this discussion, however, I want to provide a brief explanation about how and why I became interested in a critical poststructuralist approach. In the Foucauldian genealogical spirit,[2] I provide this "backstory" not for history's sake, but because it provides an important context for evaluating my continued use of this approach today.

Moving Toward a Critical Approach: The Backstory

My early emotion labor research with 911 call-takers – which provided ethnographic detail on the ways employees use communication to manage emotion work when in crisis – was almost paradigmatically interpretive in nature.[3] It was not until I tried to make sense of my (auto)ethnographic work on a cruise ship that I began a foray into critical theory. Over the course of eight months, I served as assistant cruise director on the *Radiant Spirit* luxury cruise liner (a pseudonym). My job was to smile, make conversation, lead activities, greet passengers, and generally be an ever-cheery hostess on the ship. Uniforms and nametags were required in all passenger areas and I worked every day, up to 15 hours a day, without a single full day off. Not only were cruise staff expected to be emotionally on stage in passenger areas, they also did emotion work in the cruise staff office, the officer mess, crew bar, and sometimes even on the street or in restaurants in port cities. As such, the only consistent backstage areas were our 10 by 12 foot (windowless, shared) cabins. During my reign on the *Radiant Spirit*, I personally experienced high levels of burnout, stress, emotion labor, and self-alienation.[4]

My burnout and difficulty with emotion labor was perhaps no more poignant than in the following situation. During an afternoon off in Cabo San Lucas, I stood waiting in line behind other crew members at one of the few payphones. Just before the ship was to leave port, I made a static-filled call to my father in Wisconsin. While I envisioned a quick and lighthearted hello, I instead learned that my grandmother had died the evening before. As I raced back to the ship to prepare for the evening on stage, I tried to make sense of the somber and surprising information. However, with little time for contemplation, I hurried to my cabin, hastily shared the news with my roommate, showered, and changed into the night's festive costume. Immediately after the stage show, I jumped into pajamas and ran up to the passenger disco to host the pajama party theme night. I went ahead and held up a pretty convincing performance for the entire evening, which also included sitting and chatting with a couple of passengers who said they *had* to buy me a drink.

Later that night, I wrote in my journal about the range of emotions I experienced that evening – including happiness at helping passengers enjoy themselves, sadness for my father, irritation that work seemed to be a higher priority than personal life, and confusion as to how I should best jump among these conflicting emotions. To ease my conflicted emotional state, I had intermittently run over to a couple of crew member friends sitting in the disco, who knew about my grandmother's death, and explained how "I'd rather be doing anything right now but dancing." I felt proud of my performance, but also somewhat guilty that perhaps I should be showing more sadness.[4] These intermittent disclosures to my friends represented a desperate attempt to manage the expectations about the various emotions I should be performing.

Six months later, when I got off the ship (and back to graduate school), I tried to figure out why this particular situation, and why emotion labor in general, was so difficult and stressful on the *Radiant Spirit*. I naturally turned to the existing literature on emotion labor and burnout. What I found, though, was somewhat disappointing. It focused primarily on the individual – how the employee could better deal with burnout through things like deep breathing; how an individual's acting method related to self-alienation. Extant theories, as I'll discuss in more detail below, would suggest that the preceding situation was difficult because I was faking one emotion (cheeriness) while *really* feeling sadness. However, given the range of *real* emotions I experienced that evening, I felt unsatisfied with the "emotive dissonance" explanation. At the time of the incident, I had the intuitive sense that, surely, the organizational structure and norms on the *Radiant Spirit* had something to do with the difficulty of doing emotion work. However, I found very little in the existing literature that focused on larger organizational issues that played a role in exacerbating issues of burnout and emotion labor.

During this time, I also happened to be taking my first class in critical and postmodern theory in organizations from Stanley Deetz at the University of Colorado. In short, over the next few months I learned that a critical poststructuralist approach, inspired by Michel Foucault, would help to usefully explicate how structural issues and discourses of power exacerbated issues of burnout and emotion labor.[2] For instance, a genealogy of the cruise industry helped to explain why emotion labor was normalized and unquestioned. The total institution aspect of the cruise ship made it difficult to escape its suffocating norms.[5] The lack of a backstage made it all but impossible to express important (but not organizationally prescribed) emotional facets. Cruise ship employees' lack of power and self-subordination discouraged any questioning of the organizational expectations. Indeed, as illustrated in the above example, I never even entertained the idea that it might be appropriate to ask for an evening off. Critical poststructuralist theory helped explain how employees regularly self-subordinate to organizational norms and make panoptic control structures their own.[6]

So, I turned to a critical approach not because of an a priori goal to examine injustice and power. Rather, I found it simply to be a great way to better shed light on problems with emotion labor and burnout that the existing literature had not yet thoroughly explored. In what follows, I discuss the limitations of examining emotion labor and burnout from individual and psychological approaches. I then turn to a case study of correctional officers that aims to illustrate the utility of a critical poststructuralist approach.

Limitations of Extant Burnout and Emotion Labor Literature

Taking a critical approach means that commonsense assumptions must be questioned and used for social change. Furthermore, critical theory alerts us that things aren't always what they seem. Here I provide an overview of important concepts in the emotion labor and burnout literatures as well as question several past assumptions about these issues.

Emotion labor

Emotion management is generally considered to be the effort people put into making sure their private feelings are expressed in a way that is consistent with socially accepted norms, such as looking happy at a party and somber at a funeral. When emotion management is commodified as something to be bought and sold in the workplace, it becomes *emotional labor* – or what many scholars including myself have shortened to call *emotion labor*.[7] Employees engage in emotion labor when they create an emotional "package" through their facial and bodily display that serves as part of the organizational product. Emotion work has a number of faces[8] – bill collectors create alarm, supermarket cashiers cheerfully greet customers, theme park employees exude excitement, and caregivers show concern. Emotion work not only involves the inflation of emotions, but also the suppression of organizationally inappropriate feelings.[3] Call-takers at 911 suppress anxiety and alarm; high-beam steel workers hide fear; professors camouflage distress; healthcare workers swallow disgust; and police officers conceal weakness.[9]

Emotion work is important to organizations for several reasons. For many employees, such as waiters or flight attendants, a cheery emotional front is part of the product bought and sold. For other professionals, emotion labor is an embedded activity that facilitates their service; by hiding their fear, for instance, doctors are better able to deliver medical treatment. Researchers have examined how emotion labor can affect sales, influence clients, improve customer service, increase receptiveness to organizational change, and create emotion or calm in others.[10] For these and other reasons, emotion labor is considered integral to the success of many organizational endeavors.

Some research suggests that emotion labor can be emotionally healthy, pleasant, and even fun.[11] However, the lion's share of research links emotion work with a number of negative psychosocial effects.[12] Research has connected emotion labor with burnout, depression, cynicism, role alienation, emotional numbness, job tension, and emotional exhaustion. Why can emotion labor be so difficult?

The majority of research focuses on *individual psychological* causes for this pain, suggesting that the discomfort of emotion labor arises due to "emotive dissonance" or a clash between *actual* inner feelings and outward expression.[7] From this point of view, emotion labor obstructs an employee's ability to reconcile *true* feelings with an organizationally mandated *false* display of emotion. This viewpoint suggests the pain of emotion work is primarily about employees' individual acting methods. *Deep acting* – when members internalize the prescribed emotions and make them their own – supposedly leads to alienation and burnout. *Surface acting* – in which employees do not change their inner feelings, but change their outward emotional expression to fit organizational norms – is not supposed to lead to feelings of estrangement, but may make employees feel phony. Workers who believe that offering certain prescribed emotions should be part of the job, or *fake in good faith*, purportedly do not feel as much psychological discomfort as those who do not believe the false emotions should be part of the job, or *fake in bad faith*.[13] Other researchers have argued that emotive dissonance results in less emotional exhaustion and higher job satisfaction when employees internalize their work duties and make the role their own.

These theories provide a strong basis for understanding the discomfort of emotion labor. However, I argue that the concept of emotive dissonance suffers from an over-reliance on individual and psychological explanations.[10] It suggests that feelings are individual, personal, and internal and are then made fake either through surface acting or deep acting – processes considered to be ultimately separate from a real self.[7] The presumption that emotion has a "truer" existence before it is constructed and constrained through organizational norms is problematic because it underestimates the role of communication in constructing emotion.[14] Emotion develops in light of communication terms operative within the local moral order. Indeed, it is difficult to feel and express emotions for which there is no word or label. Societal and organizational discourses shape the very notions of emotions.

A critical poststructuralist point of view maintains that identities, including emotional identities, are not singular or dichotomous, and not real or phony. While individuals may talk in terms of having a real self vs. a fake self, a poststructuralist viewpoint suggests that the self is "crystallized" with a number of facets.[15] The identities and emotions of employees are constituted through overlapping discourses of power. As such, emotions are neither wholly real nor fake, which in turn suggests that we must look beyond individuals' emotive dissonance and different methods of faking it to understand the discomfort associated with emotion work. Rather, discourses of power and prestige mark some emotional expressions as more powerful than others. Certainly, different organizational environments foster different notions of the most powerful or preferred emotional states. However, in many Western cultures, feminized emotional expressions such as nurturing, caring, and serving are seen as less powerful, and less preferred than those of toughness, stoicism, and emotional detachment.[16] A critical approach suggests that researchers go beyond a focus on internal psychological states to consider how external discourses and norms affect the difficulty of emotion work.

Burnout

Burnout is a three-dimensional concept characterized by: 1) emotional exhaustion (or a "wearing out" from a job); 2) depersonalization or a negative shift in responses to others, such as clients; and 3) a decreased sense of personal accomplishment.[17] As we enter the twenty-first century, burnout and stress – terms that are often used interchangeably – seem endemic to work. Burnout management training sessions are commonplace and the popular press is filled with articles about how to avoid, beat, and handle stress. However, stress and burnout are fairly recent concepts. Much of the stress research developed during World War II to test and select soldiers who would be the most "stress fit."[18] The primary concerns of early researchers in this area were with instincts, the fight-or-flight response, and the individual physiological reactions when certain stressors were placed on people. While today's organizational stressors are quite different and more varied than those faced by soldiers, this early research set the stage for later work.

As such, it perhaps should be of little surprise that most organizational research and training still treat burnout and stress as *individual* pathologies rather than organizational, structural dilemmas. Employees are trained to identify and tackle their stressors using tactics such as biofeedback, meditation, and relaxation techniques. Furthermore, when workers are considered to be too stressed out to do their work effectively, they are often referred to employee assistance programs (EAPs). These individualistic stress interventions may assist with personal coping, but they oftentimes miss the *working patterns* that contribute to and define stress.

In contrast, a critical poststructuralist approach treats stress and burnout as *organizational structural problems* – having much to do with collective social support, discourses of power, and larger organizational work structures. Individual remedies such as meditation and muscle relaxation do more to focus on the *symptoms* of burnout rather than to critically examine the *job stressors* themselves. Furthermore, individual approaches often relegate the working out of emotional difficulties to back-stage or off-stage areas (such as EAPs). In doing so, the organization effectively seals off issues of stress and burnout from the larger organization. This makes collective coping more difficult. Furthermore, EAPs unfortunately tend to be stigmatized and, thus, underutilized. This is due to their privatization and because, historically, EAPs have been associated with alcoholic or deviant employees.[18]

Ironically, individualizing these issues is largely disempowering to practitioners who actually want to do something about stress and burnout. Organizational administrators have very little control over employees' ability to apply meditation, biofeedback, or exercise advice. However, they do have some control over certain organizational structures that play a role in creating stress and burnout in the organizational atmosphere – things like organizational contradictions, limited opportunities for employee social support, or organizational cultures that make employees feel powerless. This does not mean that individual differences are completely irrelevant. However, it does suggest that we need to do more to analyze the collective nature of people's adaptation to the work environment. As illustrated in the following case study of jail and prison correctional officers, organizational burnout and the pain of emotion labor are exacerbated by structural issues including discourses of power and prestige, organizational contradictions and paradoxes, and a lack of social support.

The Case of Correctional Officers

Over the course of 11 months – May 1999 through March 2000 – I researched the work life of correctional officers. I interacted with 109 research participants (72 male, 37 female) who were employed at a county mixed-gender jail, Nouveau Jail, and a state women's prison, Women's Minimum. I engaged in a "tracer" form of ethnography, where the investigator follows people and their movements over time, *in situ*,[19] and immersed myself in the correctional scene, observing everyday activities and collecting in-depth narratives and explanations from officers. A guiding research question was "why are correctional officers burned out, and how is this related to expectations for emotional control in the workplace?"

The primary source of data was fieldnotes from 80 hours of shadowing correctional officers in their day-to-day work and 33 hours of serving as a participant or participant-observer during training sessions. Additionally, I examined a number of training documents and conducted 22 in-depth recorded interviews with correctional employees: 10 with Nouveau Jail officers, nine with Women's Minimum officers, and three with organizational supervisors, including the prison warden, jail captain, and Nouveau city sheriff. I logged a total of 171 research hours yielding 722 single-spaced, typewritten pages of raw data.[10] I conducted a grounded interpretive analysis of the data, reading and rereading fieldnotes, documents, and transcribed interviews for recurring patterns. Emergent themes included emotion labor norms; emotional performances; and issues that mitigated the difficulty of emotion labor and contributed to burnout.

Pictures of burnout behind bars

As a population, correctional officers are burned out.[20] Past research, most based on one-time survey studies, suggests that officers experience role conflict, danger, strained relations with inmates, administration, and co-employees, lack of influence, over-crowding, inadequate staff, and a negative personal image.[21] About half of officers view their jobs as stressful, and about a third report having problems with burnout. Part of my quest in doing ethnographic immersion research was to paint a picture of what burnout can look like in a correctional setting. Among other ways, I found that burnout manifested itself in correctional officers through symptoms of paranoia, withdrawal, literalism, toughness/coldness, an us–them mentality, and embarrassment of the job and themselves.

First, I found that many employees were paranoid, and largely for good reason. Not only did officers mistrust inmates, but also they mistrusted administrators and each other. As discussed in more detail below, they were afraid because administrators often took inmates' word over their own. Officers also cited confusion over whether or not they could trust their fellow officers. This paranoia traveled with them outside of the workplace and into private life as they visited discount stores, fast food places, and football arenas. While I heard no evidence of officers being assaulted outside of work, they were consistently wary that an ex-inmate might seek revenge. One officer explained, "I find myself fighting to not be so paranoid. I'll go to the store. I'll go to Kmart or Target . . . and I'll look at somebody and think, 'he looks like an inmate.' I have no idea where it comes from."

Officers were also largely withdrawn, quiet, and unquestioning of organizational norms. In the training sessions I attended, the leaders did not encourage participation, and when trainers did ask if officers had questions, they would usually remain quiet. One officer yelled out after a particularly long training session, "No questions 'cause we're so satisfied sir!" Indeed, many officers evidenced a literalistic "I'll just do what you tell me" mentality. As such, they sometimes evidenced a lack of complex thinking, and arbitrarily followed the rules. An interview excerpt with a correctional officer illustrates this:

> They want someone who's like a robot. . . . If you think, you get into trouble. The one who would make a perfect officer . . . is the one that can stare at a wall for five hours and it won't faze him. You have to follow the rules . . . if you don't know what it is, look it up. It's right there. "What do I do?" It tells you what to do in every situation, so there's no room for you to think.

Officers also developed an us–them mentality. Officers exuded excitement when they caught inmates in wrongdoing, saying things like, "There's nothing better than a good bust." Indeed, they often saw an inmate "win" as a correctional officer "loss." For instance, visitation officers expressed disappointment on Christmas Day for the nice weather, as it would bring out a lot of visitors and make their job more hectic. Officers' comments and behaviors also reinforced an us–them boundary even in scenarios in which it was not obvious that an inmate's gain was an officer's loss. The following example is typical. I once observed an officer sorting out the inmates' dinner and filling up their Kool-Aid glasses. He tasted one of the batches of Kool-Aid and said, "Yuck, this one doesn't have sugar in it." Then he muttered to himself, "Do you think we should give them [inmates] the good Kool-Aid or the bad Kool-Aid?" He continued, "I think the good stuff for us, the bad stuff for them." The inmates' loss was the officers' gain – even though there was enough of the good Kool-Aid for both the officers and most of the inmates.

Furthermore, over time, officers appeared to become increasingly cold and dismissive, not only to inmates, but also to other outsiders and in personal situations. One officer explained how, since taking the job, she was much less fazed by violence, whether in the prison or on the street. A Nouveau Jail officer explained how officers became cold over the course of their career:

> When they're hired as a new recruit, it's "I'm so happy to be here and I love everybody." And then after a couple of years, it's "Everybody's an asshole but me and the sergeant and you guys and the sheriff." And a year or two later, it's "Everybody's an asshole except me and the guys and the sheriff." The sergeant's an asshole too by that time. And then it's just "me and my partner." And that's a pretty normal progression.

Another officer near retirement appeared somber and regretful as he summed up how his emotional demeanor had changed because of the job, saying, "I guess I grew hard and cold about a lot of things. The biggest thing that doesn't affect me is injuries and death. I just don't have the same feelings I used to have."

So, in summary, past research as well as my ethnographic research, suggests that officers are largely burned out, manifested in a correctional mentality that is paranoid, withdrawn, literalistic, and hardened. This, in turn, can lead to a number of organizational and personal problems. Organizationally, when employees have an us–them, bossy mentality toward inmates, they are less likely to be interested in rehabilitation and care. On the flip side, if they feel alone and depressed, they may be more easily swayed to go to the inmate side and seek inappropriate relationships with the criminals they are supposed to be watching. Furthermore, when officers are literalistic and withdrawn, it is more difficult to be flexible in the workplace, and inflexible officers cannot deal with the day-to-day details of watching over inmates.

Officers also cite difficulty in being able to turn off their institutionalized personality when they go home. As one officer told me, "This job will change your mindset. My ex-wife used to tell me I was a jerk. She said that, about an hour before work, when I would get into my uniform, I'd start *telling* rather than *asking* and get louder and totally unsympathetic." Officers have a divorce rate that is twice as high as the average worker, tend to have elevated problems with domestic violence and alcoholism, and a life expectancy of 59 years.[22] This is not only problematic for the officer, but also for the organization because it leads to increased sickness, absenteeism, and turnover.

Toward a structural remedy

So, the question arises, why are officers so burned out, and what might be done to remedy the problem? The current practice in most correctional organizations is to deal with burnout as a personal problem, teaching employees to engage in individual relaxation techniques when they get stressed out. And when employees get too burned out to do their job, they are directed to the (oftentimes stigmatized) employee assistance program. While these approaches might be helpful for meeting the effects or symptoms of stress, they do little to tackle its causes. A critical poststructuralist approach would suggest that these problematic pictures of burnout are fruitfully addressed by examining structural issues that exacerbate burnout and make it difficult to provide emotion labor to convicted criminals. Here, I point to four such issues: low prestige, correctional contradictions, feelings of powerlessness, and a lack of social support.

Battling societal discourses of low prestige

During the course of my research, it became very clear to me that correctional officers do extremely important but very difficult work. Unfortunately, officers tend to hold their job and themselves in fairly low esteem. Punishment is the most hidden part of the penal process, and facts about prison life are largely silent and invisible.[2] When information about jails and prisons is covered in the media at all, it is usually only when something goes wrong, such as an escape or sexual abuse. Correctional officers feel misunderstood and denigrated by a variety of audiences, even by other law enforcement professionals.[23] Officers said: "We are considered the dregs of the police department," "Police officers don't consider us to even be in their same category," and "Corrections is like the crappiest job in the criminal justice system." Many officers compared themselves to "babysitters" – a label that connotes low-status, feminized work.

Officers also dealt with the "contagion" effect.[24] The stigma associated with criminals rubs off onto workers, and correctional officers are sometimes regarded by outsiders to be not so different from the population they control. As one officer explained, "They think that we're part of the punishment, that we're uneducated, big mean people barking out orders. You know, I've even had people ask me if we *beat* people!" Another said, "In movies, they depict us as brutal, disrespectful to them. We hurt them, we beat them up."

This low regard also emanated from friends and neighbors who assumed correctional officers were stupid and that the job was easy and mindless. As one officer said, "A lot of times my family thinks I get paid for doing nothing. . . . They say, 'God, you get paid all that money and you watch TV and play video games all night.'" Another officer said her friends thought she got paid for "pushing buttons and doors are sliding and that's all there is to it."

Because of this public misunderstanding and denigration, officers are unable to go home and make sense of their jobs in the same ways as do other employees. Therefore, they oftentimes try to leave "work at work" but, by doing so, are prevented from making sense of their world in the same ways as are offered to people who work typical nine-to-five type jobs. Some correctional officers internalized the low opinions of their job and felt depressed about their work. Others felt emotionally frustrated and exhausted in the battle to continually combat negative opinions and misunderstandings, trying to prove to others (and themselves) that the job was indeed significant and moral.

Managing low status emotion labor in a tension-filled organizational environment

Officers also felt strain as they attempted to provide the expected emotion labor to inmates.[10] They were expected to be respectful by calling inmates by a title and opening their doors. While not hired as counselors, officers were also expected to be nurturing, listen to inmates, help them think through problems, and prepare them for life outside the barbed wire. Furthermore, they were expected to use their judgment, and be fair and flexible. Officers who strictly followed the rules were negatively labeled as "badge happy."

At the same time, officers received even stronger norms that they should never trust inmates, and that they should be tough, unaffected, and unemotional. Training manuals warned officers in no uncertain terms that they should not "get personal" with the inmates. Officers reiterated the importance of toughness in their informal talk, making fun of those who got "sucked in" by inmates. A good officer was described as "not a chocolate heart" – a metaphor that suggests that officers should not melt or be sweet-talked by inmates. Rather, good officers were described as strict, disciplined, and consistent. One officer proudly described herself as "just like a drill sergeant."

Most officers did an admirable job of holding up these emotion labor expectations, at least to some extent. However, officers (especially male officers) appeared more able to be tough than be nurturing – especially when they were required to engage in subservient activities such as serving food or picking up laundry. Similar to how I experienced tension on the cruise ship when my grandmother died, officers expressed conflict about negotiating contradictory emotion displays, such as being respectful, but suspicious, and nurturing, yet disciplined. While all organizational environments are marked with tension and contradiction, when discourses of power dictate two different emotional performances, employees evidence confusion about how best to attend to both expectations.[25]

In the case of correctional officers, larger societal discourses (as well as some discourses within the organization) suggest that men should be strong, tough, and better than a convicted criminal. However, in the moment, these officers expected to provide feminized service (e.g., laundry pick up, Kool-Aid delivery) to criminals – people that society has hidden away and marked as deviant. In these paradoxical situations, in which officers were expected to show low-status emotional fronts, they could become sarcastic, detached, and caustic. This difficulty associated with the emotion labor, though, is not necessarily caused by emotive dissonance (feeling one *real* emotion such as toughness and having to show another *fake* emotion like respect). In fact, when asked whether they had to fake emotions, correctional officers mentioned that acting like a jerk oftentimes required a fair amount of emotional effort. Rather, a critical poststructuralist approach suggests that it is difficult to perform a nonpreferred low-status emotion in the face of discourses of power that define the preferred officer as tough and "not a chocolate heart." It is no wonder that, in such situations, officers sometimes engaged in practices that would "accidentally" punish inmates – such as serving them the "bad" Kool-Aid.

It is also difficult to navigate contradictory emotion labor norms. Officers must respect inmates, but also be continually suspicious. They must nurture, yet be tough and maintain detachment. They must follow the rules, yet be flexible. Unfortunately, correctional officer training does little to nothing to address these dilemmas, or provide a space where administrators and employees can acknowledge their existence and try to work through them.

Past research suggests that, when confronted by contradiction, people usually respond with a combination of confusion, displeasure, and anxiety.[26] This is exacerbated when contradictions are not talked about and individuals feel as though they cannot "escape" or make sense of the contradiction through talk.[27] Jails and prisons are "total institutions"[5] and separated from most people's life paths. Furthermore, the routine and pace of prison life is so different from the "outside" that few correctional employees feel comfortable bringing their work home with them. As such, employees can find these contradictions suffocating and impossible to avoid. In these cases, employees can feel like they must be misunderstanding something, or that they are crazy. Indeed, past "family systems" theory research tells us that the emotional reactions of paranoia, literalism, and withdrawal (pictures of burnout among correctional officers) are common in children who are faced with paradoxical messages from a parent.[27]

So, we see that burnout can be connected to the contradictory atmosphere and larger societal discourses that paint correctional officers as low status. Furthermore, their work asks them to be respectful to alleged criminals. Therefore, when discourses of power ask for emotion labor that counters a nonpreferred identity, it becomes difficult.

Creating spaces for social support and communication about the contradictions

How can we help officers avoid framing organizational tensions as paradoxes and evidencing unhealthy emotional reactions? How might we provide a respite that could attend to issues of low prestige and the threatening nature of showing low-status emotions? My research suggests that correctional organizations should do more to acknowledge and help employees make sense of organizational tensions, and create spaces and places in which officers can have more camaraderie and social support from each other.

Currently, officers are largely left to make sense of the organizational tensions on their own. Communication theory tells us that talking with others about contradictions is one way to "escape" paradoxes.[27] Communication does not reconcile or eliminate contradiction – it just allows people to make sense of it and make it less of a mystery. Discussion allows people to realize they are not the only ones experiencing these tensions in their work. One way correctional administrators might approach inclusion of metacommunication about organizational tensions would be to introduce role playing of dilemmatic scenarios (e.g. wherein an officer must be nurturing, yet still watchful) in training sessions.[25] To encourage questioning and an acknowledgment of the complexities inherent to the job, scenarios could illustrate the range of ways that officers can deal with similar situations effectively. This approach could also encourage a discussion on the advantages and disadvantages of different paths of action.

As noted, officers often face disdain and lack of understanding about their work. This can be particularly problematic because research suggests that extra-organizational factors – such as the views of family, neighbors, and the community at large – are at least as important as intra-organizational factors in determining people's attitudes to their jobs.[28] Unfortunately, the regimen and isolation of correctional officer work exacerbates the potential utility of support from family or friends. Traditional external sources of social support may not ameliorate employee stress when these groups do not understand or have a negative perception of the work that employees do within total institutions. As we can see, officers have a difficult time trying to get social support from traditional sources such as friends and family. Unfortunately, officers also face obstacles to receiving social support within the correctional atmosphere.

Correctional officers work within an environment of wariness and mistrust. While they are hired to be watchers, they are ironically the most watched of any group in the penal system. They are gazed at, and thus disciplined, by inmates, administrators, and each other. Because of this structural feature of the job, officers largely mistrust management and sometimes each other as much as inmates. Officers said things like: "You can do a great job for ten years, then you screw up once and you get fired," "They can find out anything about you and that makes it very scary," and "Lots of times, management will trust an inmate's story over your own." One officer even discussed how this lack of trust permeated her dream world: She shared a dream in which she fell on some ice and, when she called for help, the sergeant on duty refused to come because he was in a meeting. Many officers also seemed wary of each other, and various shifts of employees were almost combative and competitive with one another.

In addition to this lack of trust, the mere structure of most correctional organizations makes it difficult, if not impossible, for employees to talk to each other. The only time they are all together is during the announcement-saturated, 15 minute pre-shift briefing. Furthermore, most officers work on their own as they watch over a certain housing module or pat-down inmates as they enter various areas of the facility. The fact that employees are largely cut off from one another is especially unfortunate considering that social support is considered to be most effective when it comes from like-minded others.

So, officers work in an environment of mistrust and face a situation in which they have difficulty gaining social support from their family and friends, their managers, and their co-workers. This is problematic in any job, but may be especially devastating when employees must do low-status "dirty work" work that threatens their identity.[23] In contrast to flight attendants, for instance, who are able to retreat briefly to the galley to collectively make fun of a rude passenger, or in contrast to paramedics, who can together decide it is not their fault if they cannot convince a whacked out drug addict to go to the hospital, correctional officers have few opportunities to commiserate with like-minded peers and re-create their self-image in preferred ways. This helps to explain why engaging in low-status emotion work can be so difficult among correctional officers – they are asked to be respectful and nurturing to clients that societal discourses paint as deviant and bad. And, then they face the additional burden of structural obstacles that make it all but impossible to rebuild a secured and preferred sense of self.

Given these challenges, correctional organizations need to consider how they could provide officers with more backstage, collective spaces for peer social support. This might include increasing the amount of time of spent in pre- and post-shift briefings or providing collective break times. Organizations should also consider ways officers might be able to work in pairs, at least for part of their shift. I found that when employees worked together, they were better able to provide the respectful and nurturing emotional performances required of their job. In such situations, officers were able to vent about the low-status performances and communicatively reconstruct themselves in preferred ways.

In contrast, when employees work without peer support, they often feel limited by the options available to deal with the paradoxes, emotion work, and low prestige that characterize their everyday work. First, and most common, they can absorb and internalize the identity threats of their work, and process them on their own. However, my data suggest that, over time, doing so can deteriorate employees' sense of self-worth, lead to a cold dismissive mentality, and ultimately result in burnout. Another (problematic) option is for officers to garner social support from the only other audience available to them – inmates. Of course, confiding in inmates is completely against the rules and can result in costly repercussions; when officers turn to inmates for social support, they are more liable to get sucked in by inappropriate relations or ruses. In turn, the organization may be faced with lawsuits, officer hearings, and increased turnover. Given these costs, it makes sense to consider creative organizational changes that would allow officers to more often work with one another.

Providing opportunities for power

Another issue that exacerbates challenges with burnout and emotion labor is officers' feelings of powerlessness. As mentioned, officers face societal discourses that paint their job, and correctional institutions in general, in a negative way. Given that officers talk about themselves as "glorified babysitters," the "scum of law enforcement," "maids," and "camp counselors," it is clear that many of them have internalized the idea that they hold low-status, low-power positions. This is only worsened by the ways internal structures preclude officers from feeling powerful in their work environment.

While we might presume officers have legitimate power due to their formal position and their badge, this is not necessarily the case. Although inmates agree with officers' rights to give orders, inmates generally don't feel an obligation to obey.[29] Furthermore, officers oftentimes feel as though their ideas are not heard or appreciated by managers. As one said:

> I think your frustration comes out when you . . . see that there might be a better way to do it. You present it, and it's like, "You fool, what do you mean 'a round wheel'? We've been using the square wheel for years. Are you crazy?" You're hated for bringing it up.

Second, despite the brutality portrayed in sensationalized, Hollywood depictions of prisons and jails, today's penal institutions do not condone punitive (or punishment) correctional philosophies.[30] In moving toward "kinder and gentler" correctional approaches, however, officers have lost punishment and coercive power. One officer discussed his frustration with the lack of coercive power. He summed up the worst part of the job, saying:

> Dealing with some of the assholes and not being able to strike back . . . If I don't do anything, then I look like an idiot, and if I *do* do something, then I'm a badge-heavy jerk who just wants to beat people up. That's not me and sometimes you just need to swallow whatever they're giving you and you've got to take it and just say, "you son of a bitch," and there's nothing you can do. That's very, very frustrating.

Officers not only are limited in their power to punish. They also have very little power to reward inmates. Correctional administrators and a faceless "system" make decisions about inmate classification, privileges, and early release. As such, officers often feel as though they serve merely as messengers and enforcers.

At the same time, officers feel quite frustrated with their inability to enforce rules. For example, an officer caught an inmate with contraband tobacco in her cell, but because he forgot to write her cell number on the write-up form, the bust was thrown out by management. This officer expressed irritation saying, "Why bother with it? If they're going to throw it out for some thing like this, you know, when we found the tobacco right on her, what is going to get busted?" Another explained, "It's frustrating because you write them up and then they just let it go. And then the inmates just laugh at you . . . Why should I care? But then that's not good for us to get . . . lax in our work." For this officer, there was no easy answer – he did not want to be lax, but he also did not like feeling embarrassed and powerless when his write-ups were thrown out.

Furthermore, officers are told they are not inmate counselors and should not act as experts or give advice to inmates. This strips away from officers any potential feelings of power and satisfaction that come from being an authority or specialist. Indeed, a number of the correctional officers took the job because they hoped to make a difference, and became disillusioned when they learned that they were not formally allowed to give advice. Furthermore, because inmates live in the institution 24/7, and officers cycle in and out during three shifts, inmates often know more about the (ever-changing) rules and regulations of the institution than do officers. As such, officers also have very little expert power.[29]

Last, let's look at referent power granted based on respect and admiration. My data supported past research that suggests that officers who are fair and evenhanded in their relations with inmates, who display respect, and fulfill their promises do garner some respect. However, because officers are *expected* to be respectful to inmates, doing so no longer necessarily triggers surprise, admiration, or affinity, thus mitigating it as a space for referent power.

To address correctional officers' feelings of powerlessness, correctional administrators could consider several different practices. First, from a critical poststructuralist viewpoint, it is important to remember that power is a fluid process, not a product. From this point of view, administrators need not believe that by creating organizational practices that provide officers with more feelings of power they must give away their own power. For instance, officers would likely feel more expert if administrators simply provided explanations of rule changes and why, for example, a particular inmate was not punished for a certain offense. This would allow officers to at least seem "in the know" when they had to enforce different policies. Administrators might also consider placing several correctional officers on administrative boards – if nothing else, so inmates feel as though officers do have a say in creating rules. As it stands, officers' relative feelings of powerlessness lend themselves to decreased respect from inmates and officers feeling burnout and a lack of pride in the job.

Conclusion

In this chapter, I have explained the ways that burnout and the pain of emotion labor are usually treated as individual employee problems that workers should try to tackle on their own. Typical "cures" usually include meditation, muscle relaxation, biofeedback, and siphoning off the "sick" employees to employee assistance programs. While examining burnout and stress as individual problems may be helpful in some ways, it is problematic considering that EAPs are oftentimes stigmatized by workers and thus are underutilized. Furthermore, focusing on the individual obscures the ways stress and burnout are largely due to organization-wide practices and norms. In contrast, a critical approach sheds light on larger discourses of power and structural issues that exacerbate emotion labor and burnout. By taking such an approach, organizations are better able to address some of the root causes of employee stress and burnout.

As illustrated in this case study, correctional officers face several structural issues connected to burnout. They face societal discourses of low prestige that denigrate correctional institutions. They also work in total institutions, marked with contradictory organizational norms; they are asked to do low-status service work for convicted criminals, feel powerless, and face significant challenges in garnering social support. These issues help explain why so many officers feel alienated, depressed, perplexed, and burned out with their work. Clearly, officers themselves have very little control over these matters. They cannot, for instance, solve structural contradictions or low prestige by going home and taking a hot bath, or by talking it out with an employee assistance counselor. However, the good news is that, by identifying structural concerns that contribute to burnout, administrators and societies can begin to address ways that institutions might be changed so that their employees could have more fulfilling and functional jobs. Whether it be a correctional institution or cruise ship, it is important to recognize that there are a number of organizational practices that can be shifted in order to help employees feel better and less burned out in their work. These include providing space for like-minded peer employees to communicatively construct a preferred identity, engaging in practices that educate clients and outsiders as to the worth and morality of employee work, and acknowledging and helping employees make sense of the tensions that mark their organizational endeavors.

This case also extends theoretical understandings of emotion in organizations. A critical approach suggests that the difficulty of performing emotion is largely based on societal and organizational discourses of power. Emotion norms are easier to uphold when they prescribe emotions that discourses condone as part of employees' preferred identity. This is why emotion labor can be fun and electrifying in some situations (e.g. when officers get to act tough around inmates), and degrading, alienating, and miserable in other situations (e.g. when officers have to engage in low-status, feminized activities like serving Kool-Aid). Faking low-status emotions that contrast with a preferred identity is much more difficult than feigning those that paint an employee in ways that align with dominant organizational discourses. Furthermore, members can more easily feign low-status emotions when they can also interact with one another backstage and rebuild their identity through interaction with their peers.

I believe there is still much to explore in regard to how larger societal and organizational discourses affect burnout and emotion labor. A critical poststructuralist viewpoint suggests that discourses of power are central to the ways that identity and emotion are constructed, constrained, and interpreted. Indeed, employees' "feelings and emotions . . . are tied to the patterns, tensions, and contradictions of the varied role, power, and structural arrangements."[31] Identifying and making sense of these structural challenges is an important first step in moving toward transformation and disrupting organizational practices that constrain employees' identities in emotionally unhealthy ways.

References

1. Thomas, J. (1993) *Doing Critical Ethnography*. Newbury Park, CA: Sage.
2. Foucault, M. (1977) *Discipline and Punish: The Birth of the Prison*. New York: Vintage Books.
3. Tracy, S. J. and Tracy, K. (1998) Emotion labor at 911: A case study and theoretical critique, *Journal of Applied Communication Research*, 26, 390–411.
4. Tracy, S. J. (2000) Becoming a character for commerce: Emotion labor, self subordination and discursive construction of identity in a total institution, *Management Communication Quarterly*, 14, 90–128.
5. Goffman, E. (1961) *Asylums*. Garden City, NJ: Anchor Books.
6. Deetz, S. (1998) Discursive formations, strategized subordination and self-surveillance. In McKinley, A. and Starkey, K. (eds) *Foucault, Management and Organizational Theory*. London: Sage, 151–72.
7. Hochschild, A. R. (1983) *The Managed Heart: Commercialization of Human Feelings*. Berkeley: University of California Press.
8. Fineman, S. (2006) Emotion and organizing. In Clegg, S. R., Hardy, C., Lawrence, T., and Nord, W. (eds) *The Sage Handbook of Organizational Studies*. London: Sage, 675–700.
9. Miller, K. (2002) The experience of emotion in the workplace: Professing in the midst of tragedy, *Management Communication Quarterly*, 15, 571–600.

10. Tracy, S. J. (2005) Locking up emotion: Moving beyond dissonance for understanding emotion labor discomfort, *Communication Monographs*, 72, 261–83.

11. Shuler, S. and Sypher, B. D. (2000) Seeking emotional labor: When managing the heart enhances the work experience, *Management Communication Quarterly*, 14, 50–89.

12. Wharton, A. S. (1999) The psychosocial consequences of emotional labor, *Annals of the American Academy of Political and Social Science*, 561, 158–76.

13. Rafaeli, A. and Sutton, R. I. (1987) The expression of emotion as part of the work role, *Academy of Management Review*, 12, 23–37.

14. Waldron, V. R. (1994) Once more, with feeling: Reconsidering the role of emotion in work. In Deetz, S. A. (ed.) *Communication Yearbook*, 17, 388–416.

15. Tracy, S. J. and Trethewey, A. (2005) Fracturing the real-self–fake-self dichotomy: Moving toward "crystallized" organizational identities, *Communication Theory*, 15, 168–95.

16. Mumby, D. K. and Putnam, L. L. (1992) The politics of emotion: A feminist reading of bounded emotionality, *Academy of Management Review*, 17, 465–86.

17. Maslach, C. (1982) *Burnout: The Cost of Caring*. Englewood Cliffs, NJ: Prentice Hall.

18. Newton, T. (1995) *"Managing" Stress: Emotion and Power at Work*. Thousand Oaks, CA: Sage.

19. Fineman, S. (1993) An emotion agenda. In Fineman, S. (ed.) *Emotion in organizations*. London: Sage, 216–24.

20. Tracy, S. J. (2004) The construction of correctional officers: Layers of emotionality behind bars, *Qualitative Inquiry*, 10, 509–33.

21. Huckabee, R. B. (1992) Stress in corrections: An overview of the issues, *Journal of Criminal Justice*, 20, 479–86.

22. Cheek, F. E. (1984) *Stress Management for Correctional Officers and their Families*. College Park, MD: American Correctional Association.

23. Tracy, S. J. and Scott, C. (2006) Sexuality, masculinity and taint management among firefighters and correctional officers: Getting down and dirty with "America's heroes" and the "scum of law enforcement," *Management Communication Quarterly*, 20, 6–38.

24. Brodsky, C. M. (1982) Work stress in correctional institutions, *Journal of Jail Health*, 2, 74–102.

25. Tracy, S. J. (2004) Dialectic, contradiction, or double bind? Analyzing and theorizing employee reactions to organizational tensions, *Journal of Applied Communication Research*, 32, 119–46.

26. Putnam, L. L. (1986) Contradictions and paradoxes in organizations. In Thayer, L. (ed.) *Organization-Communication: Emerging Perspectives*, Vol. 1. Norwood, NJ: Ablex, 151–67.

27. Watzlawick, P., Beavin, J. H., and Jackson, D. D. (1967) *Pragmatics of Human Communication: A Study of Interactional Patterns, Pathologies and Paradoxes*. New York: W. W. Norton & Company.

28. Drory, A. and Shamir, B. (1988) Effects of organizational and life variables on job satisfaction and burnout, *Group and Organization Studies*, 13, 441–55.

29. Hepburn, J. R. (1985) The exercise of power in coercive organizations: A study of prison guards, *Criminology*, 23, 145–64.

30. Schlosser, E. (1998) The prison-industrial complex, *The Atlantic Monthly*, 282 (6), 51–77.

31. Fineman, S. and Sturdy, A. (1999) The emotions of control: A qualitative study of environmental regulation, *Human Relations*, 52, 643.

CHAPTER 4

CRISIS WORK

Rape Work: Emotional Dilemmas in Work With Victims

Patricia Yancey Martin, Douglas Schrock, Margaret Leaf, and Carmen Von Rohr

This chapter explores how *rape workers* – people whose job requires work with rape victims or their cases[1] – experience emotions due to the obligations of their jobs and the contexts in which they work. Just as jobs are located in organizations, organizations are located in *spatially extensive* and *temporally persisting* institutions that provide them with missions, legitimacy, resources, and obligations.[2–4] In the US, most rape work is performed by people situated in one of three institutions (legal, medical, and gender), five organizations (law enforcement, prosecution, the courts, hospitals, and rape crisis centers), and nine occupations (police officer, victim advocate, nurse, physician, rape crisis worker, prosecutor, defense attorney, judge, and juror).[1] This chapter describes the *emotion culture* of these institutions, organizations, and occupations to assess how their feeling and display rules affect rape workers. Its aim is to identify the problematic emotions that workers feel when performing rape work and to show how they are produced by work conditions and dynamics.

One arena where rape work is done is the *legal institution.* This institution legitimates law enforcement, prosecutors, judges, defense attorneys, and jurors to investigate rapes, arrest rapists, sentence rapists, question victims, prosecute rapists, file legal charges, and judge rapists' guilt. The *medical institution* legitimates physicians and nurses to treat injured and sick "patients" and to examine, touch, and remove evidence from the bodies of rape victims. Finally, the *gender institution* legitimates rape crisis centers to mobilize public opinion and action against rape, pressure mainstream organizations (those embedded in the legal and medical institutions) to improve and make rape victims' welfare a top priority.[i] Organizations embedded in the legal and medical institutions have many goals and obligations whereas rape crisis centers, stemming from the *second wave women's movement,* focus narrowly on rape.[5] Rape crisis centers' focus on rape cases and victims is an institutional product, as is mainstream organizations' relative inattention to rape and victims.[ii]

Rape – the forcible perpetration of sexual violence by one person against another without the latter's consent – is emotionally unsavory and discomfiting to all who hear about it, much less experience it. Yet, it is not uncommon. We hear many reports of gang rapes in war-torn nations and of celebrities who rape admiring fans. However, most rapes are committed by people the victims know, not strangers who jump out of bushes in the dead of night, nor even military personnel or celebrities. For many reasons, knowing the true scope of rape of even one nation is difficult. The most reliable data in the US come from police departments that report the annual number of reported forcible sexual assaults to the Federal Bureau of Investigation. Between 1980 and 2000, these data show the US rape rate ranging from 37 per 100,000 inhabitants in 1980, to 41 in 1990, to 32 in 2000.[6] Thus, despite a modest decrease, rape remains pervasive. Furthermore, although the US reports more rapes than its industrialized counterparts, the rates for them are also high. For example, in 2003, the US rate was 32 per 100,000, while rates for England were 25, France 17, Austria 15, and Ireland 12.[7]

Despite the accomplishments of rape crisis centers and the advancement of legislation spurred by the second wave women's movement, rape remains underreported and all too prevalent. The situation is extreme in many parts of the developing world, where protective legislation and rape crisis centers are nonexistent. Especially alarming is the predicament of women in cultures characterized by severe oppression. Bride burning, honor killings, sexual trafficking, and virginity examinations are only a few of the crimes routinely perpetrated against women in such societies.

Most known rapists are men and the vast majority of victims are women or girls. The conflation of these patterns with myths about rape and stereotypes about women, men, and sexuality prompts a shift in blame away from rapists to victims, with a routine focus on what victims do to *cause* themselves to be raped. Many women fear men as potential rapists[8] and men, in turn, feel defensive about women's fear of them. In work settings, where gender is allegedly irrelevant,[9,10] our evidence suggests that gender stereotypes and beliefs affect how rapists and victims are viewed and treated and how rape work is done. Emotions associated with gender norms and stereotypes affect who does which kinds of work and how they perform and react when doing it.

The organizations and occupations in our study are organized in accord with gender.[1,11,12] That is, top officials in police departments, prosecutors' offices, and court settings are predominantly men and most lower-level workers (e.g., support staff) are women. Rape crisis centers are, as a rule, women-only organizations. In police departments, most "sworn" or armed positions are occupied by men and most victim advocate positions by women. Most prosecutors are men and most support workers, including victim advocates, are women. Most judges are men as are most defense attorneys. In hospitals, most physicians are men and most nurses are women. In short, ultimate authority in most rape work settings is wielded by men.[1:ch.2] While these conditions need not produce particular outcomes, their pervasiveness in interactions suggests that where gender is present, it often has an impact.[13] Given rape's gendered character, and the gendered composition of rape work organizations and occupations, expectations associated with gender compete with alleged "gender-free bureaucracy" as a basis for organizing rape work, including its emotional features.[14]

Data for this study were collected through interviews with over 200 rape workers employed by 130 organizations in Florida between 1983 and 2004.[1] The early project, which addressed organizational and community influences on workers' practices and perceptions, paid little attention to the emotional aspects of rape work. After encountering strong emotional reactions – and nonreactions – from our informants, additional interviews were done to explore workers' emotional experiences and views of victims' emotions.

Organizations and Emotion Cultures

Emotion scholars refer to *emotion culture* as "widely held views about how people in a society should express and interpret situated emotions."[15] Views about emotions are conveyed through "language, rituals, art forms" and similar means.[16] We suggest that organizations, like societies, have *emotion cultures* that consist of language, rituals, and meaning systems, including rules about the feelings workers should, and should not, feel and display. Barbalet[17] and Martin[18] discuss organizations' *emotion climate*. For example, service workers are routinely told to avoid displaying anger at work because it risks losing customer loyalty and/or profits.[19–21] Nurses and police officers are told to display caring, concern, and diplomacy toward patients and crime victims for purposes of being helpful and/or to maintain positive relations with the public.[22] Although rules instruct workers about the feelings they *should* have and display to victims (and others), rape workers regularly experience and sometimes display proscribed emotions. For instance, nurses and police officers often feel fear, rage, disgust, sadness, and anxiety – emotions that are difficult to manage and that can hinder effectiveness.

An organization's emotion culture specifies particular activities and practices as well as feeling and display rules for its members and an *emotional discourse* that accounts for its rules and activities. An organization's emotional discourse "makes sense" of emotional requirements. Yet, as Martin and Powell[23] note, some organizational rules contradict others and, even when they are consistent, individual workers may interpret them differently. As a result, conflicting feelings and emotional encounters between workers and their clients, and among workers, are not unusual. In short, the emotion cultures of organizations routinely foster conflicts and also fail to provide their workers with the means for managing them.[24] Workers thus routinely experience emotional dilemmas. When their expectations or obligations are frustrated, they may feel "forbidden" emotions that they are unable to manage.

An organization's emotion culture is often conflated with workers' gender.[10,13,25,26] That is, women regularly do more emotion work than men, due to the jobs they hold and to gender-related norms and stereotypes that frame women as "emotional experts," particularly when upsetting and/or softer emotions are involved.[11,27,28] Some emotions are acceptable in men but forbidden to women (e.g. anger and aggression), while other emotions are allowed in women but are strongly disapproved of in men (e.g. giggling and crying). An example of this dynamic is reported by Heimer and Stevens[29] in intensive healthcare units where physicians, most of whom were men, delegated work with distraught family members to social workers, most of whom were women. Susan Martin[11] found that male police officers' "felt need [sic] to be emotionally constrained" prompted them to transfer tasks to women when they thought they might evoke "soft emotions" like sadness or empathy. Sucher[30] found similar patterns among victim advocates in police departments and prosecution offices and Martin[13] documented them among rape workers generally. Based on this background, we address how the institution of gender[4] shapes the emotions of rape workers.

Emotion Cultures and Rape Work

In general, medical and legal organizations prize rationality and instrumentality, including emotional distance between workers and "clients." As a result, rape workers in these institutions are required to display a "caring manner" but not to feel genuine warmth or compassion toward victims. Rape crisis staff, in contrast, are instructed to feel and express genuine warmth and compassion.[1] Conflicts regularly arise when workers with these differing orientations encounter each other. Conflicts also develop when an individual worker is told to, at once, follow rules that require rational instrumentality *and* emotional closeness. This dilemma occurs regularly for victim advocates in law enforcement and prosecution settings, as we describe shortly.

We now review the emotion cultures of organizations in three institutional arenas to show their effects on rape workers and victims.

The legal institution: organizations, jobs, and emotion culture

The legal institution has many goals and obligations – from questioning victims to judging rapists' guilt. As far as the victim is concerned, legal-justice organizations are primarily interested in her credibility as a witness to a crime, and less interested in her emotional, psychological, and physical well-being as a victim. Ultimately, the organizational obligations, institutional frames, and emotion culture of the legal institution encourage its workers to collaborate with rapists and settle cheap rather than to help victims recover and obtain justice.[1]

Dilemma: victim or witness?
Legal workers face a situational dilemma in work with rape victims that stems from the victim of the crime also being the (usually only) witness to the crime. Cultural expectations for these statuses differ sharply. "Good victims" are framed as deserving sympathy[31] while "good witnesses" are framed as needing to provide a coherent, logical, credible account of their experience.[1] Rape victims may be problematic on both counts. As Clark[32] notes, rape victims are often presumed to have prompted their attack, thus their status as good victims is in question. A good witness is one who provides an account that helps legal officials *win*. Koss[33] concludes that rape victims need to be believed and supported, not challenged and forced to recount their story again and again. Rape victims need acceptance while rape witnesses need to provide an account that is instrumentally useful.[34]

Legal institution discourse thus orients rape workers to collect and preserve evidence, "build cases," prove cases, defend the accused, and judge the accused. It does not orient them to view and treat rape victims primarily as victims, at least after initial encounters. Having victim and witness in the same person creates emotional dilemmas for rape workers. Feeling and display rules appropriate for interacting with a victim – sympathy, gentleness, empathy – contradict those appropriate for interacting with a witness – skepticism, neutral affect, emotional distance. The emotional dilemmas stemming from this condition are now reviewed for six categories of legal institution workers.

Law enforcement officers

Most legal work on rape cases is done by law enforcement employees. As Campbell et al.[35] report, most victims never get their day in court. One reason is that only a minority of cases reported to the police go beyond the reporting stage; that is, they are not forwarded to the prosecutor for legal processing.[iii] Police officers' obligations prompt them to focus on determining probable cause, investigating reports of rape, making arrests, and "building good cases," and the feeling and display rules of law enforcement organizations prompt them, in a stereotypically masculine way,[26] to be emotionally inexpressive.

While embedded in an emotional discourse that centers on rationality and a charge to collect and protect evidence, police officers are regularly confronted with emotionally evocative situations. Law enforcement personnel spend substantial time with rape victims, thus having opportunity to observe the variety of forms that rape takes, the variety of victims subjected to it, and the range of victims' reactions. Typically, they encounter victims shortly after the rape while they [victims] are upset, vulnerable, in shock, or out of control. Hands-on experience with victims of all ages shows them that rape is not romance that has got out of hand but a violent action involving domination.[36] And, yet, their emotional reactions to rape victims are often ambivalent.

Under such conditions, it is not surprising that police officers have difficulty remaining calm and somewhat distant when doing rape work. Some experience strong feelings of sympathy, especially toward victims they define as "100%" or "real." When they frame a victim as someone who deserves empathy and support, they may feel affection or pity and a desire to "exact revenge" on a victim's behalf. Even when an agency's feeling rules proscribe such emotions, police officers work in situations that regularly evoke strong yet institutionally unsupported emotions. In other words, law enforcement's emotion culture is contradictory. When the conditions of work induce feelings that are forbidden by organizational feeling rules, emotional dilemmas arise.

Organizational discourse that emphasizes rationality and evidence provides a way for officers to "cut off" or constrain compassion for victims and focus on the instrumental tasks of collecting evidence, protecting the scene of the crime, finding a suspect, and so forth. Yet even this work and discourse can evoke emotional dilemmas. When officers perceive victims as reluctant to answer questions or as not telling the whole truth they may become angry. An institutional discourse that orients them to define victims as witnesses, rather than as survivors of traumatic violence, can protect them from feeling empathy while making them vulnerable to emotional outbursts, including anger and rage, which they are told to avoid. A rape crisis worker describes this dynamic:

> What I've seen over and over again . . . especially in a hospital setting when I'm going there to provide outreach to someone who has just been raped and [she] may be flip-flopping on whether to report. I see the law enforcement officers say this and the victims say that and it just gets harder and harder for them to communicate. . . . More than once I've said [to the police officer], "OK, whoa! Let's leave the room and just talk for a minute. . . . [T]here is all of this anger and all of this stuff that is going on and no one has any idea of what she wants at that point. . . . But pushing doesn't get you anywhere." [Q: Have you observed a police officer argue with a victim?] Yes. [Q: About what?] *Like over whether or not she was being cooperative* [emphasis hers]. I've heard police officers say things like, "You know I had to get out of bed in the middle of the night to come here to the hospital." While she was sort of flip-flopping on, "I don't know if I can talk to you right now" sort of thing . . . "I don't know if I want to do this." (Rape crisis worker, white woman, age 28)

Organizational discourse and obligations can thus lead police officers to act in ways that make it difficult to gain information about the rape and create miscommunication. Victims may be "uncooperative" in part because of organizational obligations and discourse that shape officers' practices. Ironically, law enforcement's emotion culture may prompt officers' anger, which has an unintended consequence of undermining their ability to achieve organizationally mandated goals – that is, gaining the cooperation of victims to "build a good case."

Victim advocates

Victim advocacy (also called victim-witness-advocacy) is a fast-growing occupation in US police departments and prosecution offices. Victim advocates' mandate is to help police officials and criminal prosecutors manage crime victims and develop "winning" cases. They perform many emotionally intense tasks, such as informing parents of the death of a child, calming children who witness domestic violence or murders, helping victims of domestic violence escape, and comforting rape victims. The creation of this occupation represents a division of emotional labor in legal organizations. Workers who do this job are nearly all women, thus illustrating one way that the emotion cultures of legal institutions are gendered. As a rule, *women* victim advocates have the obligation to "absorb" crime victims' emotions, thus providing emotional protection to *men* police officers and prosecutors.[13,30] Despite considerable "sex integration" in many US jobs, over 80 percent of uniformed (or higher ranking) law enforcement officers and of criminal prosecutors continue to be men.[37] Weed[38] and Sucher[30] claim that 95 percent or more of victim advocates are women.

While victim advocates provide "emotional first aid" to victims, as one interviewee said, they work within a legal institution that requires them to help police and prosecutors develop and win cases. They spend much of their time comforting and soothing victims, yet their chief instrumental assignment is to gain victims' cooperation to "build a good case." Victim advocates walk an emotional tightrope when told to genuinely care about rape victims *and* to assure their cooperation and effectiveness as witnesses. They can become emotionally wrapped up in some victims' trauma, yet they must manage both victims and themselves. Also, they must deal with officers who prefer to remain emotionally distant and whose actions are constrained by bureaucratic rules. The following quote illustrates victim advocates' emotional dilemma with regard to trying to "bridge the gap" between emotionally distraught victims and presumably "nonemotional" legal system workers.

> I think bridging the gap between social work and law enforcement can be difficult at times. . . . Even though we're here to serve the victims and the community, we have different goals, different missions. There are times we'll get into it with some of the investigators because we feel very passionate about something, whereas they're not quite sure. I mean, like when they're doing an investigation and they have certain things to meet to get a warrant for an arrest . . . [sometimes] it [a case] just doesn't meet their standards of the law . . . whereas we see the victim and all the things that this person's gone through and the frustration . . . and the, you know, not getting the system to work for them. We're advocating all that for the person to have and it still doesn't work. That gets very frustrating at times.

Because of their duty to absorb rape victims' emotions, victim advocates are often moved by victims' trauma and become more deeply committed to obtaining justice for them. But absorbing victims' emotions, as the above quote shows, also sets them up to become angry and frustrated with officers, as well as the entire legal institution, when justice is thwarted.

In a somewhat contradictory fashion, legal institution discourse sets up victim advocates to experience anger and resentment toward any "victim" they believe is less than "100%" – that is, who is not being truthful. For example, one advocate described her feelings of outrage when working with a victim whom she thought was lying. The quote shows (her belief) that she never stopped displaying nurturance and sweetness, even though she felt intense anger.

> There was a rape victim who came in who wasn't really raped. And I got very angry about it because I was, like, you know, you're hurting so many women by doing this, by claiming rape when it was not rape. And I got very angry and the whole time I was just very nurturing towards her, very sweet, and I got out of there and said, "Jane [her supervisor], I can't believe she would do something like this," and I was so angry. . . . I was very angry about it and I had to do some serious processing [sic]. I'd talk about it and it would come up again and again. . . . I asked Jane, "How do you deal with this? How do you deal with these people who are lying about this? And you've got women who are being [truly] raped all the time." (Victim advocate intern, white woman, age 22)

Here we see how victim advocates' complex obligations – to be nurturing toward victims and help legal officials build cases – can conflict with each other. More specifically, when victims appear unable to help build "a good case," victim advocates question their claims to victim status,[31] which evokes the advocates' anger. But expressing anger is a violation of the feeling rules that victim advocates are instructed to follow. They are thus forced to hide those emotions when interacting with women whom they define as nonvictims.

Prosecution

Prosecutors spend substantial time on the rape cases they accept for prosecution. They accept few cases and the ones they choose are selected based on the odds of "winning"[1] – that is, they "cream" the best cases. Once they accept a case, they have the ability to interview victims in their offices and let them tell their story in unfettered, unstructured ways. And yet, prosecutors' interpretations of victims' accounts are filtered through the legal institutions' discourse, which shapes their feelings and reactions. That is, prosecutors' compassion is conditional upon rape victims' ability to present themselves in ways that presumably will sway a judge and jury. They define the feeling rules that victims must follow in order to get their full commitment and effort.

Prosecutors are most likely to feel good about victims who can help with their cases or, as one prosecutor said, "have moxie."

> The victim must be enraged . . . mad at her assailant . . . furious at what he did to her. If she has any guilt, we have to get that out [of her]. She has to let that go. She has to feel that this is an awful . . . an outrageous thing that has been done to her. If she has doubts, if she hesitates or looks guilty, the jury picks this up. . . . This girl [a 19-year-old who was recently raped] has moxie. She is mad and she wants to put this guy in jail. She is all right. . . . The victim must be sure of herself, almost cocky with the defense attorney, and [able to] hold her own under grueling questioning. She has to be a *good witness*. (Assistant state attorney, white man, age 58)

As this prosecutor implied, prosecutors let victims know that they cannot express guilt and must express righteous indignation at their rapists. Prosecutors' affirmation and own positive emotional expressions in response to such displays, regardless of their intentions, teaches victims how to express emotions that will gain prosecutors' support.

While prosecutors' own emotional well-being is dependent on victims' righteous indignation, the rational discourse of legal institutions nonetheless demands logically assembled evidence to make a winning case. As a result, if victims cannot produce a rational and convincing victimization story, the prosecutor may frame them as "bad victims" and they themselves get righteously indignant. A former prosecution office advocate described this dynamic:

> I used to be a victim advocate with the state attorney's office. I interned there for a year and then they hired me [in the] summer before graduate school for about three or four months. *I know they get very angry at victims.* I couldn't work there. I think there is sort of this false sense of victims trying to manipulate people in the system. My reading is that it is false. I think [prosecutors] read people's needs, people's pain . . . what people are going through as some sort of manipulation of them or the system, which I think is just false. Maybe that is where that anger comes from. [T]hey need that [a rational, coherent story] and so when they aren't getting that it's like you are a *"bad victim."* (Rape crisis center worker, white woman, age 28 (our emphasis))

Prosecutors thus use the rational discourse of legal institutions to negatively judge victims' flawed accounts of rape, which, in turn, evokes their anger towards victims.

Expressing such anger, even if merely in the guise of a skeptical comment, likely also teaches victims how they are supposed to construct their rape stories. It thus appears that the victims are the ones being manipulated in such cases.

The prosecutor's role in preparing victims for trial involves not only trying to shape how victims construct stories but also how they deal with defense attorneys' emotionally disturbing questions. Such work requires prosecutors to suspend compassion for victims to "toughen them up." As one prosecutor said:

> Our job is to prosecute, if at all possible. We can't be emotional. We would be hard-hearted bastards if it [the victim's vulnerability] didn't affect us but we have to stay objective. We have to prepare the woman for what is to come in court. Sometimes this makes it seem as though we are being unnecessarily rough and uncaring but she has to be prepared for how the defense attorney is going to treat her; how they will drag in every piece of dirt they can find . . . Sometimes the victim advocates get on our case because they think we are being too rough with the victims. We aren't trying to be rough. We just need to get them ready for the defense attorney who's going to ask questions like, "Isn't it true you wanted it?" or "Did you have an orgasm?" (Assistant prosecutor, white man, age 62)

The gendered emotion culture of prosecution offices not only involves delegating nurturing interpersonal emotion work to women victim advocates but also delegating to men prosecutors the job of performing confrontational or hostile emotion work with victims. Thus, in contrast to victim advocates who are supposed to feel empathy for victims, prosecutors are supposed to abide by a feeling rule that in effect proscribes empathy. For example, when asked if "prosecutors become emotionally involved with the victims," one victim advocate responded:

> No . . . they don't. They can't afford to. They are supposed to stay objective and concentrate on the victim so we can help them. They don't become personally that involved. It's not really their job. And they wouldn't be very good at their job if they did. [Q: So the victim advocates help them?] In a way. They tell us to tell the victim something or find out something. So we're the ones always in touch. Their job is to look at the facts and see what they have and prosecute. (Victim advocate, white woman, age 46)

While there is an implicit rule against feeling empathy with victims for prosecutors, they nonetheless have such feelings, although they rarely talk about them. Prosecutors believe rape cases cause burnout due to "emotionally volatile" victims and the low odds of "winning." One public defender who said rape cases are an emotional burden alleged that a sexual assault unit was dissolved because the work was too "exhausting and draining" for the prosecutors. Many prosecutors expressed a preference for taking on other types of cases, including murder, because they are less emotionally demanding. As one prosecutor noted:

> I prefer homicide because the victim is already dead. The emotional toll of dealing with the case is much less. Lots of prosecutors don't like sexual battery cases because of the emotions. (Assistant prosecutor, white woman, age 35)

Defense attorneys, judges, and jurors

To a considerable extent, defense attorneys, judges, and jurors view rape victims in the abstract, based on assumptions, myths, and generalized conceptions of rape and rape victims. They have few opportunities to become acquainted with a victim because they are located far away "in the system." For a rape case to reach them, a victim must have reported (and, typically, cooperated in developing) the case, a rapist must have been apprehended, and a prosecutor must have filed criminal charges. Even then, their contact with victims is constrained. Judges, defense attorneys, and jurors cannot talk with a rape victim outside the court/legal context unless she agrees; thus, there is no opportunity for her to tell her story, unchallenged, as she wants to tell it.[39]

As a result of this structure, attorneys, judges, and juries rarely grasp the subjective experience of rape victims. To illustrate, a public defender sees no difference in being raped versus robbed:

> I don't see rape cases [as] any different than any other case. We have all kinds of crimes, all kinds of victims. It's my job to make the state prove its case. . . . I don't want anybody to be a victim of a crime but I also don't think anyone should be singled out because of the *type* of crime. All the special attention sexual assault victims and spouse abuse get these days is not right when there are other equally harmed victims, like robbery, that don't get as much attention. Sexual battery, crack, and spouse abuse are the in-crimes right now. (Assistant public defender, white man, age 43 (emphasis his))

Judges often appear to accept rape myths, such as rape is romance gone awry. Some accuse victims of leading on a man or not being pretty enough to be raped.[1] Like defense attorneys, they see rape cases as like any other case and, consequently, profess few positive emotions toward victims. Most are emotionally indifferent although some are hostile, alleging that rape victims get special treatment. As Maryland Judge Bollinger said, a young woman raped by her supervisor from work while passed out "led him on" in an inappropriate way, thereby "facilitating" her rape, and a Florida judge said that a 50-year-old woman who was raped repeatedly by a much younger man was too ugly to be raped. Some of this apparent misconstruction is prompted by a legal system that is oriented to protecting the rights of the accused, while giving minimal attention to the rights of victims. In addition, because most judges are men and have experienced little if any fear of rape, they are less likely to understand rape or construct victims empathetically.[40] Thus their work conditions and gendered biographies promote, at best, emotional indifference toward rape victims.

The medical institution: organizations, jobs, and emotion culture

Most US communities require medical professionals and hospital emergency departments to examine anyone who reports being raped. In the usual case, a law enforcement officer drives a victim to the hospital where a rape examination ("exam") is conducted by a nurse and/or physician.[1,41,42] Rape exams are primarily forensic procedures aimed at collecting evidence from a victim's body for use in a potential legal case. Hospital staff resist rape exams for many reasons, not least of which is the paperwork they entail, the time they consume, and the necessity to control evidence in accord with police department procedures.[43] To show their displeasure, some medical professionals avoid rape exams by playing the laggard, doing them improperly, and refusing to talk to victims. Due to the fear that rape exams will involve them in time-consuming and unpleasant legal procedures, Martin[1] depicts medical professionals and hospital emergency departments as *reluctant partners* in the community systems that process rape victims.

Dilemma: victim or patient?
Hospital staff experience emotional conflicts in relation to rape work due to a perception that rape victims are not "real patients."[1:ch.4] When a victim is physically injured, she qualifies as a "real patient" and receives medical care. If she is uninjured in the ways emergency medical procedures routinely address, staff resist involvement.[iv] Physicians and nurses resent being forced to perform an exam that does not require their diagnostic and treatment skills, even though invasive bodily procedures such as examining vaginas and rectums are the normative purview of medical professionals. Awareness of this point prompted a nurse to depict rape exams as "medical-like" and assert that this is why they are done in hospitals rather than elsewhere (e.g. in police departments).

Medical-institution frames orient physicians and nurses to view involvement in rape exams as improper and unpleasant. As Resnick et al.[44:1325] note, the emergency room practice of "treating existing injuries" in "short visits" discourages the focused, sensitive, unhurried attention that rape victims need. Furthermore, emergency room physicians are seldom trained in the purposes or practices of rape exams and many do not know how to perform them. They also know little about how to talk to or treat victims or the humiliation victims feel after being raped. While the state can force emergency room personnel to perform rape exams, it cannot make them behave in comforting or even competent ways. Physicians and nurses have many emotional reactions to rape exams and victims, some of which influence them to treat victims harshly, as the following quote from a physician illustrates:

> They are afraid of going to court and they don't want to get involved. You know, our residents think they have to determine if a "real rape" occurred. We tell them they don't, but they *hate* these cases. They [rape cases] make us all uncomfortable . . . I always had a feeling [when he was doing rape exams himself] when I walked into the victim's room that I was not wanted, needed maybe . . . but not wanted. I felt like it was an intrusion at a very sensitive time. We all dislike the rape exam; it's a distasteful time. (Chief resident of hospital obstetrics/gynecology, white man, age 31)

Medical personnel thus dislike the emotions they feel when dealing with rape victims while fearing legal entanglements. Conditions in emergency rooms and the training of emergency room personnel fail to orient them toward sympathy or the expression of positive emotions. As a result, they may doubt a victim's credibility as a "real" patient/victim:

Many of our cases are *suspicious* and we don't feel really good about it. . . . Some of them [victims] seem more like teenagers trying to get away with something than, you know, real rape victims. That makes it harder for our staff to stay motivated. (Emergency room nurse, white woman, age 35 (emphasis hers))

Some medical personnel expressed resentment more overtly. As one obstetrician-gynecologist put it:

Why should I be called out in the middle of the night to examine a stranger, someone I don't even know, who doesn't want to see me and I don't want to see? They pay a measly $35.00 and the exam sometimes takes two hours. . . . [I]f you go to court, they don't pay anything and it disrupts my practice for days and sometimes weeks. . . . I think they should get nurses to do it, like they did in [another state] where I was before. . . . Don't get me wrong; I don't hold it against victims but it's not a good situation and such a waste. (Obstetrician-gynecologist in private practice, white man, age 45)

Overall, the conditions of work evoke in medical personnel emotions such as discomfort, fear, and resentment, which they are not supposed to display to patients. Simultaneously, the emotion culture of medical organizations hinders compassion for rape victims. Such conditions may be the reason why medical personnel often try to avoid dealing with rape victims. As a chief resident of a hospital obstetrics/gynecology unit said, staff ". . . will dilly dally for hours waiting for a shift change or someone else to maybe do it [rape exam]." Similarly, an emergency room nurse said some physicians ". . . will see a child with a cold before a rape victim."

The gender institution: organizations, jobs, and emotion culture

As noted earlier, gender is more than norms, stereotypes, and a social status regarding what boys and girls, women and men are like and/or should do. We view it as a social institution with many complex dimensions and dynamics that both affect and reflect the emotions of work in rape crisis centers and other organizations.[4,9,10,44–46] Framing gender as an institution helps us understand how it shapes the emotion cultures of workplaces[9,19,25,47] and partially explains the feminist stance that many rape crisis centers take when working to support victims in the community.[1,48] Rape crisis centers, as products of the second wave women's movement, are more aware of gender-based inequalities and dynamics and more willing to mobilize on victims' behalf.

Rape crisis personnel are oriented by organization and occupation, and by gender, to construct rape victims sympathetically.[1] They need not be concerned with their adequacy as witnesses or patients. Indeed, a basic tenet of rape crisis center philosophy is that victims should not officially report being raped nor submit to rape exams unless they truly want to. In rape crisis center philosophy, a victim's account is taken at face value; it is not questioned. She is accepted as a victim if she says she is one and she is not subjected to credibility tests. A victim merits empathy in rape crisis settings and, as a rule, receives it. Of course, some victims are more "sympathetic" than others (e.g., younger victims, victims who are physically injured, victims raped by boyfriends) but all are defined as deserving acceptance and support. Positive emotional support by rape crisis workers is thus normative in rape crisis centers more than in other organizations.

Dilemma: victim welfare vs. mainstream relations
Since rape crisis center staff are encouraged to accept victims' accounts without challenging them, they experience few emotional conflicts in their dealings with victims. Yet they often experience problematic emotions when relating to mainstream staff. Unjust treatment of victims by legal or medical workers often evokes in rape crisis workers righteous anger, which they must constrain in order to maintain cooperative relations.[1,48] Victims may not be well-served, they are told, if they display hostile emotions toward other workers. Even gentle criticism is viewed negatively by mainstream organizations, as the following account by a rape crisis worker shows:

> [Have you ever expressed anger at any other of these professionals – police, nurses, prosecutors, etc.?] The only time I *really* have [emphasis hers] has been very recently and I was really just getting so sick of my nice guy approach that I really sort of took someone on and I think I did that very carefully. . . . I was talking with a victim advocate in a department about the way one of the law enforcement officers that she worked with had handled a case. . . . I really felt that they had botched it up. It was a case where a woman had been . . . slipped some sort of thing in a glass of wine and raped by two employees of a hotel while she was staying at the hotel. So their [the officers' and advocate's] reading was that it was some sort of physical problem and no rape had occurred even though this woman was saying that she thought something had happened to her. . . . Well, later that night they had to do emergency surgery on her and found out that she had a pretty serious vaginal tear. Whereas the men's story before had been nothing had happened then all of the sudden their story changed, that it was consensual sex that they had had with her. Anyway, to make a long story short, the case did not go anywhere. The woman didn't live in [the town where this occurred]. They didn't think they could pursue. They weren't getting what they wanted out of these guys and they just let the ball drop . . . and it really upset me. I sort of took it out on the victim advocate and she was defensive with me but she sort of discussed it with me and how she felt they had done the best they could. I understand that they have a very different perspective. They are looking to "clear the case" not necessarily to take eight hours to figure out exactly what had happened. It came back to me through my supervisor that I had really ticked them off. (Rape crisis worker, white woman, age 28)

This worker expressed frustration to a police department victim advocate, who complained to the worker's supervisor. She thought she expressed her anger "carefully" but apparently even careful expressions of disapproval are not taken kindly by the organization being criticized. The story shows how a rape crisis worker's emotions of feeling support for a victim and yet distrust and disapproval of police actions can prompt interorganizational conflict. The police failed to pursue the case before the victim had emergency surgery and then, even after the surgery, failed to press forward with the case against the hotel employees. When they dropped the case, the rape crisis worker became upset. She was expected to suppress her negative feelings toward the police and display either approval or neutral affect toward them. This example of an encounter between crisis worker and police shows the delicacy of relations among rape work organizations. Failure to display positive emotions threatened goodwill and lowered the odds that cooperation would continue.

Conclusions

In her research, Meyerson[49] found that hospitals dominated by a rational discourse *devalued* emotional experience whereas hospitals dominated by a social work discourse *valued* emotions positively. Hospitals of the latter type allowed workers to experience their emotions fully, by taking time to regroup after experiencing burnout or other problematic feelings. Meyerson urges all organizations to develop emotion cultures that affirm the "emotion work" their members must do in order to thrive. To build such cultures, she advocates a feminist re-visioning of emotions in organizations that "privileges the subjectivity of the marginalized/feminized other" over the currently hegemonic masculinist, rational-technical bureaucratic ideal.[50:112]

If rape work organizations were to take this step, their emotion cultures would have to embrace more responsive conceptions of victims, including requiring members to feel genuine empathy and display affirming rather than challenging behavior toward victims. While such change may seem unrealistic, Martin[1:ch.10] argues that relatively minor organizational innovations can approximate this ideal. For example, specialized staff and units for processing rape victims in legal and medical organizations have been shown to achieve favorable results for both victims and staff.[41,42,51,52]

Our illustration of how institutional, organizational, and job conditions prompt rape workers to experience problematic emotions and impede compliance with prescribed feeling and display rules shows how work contexts set up workers to experience emotional conflicts – within themselves and with victims and other workers. Similar to work by Copp,[24] we show how organizations expose workers to conditions that prompt strong, often proscribed, emotions and yet fail to acknowledge this dynamic or provide them with ways to cope. We believe rape victims will continue to be subjected to workers' unresponsive practices until organizations that employ them reform their emotion cultures to accommodate victims' and rape workers' needs. Simply instructing workers to "be emotionally supportive" while requiring them to accomplish tasks that contradict this dictum will only create frustration and resentment. More significantly, it will assure that victims' emotional vulnerability is overlooked rather than respected for its significance and consequences.[33]

Acknowledgment

We thank Steve Fineman, Deborah Meyerson, and Robin Simon for offering editorial advice that helped us improve our chapter.

Notes

i.   See Judith Lorber[46] and Patricia Yancey Martin[4] on gender as a social institution.
ii. The medical and legal institutions are highly intertwined, with the state, in many cases, requiring physicians and hospitals to conduct rape exams, although they resist (see Martin[1]).
iii. Frazier and Haney[53] found that police pass on about 16 percent of rape cases to prosecutors – in part because a defendant must be arrested for prosecutors to proceed with a case, which generally occurs in less than one-third of rapes reported to the police.
iv. A recent US Office of Crime Victims[54] document says that 62 percent of rape victims are not physically injured to the point of requiring medical treatment. Ahrens et al.[51] in a study of two Michigan SANE programs found that over two-thirds of rape victims lacked physical injuries, with 1 percent requiring hospitalization, and Koss[33] says between 50 and 85 percent of victims are not physically injured, based on her survey of research available at the time.

References

1.   Martin, P. Y. (2005) *Rape Work: Victims, Gender, and Emotions in Organization and Community Context.* New York and London: Routledge.
2.   Giddens, A. (1984) *The Constitution of Society.* Berkeley: University of California Press.
3.   Connell, R. W. (1987) *Gender and Power.* Palo Alto: Stanford University Press.
4.   Martin, P. Y. (2004) Gender as social institution, *Social Forces*, 82, 1249–73.
5.   Schmitt, F. E. and Martin, P. Y. (2007) The history of the anti-rape and rape crisis center movements. In Renzetti, C. M. and Edleson, J. (eds) *Encyclopedia of Interpersonal Violence.* Thousand Oaks, CA: Sage.
6.   United States Department of Justice (2006) www.ojp.usdoj.gov/bjs/cvictgen.htm. Date of last access: 12/31/06.
7.   *European Sourcebook of Crime and Criminal Justice Statistics* (2006) http://europeansourcebook.org/esb3_Full.pdf. Date of last access: 01/02/07.
8.   Gordon, M. T. and Riger, S. (1989) *The Female Fear.* New York: Free Press.
9.   Martin, P. Y. (2001) Mobilizing masculinities: women's experiences of men at work, *Organization*, 8, 587–618.
10. Martin, P. Y. (2003) Saying and doing vs. said and done: Gendering practices, practicing gender in organizations, *Gender and Society*, 1, 342–66.
11. Martin, S. E. (1999) Police force or police service? Gender and emotional labor, *Annals of the American Academy of Political and Social Science*, 561, 111–26.
12. Pogrebin, M. R. and Poole, E. D. (1995) Emotion management: a study of police response to tragic events, *Social Perspectives on Emotion*, 3, 149–68.
13. Martin, P. Y. (1997) Rape processing work: gender and accounts, *Social Problems*, 44, 464–82.
14. Martin, P. Y. (1996) Gendering and evaluating dynamics: men, masculinities, and managements. In: Collinson, D. and Hearn, J. (eds) *Men as Managers, Managers as Men.* London: Sage, 189–209.
15. Fields, J., Kleinman, S., and Copp, M. (2006) Symbolic interactionism, inequality, and emotions, *Symbolic Interaction*, 29, 155–78.
16. Gordon, S. L. (1981) The sociology of sentiment and affect. In: Rosenberg, M. and Turner, R. H. (eds) *Social Psychology: Social Perspectives.* New York: Basic Books, 562–92.
17. Barbalet, J. M. (1998) *Emotion, Social Theory, and Social Structure: A Macrosociological Approach.* Cambridge: Cambridge University Press.

18. Martin, P. Y. (2002) Sensations, bodies, and the "spirit of a place": aesthetics in residential organizations for the elderly, *Human Relations*, 55, 861–85.

19. Leidner, R. (1993) *Fast Food, Fast Talk: Service Work and the Routinization of Everyday Life*. Berkeley: University of California Press.

20. McCammon, H. J. and Griffin, L. J. (2000) Workers and their customers and clients: an editorial introduction, *Work and Occupations*, 27, 278–93.

21. Rafaeli, A. and Sutton, R. I. (1987) Expression of emotion as part of the work role, *Academy of Management Review*, 12, 23–37.

22. Steinberg, R. J. and Figart, D. M. (1999) Emotional demands at work: a job content analysis, *The Annals of the American Academy of Political and Social Science*, 561, 177–91.

23. Martin, P. Y. and Powell, M. (1994) Accounting for the second assault: legal organizations' framing of rape victims, *Law and Social Inquiry*, 19, 853–90.

24. Copp, M. (1998) When emotion work is doomed to fail: ideological and structural constraints on emotion management, *Symbolic Interaction*, 21, 299–328.

25. Pierce, J. L. (1995) *Gender Trials: Emotional Lives in Contemporary Law Firms*. Berkeley: University of California Press.

26. Sattel, J. W. (1976) The inexpressive male: tragedy or sexual politics? *Social Problems*, 23, 469–77.

27. Wharton, A. S. (1993) The affective consequences of service work: managing emotions on the job, *Work and Occupations*, 20, 205–32.

28. England, P. and Folbre, N. (1999) The cost of caring, *Annals of the American Academy of Political and Social Science*, 561, 39–52.

29. Heimer, C. A. and Stevens, M. L. (1997) Caring for the organization: social workers as frontline risk managers in neonatal intensive care units, *Work and Occupations*, 24, 133–64.

30. Sucher, K. C. (1999) Second-hand feelings: emotions and gender in victim service work, unpublished MS Thesis, Department of Sociology, Florida State University, Tallahassee.

31. Holstein, J. A. and Miller, G. (1992) Rethinking victimization: an interactional approach to victimology, *Symbolic Interaction*, 13, 103–22.

32. Clark, C. (1997) *Misery and Company: Sympathy in Everyday Life*. Chicago: University of Chicago Press.

33. Koss, M. P. (1993) Rape: scope, impact, interventions, and public policy responses. *American Psychologist*, 48, 1062–8.

34. Konradi, A. (1996) Preparing to testify: rape survivors negotiating the criminal justice process, *Gender and Society*, 10, 404–32.

35. Campbell, R., Sefl, T., Barnes, H. E., Ahrens, C. A., Wasco, S. M., and Zaragoza-Diesfeld, Y. (1999) Community services for rape survivors: enhancing psychological well-being or increasing trauma? *Journal of Consulting and Clinical Psychology*, 67, 847–58.

36. Messerschmidt, J. (2000) *Nine Lives: Adolescent Masculinities, Bodies, and Violence*. Boulder, CO: Westview Press.

37. Martin, S. E. and Jurik, N. C. (1996) *Doing Justice, Doing Gender*. Thousand Oaks, CA: Sage.

38. Weed, F. J. (1995) *Certainty of Justice: Reform in the Crime Victim Movement*. New York: Aldine de Gruyter.

39. Taslitz, A. E. (1999) *Rape and the Culture of the Courtroom*. New York: New York University Press.

40. Martin, P. Y., Reynolds, J., and Keith, S. (2002) Gender bias and feminist consciousness among judges and lawyers: a standpoint theory analysis, *SIGNS: Journal of Women in Culture and Society*, 27, 665–701.

41. Ledray, L. E. (1994) *Recovering from Rape* (2nd edn). New York: Henry Holt.

42. Patterson, D., Campbell, R., and Townsend, S. M. (2006) Sexual assault nurse examiner programs' goals and patient care practices, *Journal of Nursing Scholarship*, 38, 180–6.

43. Martin, P. Y. and DiNitto, D. (1987) The rape exam: beyond the hospital emergency room, *Women and Health*, 12, 5–28.

44. Resnick, H., Acierno, R., Holmes, M., Mammeyer, M., and Kilpatrick, D. (2000) Emergency evaluation and intervention with female victims of rape and other violence, *Journal of Clinical Psychology*, 56, 1317–33.

45. Acker, J. (1992) From sex roles to gendered institutions, *Contemporary Sociology*, 21, 565–9.
46. Lorber, J. (1994) *Paradoxes of Gender*. New Haven, CT: Yale University Press.
47. Risman, B. J. (2004) Gender as a social structure: theory wrestling with activism, *Gender and Society*, 18, 429–50.
48. Schmitt, F. E. and Martin, P. Y. (1999) Unobtrusive mobilization by an institutionalized rape crisis center: all we do comes from victims, *Gender and Society*, 13, 364–84.
49. Meyerson, D. E. (2000) If emotions were honoured: a cultural analysis. In: Fineman, S. (ed.) *Emotion in Organizations*. London: Sage, 167–83.
50. Meyerson, D. E. (1998) Feeling stressed and burned out: a feminist reading and re-visioning of stress-based emotions within medicine and organization science, *Organization Science*, 9, 103–18.
51. Ahrens, C. A., Campbell, R., Wasco, S. M., Aponte, G., Grubstein, L., and Davidson II, W. S. (2000) Sexual assault nurse examiner (SANE) programs: alternative systems for service delivery for sexual assault victims, *Journal of Interpersonal Violence*, 15, 921–43.
52. Koss, M. P., Bachar, K. J., Hopkins, C. Q., and Carlson, C. (2004) Expanding a community's justice response to sex crimes through advocacy, prosecutorial, and public health collaboration – introducing the RESTORE program, *Journal of Interpersonal Violence*, 19, 1435–63.
53. Frazier, P. A. and Haney, B. (1996) Sexual assault cases in the legal system: police, prosecutor, and victim perspectives, *Law and Human Behavior*, 20, 607–28.
54. US Department of Justice (2001) www.ojp.usdoj.gov/ovc/publications/welcome.htm#r. Date of last access: 12/31/06.

CHAPTER 5

THE RECREATION CENTER

In the Gym: Peer Pressure and Emotional Management Among Co-Workers

Mary Haman and Linda L. Putnam

We cannot talk about organizations without considering the role that emotions play within them. Emotion is an inescapable part of organizational life, and scholars have done much to increase our understanding of it. Research in organizations demonstrates that emotions always exist within and shape organizational decision making,[1,2] that workplace emotions play a vital role in organizational success,[3,4] and that corporate leaders attempt to control their employees' emotions.[5,6] This final discovery prompted a host of research projects that focused on the concept of emotional labor.

Emotional labor is a type of management that individuals engage in when they modify their actual or displayed emotions to meet the demands of their job. Organizational emotion scholars have explored a variety of issues surrounding emotional labor, including such diverse topics as the social rules that shape emotional labor prescriptions,[7,8] the methods that individuals use to perform emotional labor and mitigate its outcomes,[9,10] and the consequences that performing emotional labor has on employees.[11,12] This research demonstrates that emotional labor is widespread and may be experienced within all types of occupations and organizational settings. However, it is not always experienced in the same way.

Much research focuses on emotional labor that occurs as a result of managerial control. In these situations, managers or the organizational authority monitor employee performance to determine the extent to which workers display prescribed emotions. In most cases, managers focus on whether workers display desired emotions for customers. Workers that successfully engage in emotional labor with customers may be rewarded with incentives such as preferred work schedules, salary increases, and promotions. Workers that do not properly control their emotions may be punished through undesired work schedules, denial of pay raises, or lack of promotions. Organizations may also control workers' emotions by encouraging employees to align their feelings with the beliefs and values of the company. Like managerial surveillance, this cultural control of emotional labor is also top–down.

However, managers are not the only organizational members who aim to control employees' emotions. Similarly, customers are not the only people for whom workers may be expected to direct their emotional displays. Employees' expressions of emotion may also be controlled by other workers who use peer pressure to urge co-workers to display organizationally prescribed emotions. As a result, employees sometimes monitor their emotions in front of one another just as much as they do for customers. Because few researchers focus on this type of emotional labor, scholars need to examine how this type of control is enacted and the consequences for employees.

This study focuses on emotional control and how it is enacted through peer pressures among co-workers. Thus, it examines how emotional displays are directed to other audiences, not just customers. Using interviews with employees of a university recreation center, this project offers insights about peer control that are often overlooked in traditional research. The findings hold potential to broaden critical insights about emotional labor and to offer options for managing the tensions that result from peer pressures to exhibit unwanted emotional displays.

Literature Review

Emotional labor

Emotional labor, as defined above, occurs when individuals consciously alter their emotional state or affect display to satisfy workplace prescriptions. This scholarship finds its roots in the work of Hochschild,[5,6] whose research on flight attendants led her to realize that certain jobs require individuals to express and repress emotions selectively. Her study focused on the idea that organizations may regulate employees' emotions for corporate gain. Managers create certain emotional display rules to enhance customer service, increase productivity, and raise company profits. Hochschild[6] argued that maintaining an organizationally acceptable affect display is often the primary duty of service professions. Moreover, she contended that emotional labor had a negative effect on an individual's psychological health, often causing a person to feel insincere, stressed, and burned out.

Following Hochschild's lead, organizational scholars examined the consequences of performing emotional labor. The results of these studies have been inconsistent. Although many projects confirmed Hochschild's depiction of the negative effects of emotional labor,[10,13,14] other studies found positive effects.[11,12,15] On the one hand, Van Maanen and Kunda[13] observed that emotional labor caused Disneyland workers to experience intense stress, emotional numbness, and burnout. Similarly, Waldron and Krone[14] noted that suppressing emotions heightened tension and stress levels of correction officers and damaged their interpersonal relationships. On the other hand, Shuler and Sypher's[15] study of 911 emergency call-takers indicated that employees enjoyed and sought out emotional labor to create a sense of organizational community. Similarly, Adelmann's[11] research on table servers demonstrated that performing required emotional displays increased their job satisfaction, enhanced their extrinsic work benefits (i.e. higher tips), and improved self-esteem. These inconsistent findings suggest that the consequences of performing emotional labor are not fully understood.[16,17] Part of the problem with understanding why and when different effects surface is the nature of organizational control that mandates and enforces emotional labor.

Hochschild's[5,6] conception of emotional labor focused on managerial control of workers' emotions. For her, workers relinquished control over their own emotions to the mandates of their employers or to a company's policy in exchange for some compensation. Managerial control over emotions, however, works most effectively if it is reinforced by other types of control. Emotional labor then can occur through managerial control, cultural control, and peer-based control.

Managerial control

Typically, emotional labor is aligned with overt managerial control. Overt control occurs when managers offer rewards to employees who successfully engage in emotional labor and punish workers who fail to display proper emotions. Managers may reward workers who engage in desired emotional labor through preferential treatment, salary increases, and promotions. Similarly, organizational authorities may punish workers who do not perform proper emotional labor through giving them undesirable work assignments, negative performance evaluations, or firing them. In these situations, workers are aware of the consequences that proper performance of emotional labor has on their ability to receive rewards and punishments from their employers. Specific prescriptions for emotional labor often appear in employee manuals and on performance evaluation forms that are typically reinforced in training sessions and organizational meetings. Employers emphasize that displaying prescribed emotions is critical to the job, and they directly reward and punish individuals for these emotional displays.

In managerial control, supervisors typically monitor workers to determine whether they meet the emotional labor requirements. One form of monitoring is watching employees while they do their jobs to determine whether they are displaying emotions properly. Sometimes workers know when they are being monitored through a manager's physical presence, visible video cameras, or clicking into telephone conversations. Other times, managers may tap into employees' internet use, plant spies who pose as customers, or use other employees to report on their co-workers' behaviors. In these cases, workers may not know exactly when they are being watched, but they are aware that their emotional labor is monitored, and that they will be rewarded or punished for how they perform it.

Managerial control serves as an effective way to encourage prescribed emotional displays. However, it leads to a number of problems, including requiring managers to spend time watching employees instead of doing other tasks. It also creates a workplace environment in which managers appear to distrust workers. Employees, then, may resent this supervision and loss of privacy, develop lower job satisfaction, or resist and subvert managerial requirements. For example, in Murphy's[18] study, flight attendants used a variety of practices to defy management, such as mocking organizational rules, lying to supervisors, defying the employer's mandates, and telling stories that vilified the company. Since managerial control often results in these problems, organizations have employed other forms of control, including cultural and peer-based control.

Cultural control

Cultural control occurs when employees exhibit emotional labor through embracing the symbols, values, and mission of an organization's culture. This form of control is unobtrusive in that employees monitor their own behavior. Managers do not need to watch over employees or to monitor them secretly; instead, workers who identify with the company's culture adhere to prescriptions embedded in organizational values. Thus, cultural control is control of the heart; that is, organizations control workers' actions through inculcating a sense of pride and identity with the company.

Organizations enact cultural control through socializing employees to express particular emotions. On hiring, workers learn to embrace the company ideals and emotional labor is embedded in the company's beliefs and values; thus, the culture regulates emotional expressions. For example, if a company claims that "Customer Service is Number One," then employees who believe in this value invoke emotional displays to make the customer number one. If workers buy into the culture, managers rely on the culture of the organization to guide employees in making the "right choices" about emotional displays.

Van Maanen and Kunda's study of emotional labor at Disneyland[13] provides an example of cultural control. Training sessions for new employees were filled with pep talks, inspirational films, and stories that encouraged workers to align their emotions with the values of the company – specifically, pleasing customers and connecting patrons to their inner child. Workers who identified with the organization's culture and saw their own values align with the company's beliefs accepted the edict to appear happy, cheerful, and playful while at work. Thus, when employees embraced the organization's culture, the culture regulated appropriate emotional displays. Cultural control, therefore, provided an unobtrusive way in which emotional labor prescriptions were enforced.

Cultural control, however, also affects employees in negative ways. Specifically, employees sometimes reject a company's cultural ideals, which results in cynicism and resentment about proper emotional displays. Similar to managerial control, employees may experience burnout and stress or become dissatisfied with the company's culture and actively resist emotional labor rules. Van Maanen and Kunda[13] found that emotional labor caused some Disneyland workers to undermine organizational rules by appearing joyful in helping customers while simultaneously disobeying company mandates by, for example, squeezing obnoxious customers' seat belts too tightly on rides. Cultural and managerial control may work more effectively when it is combined with peer-based control of emotional displays.

Peer-based control

Peer-based control roots emotional labor in employee relationships. Peers and co-workers reinforce the organizational culture, implement behavioral norms, and monitor each other to ensure that the rules are followed. Peer-based control is common in organizations that value employee input or enact participatory management. Thus, a worker's desire to be the "ideal employee" reaffirms and fills in the gaps for problems with managerial and cultural control. In this way, emotional labor is directed at peers in addition to management and customers.

For example, Barker's[19] study of self-managing teams in a manufacturing company revealed that workers had less flexibility and room for resistance in reporting to their peers than when managers directly controlled employees. Moreover, in organizations in which peer-based control reinforces managerial and cultural control, the norms and criteria for employee behavior are more severe than they are with managerial control alone.

Only a few studies focus on the relationship between emotional labor and peer-based control. In the cruise tour industry, Tracy[20] noted how peer pressure among fellow staff members fostered a second layer of emotional labor. Even though managers set up the rules and prescriptions for emotional labor, peers often reinforced managerial norms and deflected efforts to resist. Peers reminded their fellow workers of the norms for becoming an "ideal cruise staff member." In this respect, cruise ship workers created a virtually inescapable control system in which customers, supervisors, and peers monitored emotional labor performances. This type of emotional control led to a situation in which employees often felt trapped. This work calls for the need to understand how peer pressure contributes to emotional labor.

Emotional Labor at the Student Recreation Center

The Student Recreation Center (SRC) is a pseudonym for the main facility of a university's Department of Recreational Sports located in the United States. During the university's 2002 fall semester, 70 percent of the campus' approximately 45,000 students visited the SRC, and during the 2003 spring semester, 73 percent of students entered its doors. Recreational opportunities within the SRC include gym space for basketball, volleyball, soccer, badminton, racquetball, handball, squash, and aerobics; a fitness area with strength training and cardiovascular equipment; an indoor track; a rock climbing wall; and an Olympic size pool. The Center also offers numerous activities in which members can join for an additional cost. Examples include personal training, yoga, Pilates, t'ai chi, self-defense, and massage therapy.

To oversee these activities, the SRC employs 35 full-time workers and a large staff of part-time employees, mostly university students. Observations of full-time trainers and interviews with 13 staff employees (six males and seven females) formed the basis for this study. This case draws from comments made about emotional labor, forms of control, peer comparisons, and discussions as to what constitutes an ideal employee.

Emotional labor at the SRC typically involves displaying a cheerful countenance while on the job or "having fun." Thus, the SRC employees engage in emotional labor through both managerial and cultural control, but in ways reinforced through peer and social pressure. Managerial control is evident in an informal conversation with one of the top-ranking SRC professionals, who explains that managers strive to make sure that everyone who uses or works within the facility enjoys his or her experience. In fact, this individual talks with staff members who appear upset to help them feel better, particularly so that they do not affect clients negatively. Similarly, another top-ranking SRC staff member states, "When I evaluate staff, it [fun] does play a big role. . . . Their attitude when they come to work needs to be upbeat because we're here to serve the students." Thus, the SRC management expects workers to engage in emotional labor by having fun. Moreover, the culture of the SRC reinforces this emotional mandate through inculcating the value of "having fun," despite the fact that many employee duties are unpleasant and difficult. This overarching value is evident in employee training sessions, signs posted on the walls, and organizational practices.

Emotional labor among peers

Employees, however, could resist managerial edicts to "have fun," unless peers and co-workers reaffirm this value. Having fun, then, becomes the ideal of a good employee, one that requires co-workers to monitor these displays and to express similar required emotions to each other. Virtually all the SRC employees describe a "good employee" as someone who appears upbeat and cheerful around customers and fellow staff members. Employees need to deal with staff members "in a fun manner all the time," "display patience for each other," "encourage each other," and "keep attitudes up." Thus, good employees support each other, are outgoing people, and act as cheerleaders on the job. Cheerleaders encourage fellow workers, not just patrons of the SRC.

In contrast, bad employees are those who do not have time to chit chat, fail to celebrate each other's successes, and are not having fun. Moreover, a bad employee "takes the paycheck and leaves," "bitches all the time," "is of the old generation, in which employees don't have fun at work," and "dislikes what they are doing." These employees have low morale and "just don't fit in." Thus, peers have little tolerance for staff members who are unhappy or angry. In fact, they expect that employees will display positive attitudes at all times – even when they are really upset or frustrated with each other.

Several workers described situations in which they wanted to show annoyance or irritation with peers, but felt required to hide their feelings. For example, one participant explained that staff members must appear fun and friendly when dealing with each other. This person pointed out that, "when you actually need to approach that person [about a problem] . . . those issues don't get dealt with like they should." Another worker highlighted a situation in which a committee that he chaired did not work. This individual indicated that although he wanted to approach his co-worker about the problem, he felt unable to do so because employees are expected "to have this fun friend relationship," which made it "hard to really talk about work." This participant felt frustrated with his co-worker, yet he decided to avoid confrontation because of the requirement to appear friendly and happy with other employees.

A third employee indicated that workers were expected to appear happy all of the time – even when they were displeased with each other. She noted that, "if they've [other staff] impacted a client negatively . . . at some point you have to show the real deal." In these situations, she felt required to act happy, even though she was dissatisfied with her fellow worker's performance. In this sense, employees viewed emotional labor as preventing open and honest discussion of performance problems among colleagues. Thus, emotional labor permeated peer relationships through invoking norms of "friendliness, supportiveness, and keeping attitudes up" among fellow employees.

Peer involvement in performance evaluations (often referred to as 360 degree performance appraisal) reinforced co-worker control over emotional labor. Among other questions, the SRC performance evaluations asked employees to comment on their fellow workers' attitudes and workplace demeanor. The SRC managers read these evaluations and used them to determine promotions and merit salary. People who did not display proper emotions in front of their co-workers risked becoming targets of abuse on staff evaluations. Poor staff evaluations, in turn, could culminate in denial of promotions and pay raises. For this reason, employees might feel particularly compelled to engage in emotional labor around one another.

Peer pressure and emotional labor

Using peers to reinforce managerial control of emotional labor may be rather commonplace, particularly since it is tied to performance, promotions, and pay raises. What is less obvious is the way that peer pressure creates a culture of control that monitors emotional labor and entraps workers. Thus, peers treat fellow workers who fall into the category of "bad employees" as unable to perform the job, "not fitting in, and not having a rightful place at the SRC."

This peer pressure is exercised in two ways. First, seven of the thirteen workers in this study socially constructed emotional labor as a "natural ability," a talent, or a skill. For them, enacting the managerially desired emotions came easily because they were people oriented, had a knack for displaying emotions, and were blessed with the skill to communicate emotions. Workers who constructed emotional labor as a natural ability regarded employees who did not share their views of this labor with much disdain. These workers viewed their fellow employees who had to "work" to display feelings of fun and friendliness as disingenuous, inauthentic, or depressed. Thus, the way that workers socially constructed what emotional labor was and how it was exercised established a norm for appropriate behaviors among co-workers. Workers who viewed emotional labor as a natural ability treated other employees as if they were second-class staff.

A second form of peer pressure came from the way that respect was tied to different perceptions of acting on the job. The employees who viewed emotional labor as a natural ability looked down on the SRC workers who saw it "as having to perform a role." Performing a role meant "putting up a front," "putting aside personal issues," and "putting on a good face" to meet workplace demands. For workers who performed a role, emotional labor occurred through acting; thus, maintaining appropriate affect displays required conscious effort. As one interviewee noted, "It is difficult to feel tired, stressed, or bothered while [having fun]." But another employee commented, "You're there for the people in your class, to give them a great workout, to motivate them, to encourage them . . . that is your job . . . so you leave all your feelings at the door." Acting for these workers was necessary to be a good employee.

In contrast, employees who treated emotional labor as a natural ability saw acting as disingenuous, fake, and aligned with being a "bad employee." For them, individuals who have to act "just tell you what you want to hear" and they "can be detected." In their views, customers and fellow employees can "see through your acting" and do not respect employees who are "not being real" or who display unfelt emotions. As one employee voiced, "the ability to be yourself is one of [the SRC's] successes." "Most people here are all very natural." For these workers, being a good employee involved "myself being myself."

Also, acting could lead to unhappy employees. Workers who viewed emotional labor as a natural ability claimed that staff members who performed a role would eventually become unhappy. As one interviewee remarked, "that can get very tough on you – acting everyday. I don't think you can carry on who you are for a very long time." Workers who have to act or perform a role "don't stay very long because they're unhappy in the situation."

Thus, the second way in which peer pressure enforces emotional labor is the idea that acting is an ineffective way of doing one's job. Employees who have natural abilities view workers who "act" as dishonest, unhappy, and indifferent. Thus, employees who act out emotions are not respected because they are untrue to their own selves. If employees have to fake their emotions, they are not good workers because they are insincere and inauthentic. Through this notion of respect, one group of employees exerts pressure over another set to have fun, display patience, support staff members, hide complaints, and avoid bad moods. To be liked and respected by their co-workers, they must control their emotions in front of each other and with customers, but they must do it naturally. Employees who cannot attain this goal or who "act" in one way with their customers and in another way with co-workers are inadequate in their jobs.

In effect, peers exert control over emotional labor through monitoring the norms for co-worker interactions and peer involvement in performance evaluations. Clearly, most workplaces appreciate supportive, friendly, and fun colleagues. However, when this aim becomes confounded with a culture of "avoiding conflict," co-workers may repress emotions that aid in effective problem solving. Peers also exert control over emotional labor by aligning emotional practices with conceptions of "good" or "bad" employees. Thus, being unhappy or frustrated is equated with a bad employee while good employees are cheerleaders for each other. Peer-based performance evaluations make the links between emotional displays and the concept of an ideal employee rooted materially in pay raises and promotions. Thus, peer control of emotional labor can produce conflict avoidance through legitimating some emotions and demonizing others, instantiating emotional labor in the ideals of good and bad employees, and involving peers in assessing emotional performances.

Equally important, peers exert control over workplace emotions through aligning emotional labor with natural abilities and seeing themselves as "suitable for the job." Thus, having fun and being upbeat are talents that come naturally for some employees but not for others. In the SRC culture, peer pressure functions through the presumption that some employees "don't fit in" or "do not have a rightful place" in their jobs. Employees who have to act or fake their emotions to perform a role are disrespected because they are disingenuous or not real. They believe that the strain of acting also leads to being unhappy at work, a characteristic of a bad employee. In this sense, peer pressure reinforces managerial and cultural control by creating a workplace in which the culture of fun permeates the whole environment, including the gym floors and the staff offices.

Peers as targets of emotional labor

Even though emotional labor at the SRC is primarily aimed at customers, employees also display required emotions for co-workers and staff members; thus, fellow workers are clearly targets of emotional labor. Interestingly, employees indicate that being cheerful and motivating for patrons is less stressful than displaying the required emotions targeted at co-workers, particularly for employees who see themselves as performing a role. Most employees who see emotional labor as a natural ability claim they do not experience much stress in targeting patrons, co-workers, or management. Employees who see themselves as performing a role often experience deeper levels of acting in managing their emotions with peers than in managing displays with customers. However, employees who believe that they have a natural ability for expressing the required emotion reject any notion that they are acting with their peers.

Consequences of peer control of emotional displays

Displaying unfelt emotions of encouragement and fun among peers can raise employees' spirits and facilitate working together effectively. However, peer control of emotional displays can lead to adverse consequences. First, it creates a climate of frustration and conflict avoidance in handling co-worker relationships. Co-workers often feel required to hide emotions of frustration and dissatisfaction with employees who are not performing their jobs properly. Given that "good employees" should not complain, staff members even avoid taking their concerns to supervisors. Thus, they hide their feelings and fail to initiate issues that should be discussed to resolve problems. Issues that remain unresolved can become a source of great frustration and stress. Moreover, conflict avoidance can cause resentments to fester and can lower job satisfaction. In this sense, peer control of emotional labor may damage co-worker relationships, increase workers' stress, and lead to employee burnout.

A second consequence of peer control stems from using emotional displays to instantiate the criteria for assessing good and bad employees. Even though management typically sets these standards, employees evaluate how they are interpreted and implemented. Peers, then, assess whether co-workers are having fun, displaying patience, and encouraging each other. Through performance appraisals and peer pressures, they discipline unhappy or frustrated employees as "not fitting in." More importantly, peers reaffirm managerial and cultural requirements of emotional labor by extending these prescriptions from customer targets to co-worker interactions. Thus, emotional labor requirements permeate the entire work environment.

A third consequence of peer pressure for emotional labor stems from the dominance of one group of employees over the others. In peer control, one group of workers can emerge as privileged, typically through meeting the standards of the "good employee." At the SRC, the employees who construct their emotional performances as natural look down on those co-workers who have to act to be good employees. Thus, they create a subculture with a class system in which one group of employees emerges as accepted and fulfilled while the "outsiders" remain marginalized as "not fitting in." This type of subculture conceals subtle evaluations of performances through constructing some actions as disingenuous or inauthentic and through regarding inconsistencies in emotional displays as fake. In this way, the privileged group treats those employees who act out their emotions with disrespect. These forms of peer pressure and privilege have direct effects on turnover and job satisfaction, as is evident in the employee's remark that workers who perform a role "don't stay very long."

Implications and suggestions for change

This project contributes to the emotional labor literature and offers suggestions for change. The findings demonstrate that peers can control emotional labor through being targets of emotional displays and determining good and bad employees. Although emotional labor is typically aimed at customers, the findings of this project reveal that it is also enacted for co-workers and linked to peer control. Confirming existing research, the findings suggest that peer-based emotional labor is more demanding on employees than customer-based displays. These findings also indicate that peer control can limit employees' abilities to voice disagreements. Such avoidance of conflict may foster resentment among co-workers and increase employee stress and burnout. Thus, this study highlights the need for additional work on emotional labor in co-worker relationships.

This project also has implications for research on positive and negative emotions in the workplace. Organizations often advocate positiveness at work to attract customers and boost worker commitment, especially with a low-paid, low-power workforce. These cultures grounded in fun-at-work may actually deflect employee attention away from adverse pay and working conditions.[21] Even though the goal of "happiness management" aims to empower employees and lower their tension, prescribed fun at work can be counterproductive and serve as a smokescreen for disguising the real conflicts in organizations.[22]

Another implication of this study is that organizational members have their own conceptions of what emotional labor is and how it should be enacted. For some employees, displaying required emotions is an innate talent or a natural ability while for others these displays exhibit "performing a role." Moreover, employees who embrace the natural ability view of emotional labor differentiate themselves from and exert superiority over other co-workers who have to act out displays. Even though emotional labor scholars have a variety of views about faking emotions, levels of acting, and true feelings,[23] the findings from this study suggest that beliefs about *real* and *fake* selves are constructed within and through organizational practices.[24]

These reactions to emotional displays are also culturally rooted.[22] That is, individuals from cultures in which emotional expressions are stoic and understated may not experience tensions between natural ability versus performing a role. In these cultures, presenting "a fun demeanor and meaning it" depicts what actually occurs; hence, reactions to emotional labor and to different ways of expressing positive emotions may be culturally laden.

In general, emotional labor at the SRC is a complex phenomenon rooted in managerial, cultural, and peer control. Employees typically accept and fulfill the edict to "have fun and be friendly" on the job. They acknowledge that the culture of "having fun" differentiates them from other gyms, but they appear frustrated with emotional labor norms among co-workers and with rooting emotional labor in prescriptions of good or bad employees.

One option for changing this situation is to set up criteria for employee effectiveness, ones that are explicitly based in performance measures, such as quality of class sessions, knowledge and communication of exercise techniques, clarity of communicating routines, etc. Having a set of explicit measures for performance that are not grounded in displaying unfelt emotions might alter the image of a good employee and change the patterns of peer assessments. Also, employees need to legitimate outlets for expressing frustrations with obnoxious patrons, dissatisfaction with co-workers, complaints about job performances, and difficulties with policies. Managers need to encourage and reward employees for raising problems, voicing concerns about work environments, and expressing negative emotions. In general, managers rarely talk about the stress that employees may experience with emotional labor. Making it possible to raise these issues and discuss options for handling this stress also breaks the barrier against "acting" and makes "performing a role" acceptable.

One other suggestion would be to foster different ways of "having fun." Specifically, managers could recognize and appreciate employees who are passionate and involved as well as those who are reserved and removed from the organization's culture. Recognizing and appreciating diversity could also sanction "acting" as not necessarily fake or inauthentic. Thus, workers could realize that it is acceptable to be in a bad mood and yet provide encouragement to co-workers and patrons. Employees need to decouple the dichotomy between having fun versus complaining or between being involved versus not being passionate about one's job. By splitting up these polar opposites, employees would be less compelled to see one set of characteristics and presume that the opposites hold. In effect, employees can have fun and still complain or can be passionate at times and disengaged in other circumstances. Accepting these suggestions rests on recognizing that conflict avoidance, peer pressure, and turnover imprison some employees and eventually damage the organization.

Summary and Conclusions

Prescriptions for emotional labor at the SRC typically require employees to appear fun and friendly on the job. Workers recognize and accept these expectations as important for performing their roles. Some employees find these requirements more stressful than do others, especially for the emotional labor directed at and evaluated by peers. Peer control can be more demanding and entrapping than managerial control because of its omnipresence and its connection to co-worker relationships. Peers also contribute to judgments about which employees are acceptable and fit within the organizational culture. In participatory management systems in which employees are involved in making decisions and providing assessments of colleagues, peer control gains additional salience in the workplace.

Employees also develop conceptions about what emotional labor is and how it should be displayed. This study reveals that some employees treat displaying unfelt emotions as a natural ability while others view it as performing a role. Co-workers who see emotional labor as performing a role admit to faking their emotions to please customers and build co-worker morale. These employees explain that appearing upbeat among peers is an important part of their jobs. At some level, though, having a natural ability gains superiority over learning to perform a role. Thus, employees who see themselves as having a natural ability depict acting as being disingenuous and inauthentic, and claim that they do not fake emotions among co-workers. They also cast the consequences of acting in a negative light.

Peer control over emotional labor can result in unresolved workplace problems and inappropriate standards for assessing performance in addition to marginalizing one group of employees over another. Unresolved workplace problems stem from emotional labor norms that promote conflict avoidance among peers and discourage challenges to the ideal of a good employee. Peer control of the appropriate emotional displays also allows employees to determine who has a rightful place in the organization as well as who excels.

Emotional labor is an important aspect of organizational life. Displaying unfelt emotions toward customers and co-workers may not necessarily be stressful or harmful to employees, but developing an emotional climate that entraps some workers and leaves them feeling marginalized hurts the organization in the long run. This study suggests that employees should question forms of control that privilege some workers over others and root emotional labor in normative standards of ideals for good employees. These standards for emotional displays should be open to challenge and modification. This study also raises skepticism of peer-based evaluation systems grounded in assessing primarily employee attitudes and demeanor. It urges workers to analyze the climates and subcultures of emotional labor and to realize that diverse interpretations of emotional displays are plausible and should be valued.

References

1. Mumby, D. K. and Putnam, L. L. (1992) The politics of emotion: A feminist reading of bounded rationality, *Academy of Management Review*, 17, 465–86.
2. Putnam, L. L. and Mumby, D. K. (1993) Organizations, emotion, and the myth of rationality. In Fineman, S. (ed.) *Emotion in Organizations*. Newbury Park, CA: Sage, 36–57.
3. Martin, J., Knopoff, K., and Beckman, C. (1998) An alternative to bureaucratic impersonality: Managing bounded emotionality at The Body Shop, *Adminstrative Science Quarterly*, 43, 429–69.
4. McDonald, P. (1991) The Los Angeles Olympic Organizing Committee: Developing organizational culture in the short run. In Frost, P., Moore, L., Louis, M., et al. (eds) *Reframing Organizational Culture*. Newbury Park, CA: Sage, 26–38.
5. Hochschild, A. R. (1979) Emotion work, feeling rules and social structure, *American Journal of Sociology*, 85, 551–75.

6. Hochschild, A. R. (1983) *The Managed Heart*. Berkeley: University of California Press.
7. Rafaeli, A. (1989) When cashiers meet customers: An analysis of the role of supermarket cashiers, *Academy of Management Journal*, 32, 245–73.
8. Rafaeli, A. and Sutton, R. I. (1987) Expression of emotion as part of the work role, *Academy of Management Review*, 12, 23–37.
9. Leidner, R. (1993) *Fast Food, Fast Talk: Service Work and the Routinization of Everyday Life*. Berkeley: University of California Press.
10. Tracy, S. J. and Tracy, K. (1998) Emotion labor at 911: A case study and theoretical critique, *Journal of Applied Communication Research*, 26, 390–411.
11. Adelmann, P. K. (1995) Emotional labor as a potential source of job stress. In Sauter, S. L. and Murphy, L. R. (eds) *Organizational Risk Factors for Job Stress*. Washington, DC: American Psychological Association, pp. 371–81.
12. Wharton, A. S. (1993) The affective consequences of service work: Managing emotions on the job, *Work and Occupations*, 20, 205–32.
13. Van Maanen, J. and Kunda, G. (1989) "Real feelings": Emotional expression and organizational culture. In Staw, B. M. and Cummings, L. L. (eds) *Research in Organizational Behavior*, vol. 11. Greenwich CT: JAI, 43–103.
14. Waldron, V. R. and Krone, K. J. (1991) The experience and expression of emotion in the workplace: A study of a corrections organization, *Management Communication Quarterly*, 4, 287–309.
15. Shuler, S. and Sypher, B. D. (2000) Seeking emotional labor: When managing the heart enhances the work experience, *Management Communication Quarterly*, 14, 50–89.
16. Rafaeli, A. and Worline, M. (2001) Individual emotion in work organizations, *Social Science Information*, 40, 95–123.
17. Wharton, A. S. (1999) The psychosocial consequences of emotional labor, *Annals of the American Academy of Political and Social Science*, 561, 159–76.
18. Murphy, A. G. (1998) Hidden transcripts of flight attendant resistance, *Management Communication Quarterly*, 11, 499–535.
19. Barker, J. A. (1993) Tightening the Iron Cage: Concertive control in self-managing teams, *Administrative Science Quarterly*, 38, 408–37.
20. Tracy, S. J. (2000) Becoming a character for commerce: Emotion labor, self-subordination, and discursive construction of identity in a total institution, *Management Communication Quarterly*, 14, 90–128.
21. Fineman, S. (2006) On being positive: Concerns and counterpoints, *Academy of Management Review*, 31, 270–91.
22. Fineman, S. (2006) Emotion and organizing. In Clegg, S., Hardy, C., Nord, W., and Lawrence, T. (eds) *The Sage Handbook of Organizational Studies*, 2nd edn. London: Sage, 675–700.
23. Ashforth, B. E. and Tomiuk, M. A. (2000) Emotional labor and authenticity: Views from service agents. In Fineman, S. (ed.) *Emotion in Organizations*, 2nd edn. London: Sage, 184–203.
24. Tracy, S. J. and Trethewey, A. (2005) Fracturing the real-self–fake-self dichotomy: Moving toward "crystallized" organizational discourses and identities, *Communication Theory*, 15, 168–95.

CHAPTER 6

THE JOB CENTER

Abuse, Violence, and Fear on the Front Line: Implications of the Rise of the Enchanting Myth of Customer Sovereignty

Marek Korczynski and Victoria Bishop

A Dark Side to Emotions in Organizational Life

> Smashing windows up; smashing computers; jumping over the counter and hitting staff . . . it was actually one of the Advisers here; he beat her brother up; he used to be a Team Leader here . . . he just jumped over and started hitting him . . . He tried to get him off but because he was so violent he couldn't do anything. I mean he smashed computers up, windows, and everything. (Frontline staff, male, Caucasian, small village job center)

> I don't come to work expecting an incident but, saying that, when they happen, you're not surprised. Does that make sense really? There's an expectancy that it will be there but you never know when the next one's gonna be. In fact I only said this morning, this is my fourth week in Hantshire and we haven't yet had an incident and I was very surprised. (Frontline staff, female, British Asian, middle sized town job center)

> If you're doing a job where there's the threat of aggression or violence, you might go a whole day without it, you might go a whole week if you're lucky – but it's the fact it's in the back of people's minds all the time, that it might happen. That's the most stressful thing for staff. (Union rep., female, Caucasian, middle sized town job center)

It is clear from the experiences recounted above by job-center service, recipient facing (or frontline) staff, that there is a dark side to their emotions within service work. This is a side of service workers' emotions that is deeper and darker even than the hues with which Hochschild[1] painted the harm of emotional labor. It should be noted that the quotations are not unusual, infrequent utterances, but rather are representative of the frequent and systematic nature of frontline staff's experiences of abuse and violence within job centers in the UK. Writers situated in both academic circles and the popular press are increasingly focusing on the widespread phenomenon of customer violence and abuse to frontline staff. This particular area of interest comes as no surprise as the continued growth of the interactive service population has pushed "customer"–worker relations to center stage.[i] When discussed in the popular press, customer abuse and violence is seen as linked to a breakdown in social mores among customers, often precipitated by the consumption of alcohol. The rise in customer violence and abuse is thus discussed in terms of a meta-discourse of the wider breakdown in social mores in contemporary society.

However, a proper sociological examination of abuse and violence means that the *connections*, rather than the disconnections, of violence with social structures, norms, and mores need to be examined.[2] Abuse and violence can be seen as arising out of the nature of society, rather than out of the breakdown of society. In particular, it can be fruitful to consider how common social norms may serve as a legitimating ideology for forms of violence and abuse. This chapter lays out how notions of *customer sovereignty* can serve to legitimate and normalize customer abuse and violence in the service economy.

The chapter is structured in the following way. The next section makes the theoretical case that abuse, violence, and fear among frontline service workers should not be seen as an outcome of the breakdown of social mores, but rather as an outcome of reconfiguration of social mores around an ideology of customer sovereignty. The following three sections show the outlined process in action with regard to how notions of customer sovereignty affect management practices and frontline staff behavior in British job centers, and show how customer abuse and violence comes to be normalized within job centers. The concluding section considers the institutions and language needed to address abuse, violence, and fear experienced by frontline staff.

Customer Sovereignty and the Legitimation of Abuse and Violence

In examining forms of ideologies that can sustain abuse and violence in organizations, it is important to recall the way that feminist sociological analysis highlighted the ways in which ideologies of patriarchy legitimated, and therefore kept hidden, male harassment and abuse of women in organizational life for much of the nineteenth and twentieth centuries. It is instructive to compare male-to-female and customer-to-staff violence and abuse and their sustaining ideologies.

Table 6.1 offers a comparison of how an ideology of patriarchy legitimated, and kept hidden, male abuse and harassment towards women within organizations with how an ideology of customer sovereignty legitimates, and keeps hidden, customer abuse and violence towards frontline staff. For male-to-female abuse and violence, an ideology of patriarchy allows male perpetrators of harassment to see their actions as legitimate. For instance, it could be seen as OK for men to openly sexualize women within an organization because patriarchy allows the belief that this is simply what men do.[3] At the same time, notions of patriarchy lead female victims of harassment to see themselves as being culpable. There is a tendency for female victims to blame themselves through a consideration of the way that they acted to provoke the

Table 6.1 Comparison of roles of ideologies in sustaining male-to-female abuse and harassment and customer-to-frontline staff abuse and violence[ii]

	Male-to-female abuse and harassment	Customer-to-frontline staff abuse and violence
Sustaining ideology	Patriarchy	Notions of customer sovereignty
Implications of ideology for perpetrators of violence	Abuse and harassment of women legitimate	Myths of customer sovereignty enchant customers, but consequent disillusionment can trigger abuse; Abuse of frontline staff seen as legitimate
Implications of ideology for victims of violence	Tendency for victims to see themselves as culpable	Tendency for victims to see themselves as culpable
Implications of ideology for management actions	Management as a practice itself is implicated with patriarchy; Routine abuse and harassment elicits no action; Action on extraordinary incidents	Management as a practice itself is implicated with perpetrating ideas of customer sovereignty; Routine abuse and harassment elicits no action; Action on extraordinary incidents
Outcomes	Everyday abuse and harassment normalized	Everyday abuse and violence normalized

harassment.[4] Notions of patriarchy internalized by women lead to the belief that men are only acting legitimately and naturally when they harass. It becomes women's job to avoid provoking such harassment. They are therefore culpable themselves when they are harassed – they have failed in their task.

Management responses to abuse and violence are also conditioned by forms of sustaining ideology. Indeed, numerous studies have shown how management itself is implicated with patriarchy.[5] A management that itself is informed by patriarchy responds to routine male–female harassment by essentially doing nothing. Extraordinary or extreme manifestations of male–female violence may lead to one-off management actions, such as disciplinary procedures and a rush to institute policies, but the action on the extraordinary only serves to allow the ordinary to proceed unheeded. The outcome of these effects of the sustaining ideology of patriarchy is that everyday abuse and harassment becomes normalized.

For customer-to-frontline staff violence and abuse, notions of customer sovereignty act as forms of sustaining ideology. In an era of "consumer capitalism,"[6] there has been a "shift in power and authority from producer to consumer."[7] For instance, consider the shift in the role of the government as macroeconomic policy maker and as employer. In both spheres, there has been a marked move from a production-centered approach to a consumer-centered approach – the moves from state as guarantor of full employment to state as guarantor of low inflation to allow rising consumption, and from state as model employer to state as model service provider. These shifts are symptomatic of and underpin the rise of notions of customer sovereignty in society and particularly within organizations. Within organizational practice, *total quality management* represents one of the clearest manifestations of the rise of notions of customer sovereignty, with its central mantra of the necessity to conform to the standards that the consumer demands. To argue that there has been a rise in the consumer as a figure of authority and a rise in notions of customer sovereignty is not to suggest that customer sovereignty has become a form of "totalizing discourse" (see Fournier and Grey,[8] critiquing du Gay,[9] for this very error) or a new form of "iron cage" enclosing the service economy. Rather, it is to suggest that notions of customer sovereignty may have important organizational implications, not least in the sense that they may be able to act as important forms of sustaining ideology for customer violence and abuse.

Indeed, to sidestep the problem of setting up customer sovereignty as an iron cage that cannot be opened by its inhabitants, it is useful to conceptualize a rise in organizations offering an *enchanting myth of customer sovereignty*.[10–12] Organizations increasingly seek to portray to consumers that they are sovereign both in the sense of being in charge and in the sense of superordinancy over those serving them. In palaces of consumption, the customer, addressed as *Sir* or *Madam*, becomes mythically the sovereign. At the same time, in the search for efficiency in service delivery, organizations seek to direct customers' actions (consider, for example, the fast food assembly line followed by the customer). They appeal to customers by seeking to enchant them with a sense that they are in charge, but at the same time they seek to control their actions. Such a fine line suggests an easy movement, within the fragility of consumption,[13] for the customer from enchantment to disillusionment. For instance, Leidner[14] notes discourtesy expressed by customers to frontline workers as occurring when the bureaucratic "inflexible routines" of the production organization intruded on the service interaction.

This, then, is the first important way in which notions of customer sovereignty influence customer-to-frontline staff violence and abuse. We can see in the movement from enchantment to disillusionment a key systematic trigger for customer abuse to frontline staff. In this sharp and painful journey, it is less likely that customers will vent their anger at the architecture of the overall social situation in which they find themselves. Rather, it is more likely that this frustration will be vented at the frontline worker, the person facing them, the person apparently embodying the service organization with which they are dealing. In addition, we can see customer abuse and violence toward frontline staff also legitimated by notions of customer sovereignty. If they are in the place where "the customer is always right," what can be wrong in them abusing and threatening frontline staff? If there is a sense of guilt emerging later, after a person has sworn at a frontline worker, this guilt is assuaged by the social positioning of that person as a *customer*.

What, then, for the role of notions of customer sovereignty for the frontline staff, the victims of customer abuse and violence? As with the role of patriarchy in male–female harassment, notions of customer sovereignty can lead to victims labeling themselves as culpable. If the customer is right, if the customer is as important as management states, then perhaps it is the fault of the individual worker in triggering the customer abuse. Did they say the wrong thing or look the wrong way; did they fail to be empathetic enough? It is these questions that spring from the ideology of customer sovereignty and it is these questions that lead to a tendency for frontline staff to see themselves as culpable.

There are also important implications from the rise of notions of customer sovereignty for management actions. Crucially, management itself is implicated in the organizational presentation of enchanting myths of customer sovereignty. It seeks to enchant customers by giving them a sense of their own sovereignty. It aims to manage service interactions such that frontline staff continue to deliver to customers an enchanting myth of their sovereignty. Forced by competitive pressures to seek the customers' business, and to enchant customers, management routinely instructs frontline staff to put up with customer abuse. A number of studies have found that management's implicit message for frontline staff is that, "If a man's having a go at you . . . Your job is to deal with it."[15] Thus routine abuse and even violence[16] elicits no management actions. Indeed, any routine procedures following customer abuse and violence may actually serve to place the victims as the culpable parties (see below). As with the case of male-to-female violence, extreme or extraordinary acts of abuse and violence may lead to a management response, but again the action on the extraordinary only serves to allow the ordinary to proceed unheeded.

The outcome of the rise of notions of customer sovereignty is that customer violence and abuse becomes normalized, accepted as part of everyday life. The following three sections illustrate these theoretical points with empirical evidence gleaned from a study of job centers in the UK.[iii]

Customer Sovereignty and the Management of Customer Abuse and Violence in Job Centers

The Employment Service is a government-run public service that acts as a job matching service to the unemployed and distributes certain unemployment benefits. The Employment Service achieves this through the management of its *job centers*, which the unemployed attend in order to seek job vacancies and to collect unemployment benefits (such as money to live on, help with the rent, and help with travel costs to jobs). To qualify for these benefits, the unemployed need to "sign on" with a job center worker every fortnight and, if requested by the worker, prove that they are looking for work.

The ideology of customer sovereignty was heavily promoted within job centers. This was particularly evident in official policies and training. For example, the job centers operated a *mystery shopper policy*, where management sent a representative, posing as a customer, to assess the level of service given. The mystery shopper policy was intended to ensure a high level of customer service and to buttress the ideals of customer sovereignty. A manager noted how the mystery shopper policy was connected to the rising importance of the customer:

> We used to give people tickets and we'd time them; we'd do it all manually. Now it's the mystery shopper, which I'm all for but I don't think people take it as seriously as they should do – and they ought to – the customer should come first. (Manager, female, Caucasian, middle sized town center)

Customer sovereignty was also embodied in the Job Seekers Charter. This was a statement of "the level of service that customers could expect from the job centers." It included bullet points about the rights of customers and what they could expect from frontline staff. The Charter was hung on the walls of job centers and printed on the back of customers' paperwork. It promised that staff would wear a name badge and would give their full names when they telephoned or wrote to people. Consequently, customers had the "right" to service workers' names. In contrast, customers were usually addressed formally as Mr/Mrs, etc.

The use of a name badge was contested by the union, fearing for their members' security. They fought for staff's right to use a false name or just their first name. The outcome was that staff were permitted to do this if they requested the "privilege" from their manager. In practice, though, some managers did not approve of this outcome, and so failed to inform staff that they had a choice. The Job Seekers Charter also promised that frontline staff would be polite, considerate, open, fair, and honest when dealing with the customer, and that they would respect customers' privacy. It stated that staff who made errors would apologize and make corrections promptly.

Within training, it was stated that frontline staff had six customer service commitments:

1. I will always be helpful and friendly towards the customer.
2. I will be responsive to individual customer needs.
3. I will behave professionally.
4. I will take responsibility when I deal with customers.
5. I will earn my customers' trust.
6. I will demonstrate pride in myself, my job center and the Employment Service.

All these "commitments" reveal the stress on customer-focused service and on the "enjoyable" experience for the sovereign customer.

Within the job centers, then, the ideology of customer service underpinned all management attitudes and practices, obliging frontline workers to tolerate abuse and violence as part of their jobs. Some of these attitudes and practices will be considered in more detail.

Management attitudes

Managers often expressed the opinion that abuse or violence was largely due to frontline staff's inadequate customer service skills. For example, one manager stated that:

> I always say, treat people how you want to be treated and I do think you need to have a level of customer service, you do need to know if the customers are happy with the service that you are offering, because you can't work or improve on that. If you don't have customer service and you don't treat clients with respect and listen to their needs then that's what causes the problems. That's when you start getting aggro within the office. (Manager, male, British Asian, small inner-city job center)

And another manager explained that:

> There are times when sometimes there can be words or actions by members of staff that can provoke something that could have been diffused. (Manager, female, Caucasian, middle sized town job center)

These opinions were symptomatic of a managerial philosophy that placed the onus on service workers' actions for inciting or avoiding customer violence. It was a perspective underscoring managers' claims about how their own, superior, customer handling skills had prevented "incidents" occurring:

> If you've got a member of the public who is being quite aggressive and your member of staff is not calming them down but winding them up even further and being abrupt or rude or whatever, and you're thinking, "Oh don't do that." Sometimes you've got to jump in and calm the situation. I've had to jump in and take the customer away from the person and say, "come and sit down this end of the room" and "come and have a chat with me" just to get them out, because you can see them getting really het up and you think, "Oh, no, this is going to end up in a punch up." But definitely, if somebody hasn't got those skills . . . (Manager, female, Caucasian, middle sized town job center)

Training

Blaming frontline staff's inadequate skills was also a theme in training. In the training sessions observed, the importance of customer service was a constant refrain. For example, when briefly told how to deal with customer anger, staff were instructed to recognize anger, stay calm, use active listening, signpost the different possibilities for the customer, and to check the facts with them. The trainer detailed how performing each one "badly" could cause anger. In this way, the customer's propensity to anger was taken as a given. The trainer wrote up a pattern of "someone becoming angry" on the board, which was seen as the definitive way it would happen. She wrote:

- *Build up*
- *Then*
- *Trigger*
- *Then*
- *Escalator*
- *Then*
- *Finale*

The triggers to violence in this framing were described as "bad customer handling skills." These included poor listening abilities, poor signposting, poor confirmation of the facts, and poor labeling. Service providers were also told to familiarize themselves with the "difficult" customers, and then to change their behavior in order to avoid an "incident." It was stressed that by using good customer service skills with a difficult client a violent incident could be avoided altogether.

Union representatives and officials seemed well aware that the onus for aggressive and violent incidents was placed with the service worker, and were critical of this:

> I think, really, their approach these days is that it's all part of the job, and you will hear managers say, "Right, if you can't put up with this, you shouldn't be doing the job . . . ," and that's it; and that's a widely held view these days – which I think is true in many occupations, unfortunately. The onus is put back on the front-liner. I think that's the conclusion that we arrive at, and more often than not the staff get indirectly blamed for creating the situation in the first place – which is rarely the truth of it. (Union official, male, Caucasian)

Other organizational practices

The formal policy of recording an abusive or violent incident with a customer further contributed to the construction of frontline culpability. For example, in the official recording of violent incidents, both the manager and the service worker were required to fill in report forms. On the frontline staff's form, a question was asked as to whether the staff member had been on a "handling difficult situations course." The clear implication was that the customer violence was related to the worker's skills. In the manager's report, respondents were advised to identify the problem the member of staff was trying to solve, what triggered it, and how it was handled. Additionally, they should note if the staff member had been in an incident before, implying, once again, that the problem lay with the service provider and not with the service recipient or the work culture. The following "reassuring" view from a manager illustrates the apparent success of the approach:

> I mean we are actually doing a customer survey at the moment. . . . we obviously do provide the right sort of service because we're getting very positive feedback . . . We're professional; we're friendly; ask would you recommend your friends and colleagues to come in, and it's always yes, I've not seen a no yet. So we are doing the right things as an office and this shows; we don't have many incidents. (Manager, male, British Asian, small inner-city job center)

Frontline Staff and Culpability

Many service workers acceded to the idea that the responsibility for customer abuse and violence lay with themselves. For example, some would readily point the finger at a colleague's lack of competence in this area:

> She'll spend twenty minutes sitting down there filing, and that's gotta be really aggravating for people in the queue. When you look at Pete, he might as well have a stamp, basically sausage factory or whatever; and then you get Jenny sitting there looking at one piece of paper for twenty minutes. Both of them must annoy the customers and then if you have to deal with them after, they're already gonna be irate, before you've even said anything. (Frontline staff, female, African-Caribbean, large city job center)

In this manner, staff would appeal to their customer-handling approach in avoiding, defusing, or escalating aggression, so implicitly subscribing to the idea that customer service skills were paramount. Indeed, some would go to considerable lengths to deflect culpability away from the aggressive or problematic customer:

> No, no, no, never, never – even the people who've been aggressive here with everyone else, you know, they've been ever so friendly to me; never in my 27 years . . . none of them have been violent, they've been ever so friendly. I think it's because I turn the odd blind eye, yeah. I've been in market town, everywhere, and they've been really friendly, yeah: they just said, "Man from Social Security . . . I'm coming to see you," you know, because some of them are working on the market stalls, which they shouldn't be really – but I turn a blind eye and they say, "Look I'm going to, you know, give you good apples now"! Yeah they are all friendly, really friendly, no problems at all. (Frontline staff, male, British Asian, large city job center)

Here the frontline worker takes the customer service ideology to the extreme; the customer really *is* always right. Indeed, bending the rules to this end was a not uncommon occurrence:

> Because my experience of frontline and certain people, you have to keep the queue going down, so they keep signing them and getting them out, getting them out. They don't have a chance to spend quality time with people . . . whereas other people will spend a long time trying to get people into work and it's often the people, the long-term unemployed, that you're under the impression slightly that they're scamming the system, so certain people, and you can figure out who they are, spend a long time sort of trying to force people into work, which often causes [violent] incidents whereas other people will only make that effort if they're interested. . . . If they're scamming the system, I will just sign them and get them out, basically. (Frontline staff, male, Caucasian, middle sized town job center)

While there was evidence that many frontline workers had internalized a sense of their own culpability for customer violence and abuse, there was also evidence that this internalization was far from complete. For instance, off stage in the canteen, frontline staff often blamed customers directly for abuse:

It's very difficult to give good customer service when you're dealing with some of the notorious clients, and those that just come in to be disruptive and aggressive. Because a bank doesn't have to do it . . . comparing it with a bank, they don't have to deal with those sort of people because they don't have bank accounts. The difference between us and a lot of customer service industries is that we have got to deal with every walk of life – desirable, undesirable. (Manager, female, Caucasian, large city job center)

I suppose I would compare an office with an office, and the likelihood of an incident in an office like this is lower compared to an inner-city office. But that doesn't mean to say . . . it only needs one nasty incident and you can really shake people's self confidence, and from personal experience I never feel comfortable – you can feel the adrenalin rise straight away and you immediately think, "where's this gonna end?" Can I cope with that abuse today, which is often personal, you know – they make it personal, they'll comment about your thighs or your shape or whatever and there will be bad language. You think, "Can I really cope with that today?" "Do I deserve it?" And of course you don't. (Frontline staff, male, Caucasian, small village job center)

The Normalization of Customer Abuse and Violence in Job Centers

The outcome of the processes outlined above, underpinned by notions of customer sovereignty, was that customer violence and abuse was normalized and routinized within the job centers. In training, there were attempts, additionally, to play down the significance of the violent customer. Frontline staff were repeatedly told that theirs was not a "high-risk job." To underscore this point, the job was often compared with jobs that involved working with dangerous machinery – that is, "real danger." For example, in response to an employee's concerns about a recent violent incident, the researcher overheard one manager attempt to allay the workers' fears by explaining that, in some jobs, employees risk their health every day because of the machinery that they work with. In an interview, another manager expressed a similar sentiment:

You have to be careful, because staff, well . . . I mean, I question whether they can get the job out of proportion sometimes. . . . I always tell them to look at the stats for other jobs, you know . . . incidents can be much higher

However, this line of thinking did not always convince:

I wouldn't describe them [violent incidents] as rare. Rare to me would be something that happened once in a blue moon and that's not the case. . . . Why do they say it? Have a false sense of security, not meeting their obligations as an employer from the health and safety point of view. It's an official line and official lines are developed by people not doing the job, someone in their ivory tower sitting in London head office or Sheffield head office who's probably never actually sat on a front line and know what it's like.

They've got the theory but not the practice. (Frontline staff, female, Caucasian, middle sized town job center)

The managerial shaping of language assisted, additionally, in re-casting and de-emotionalizing abuse and violence, making them appear as more controllable, less disruptive, features of the work. For instance, the very term "incident" serves to neutralize and bureaucratize. And instead of aggressive and violent situations, front-line staff found themselves in "difficult" situations or "situations where they needed to consider their own safety." A trade union representative makes the point:

What do they call it? Reliability under pressure, adaptation to change . . . yeah, it's like in our reports, it's just absolute management bollocks . . . it just takes things away from the real issues – like violence, basically, aggression – nobody wants to use those words, because obviously it suits their means to call it something else . . . (Union rep., female, Caucasian, middle sized town job center)

Finally, in training, violent and aggressive customers were rarely directly mentioned. Instead, less innocuous phrases and concepts were used:

In training we have "challenging" customers! . . . Challenging situations – not violent customers; not drug addicts – people with "different lifestyle choices"! (Union official, male, Caucasian)

Overall, these symbolic manipulations contributed to desensitizing incumbents to both the real impact and the social/organizational causes of customer abuse and violence, making it appear a routine burden of working life that the frontline worker had, simply, to shoulder. The tyranny of the sovereign customer was thus well camouflaged.

Conclusion

While Hochschild began the process of uncovering the dark side to emotions within the service economy, a key emotional arena she neglected to fully address was that of fear and pain related to customer abuse and violence. In this chapter, we have argued that rising customer abuse and violence should be seen not so much as a result of a breakdown of social mores, but rather as an outcome of a reconfiguration of social mores around customer sovereignty. Notions of customer sovereignty can act as a sustaining ideology to underpin customer violence. Customer sovereignty ideology can legitimate customer abuse and violence in the eyes of customers; it can lead management to institute policies that lead to the systematic overlooking of customer behavior experienced as abusive or violent by frontline staff; and it can lead to frontline staff internalizing a sense of their own culpability when confronted with customer abuse or violence. The case study research used in this chapter has shown that abuse, violence, and the fear of abuse and violence were systematically present within job centers in the UK. These constituted a significant dark side to emotional life of front-line staff in these organizations, and this dark side was underpinned by an ideology of customer sovereignty.

If the outcome of the operation of an ideology of customer sovereignty is normalization of customer abuse and violence within organizations, as is suggested in the theoretical discussion and in the case study evidence, then we need to consider the public policy implications of this. If customer abuse becomes an acceptable part of everyday life in organizations, there is a need for both institutions and new forms of language to act to destabilize this everyday scene, to allow a proper questioning of it and a response to it. Here, we briefly argue that trade unions and a discourse of bullying can serve to challenge the normalization of customer abuse and violence.

At an abstract level, customer abuse and violence comes to be normalized within organizations because the customer is seen as the pivotal social actor, the basis of authority. Normalization of violence occurs because the voice of the sovereign customer overwhelms all others. Put this way, it is clear that one way to confront this situation is to raise the voice of the victims of this situation – namely the frontline workers. The most effective mode of independent worker voice articulation is the trade union. A strong active trade union presence within the service economy can act to regulate against the everyday acceptance of customer abuse and violence. To be a decent economy, the service economy needs the presence of strong trade unions. Indeed, this can represent an opportunity for the organization of service workers into trade unions. Korczynski[10] has argued that in an era where traditional union ideologies have waned, unions in the contemporary service economy can set out their aim as seeking to "civilize production and consumption simultaneously." In this way, unions can again take for themselves the "sword of justice." Through protecting the sectional interests of their members, they come to accomplish a key social good.

If institutions, such as trade unions, can be important in challenging the normalization of customer abuse and violence, so too can language. Indeed, a key contribution of feminism for organizational life was the presentation of a discourse that exposed the male-to-female harassment that had been accepted as an everyday thing. The discourse of workplace bullying represents a potential avenue for the challenging of everyday customer abuse and violence. In current practice, workplace bullying tends to refer to bullying of staff by other organizational members, most often managers. This is a rising and important discourse that has allowed the exposure of pockets of abuse, and even violence, which have been kept invisible within organizations. There is considerable evidence that the identification and exploration of the concept of workplace bullying with regard to management behavior has already had an impact on organizational practices[18,19] and has affected organizational members' consciousness[20,21]. *There is a rich potential, therefore, in renaming customer abuse and violence towards frontline staff as customer bullying.*[22] This language may serve to destabilize the everyday acceptance of customer abuse and violence. The concept of bullying highlights the illegitimacy of actions. As such, it destabilizes the concept of customer sovereignty – a concept, we have argued in this chapter, which underpins much customer abuse and violence.

Notes

i.   We use the term "customer" to mean service-recipient. Terminology is important in this
      area. The renaming of service-recipients as "customers" has occurred in a wide range of
      settings in the service economy – including job centers, where management recently insti-
      gated a change in name for service-recipients from "clients" to "customers." Our use of
      the term "customer" is not meant to endorse this process; it is used merely for ease
      of expression.
ii.   The table offers a broad comparison between two ways in which violence in organizations
      is underpinned by forms of sustaining ideologies. The table necessarily simplifies for ease
      of articulation. Crucially, we can think of ways in which the different forms of ideology
      can become intertwined, whereby a confluence of patriarchy and customer sovereignty
      can legitimate male customer-to-female staff violence and abuse.
iii. See Bishop[17] for more details on the methods underpinning the research.

References

1.   Hochschild, A. (1983) *The Managed Heart*. Berkeley: University of California Press.
2.   Hearn, J. (1994) The organizations of violence: men, gender relations, organizations, and violences,
      Human Relations, 47 (6), 731–54.
3.   Cockburn, C. (1983) *Brothers*. London: Pluto Press.
4.   Hearn, J. and Parkin, W. (2001) *Gender, Sexuality and Violence in Organizations*. London: Sage.
5.   Collinson, D., Knights, D., and Collinson, M. (1990) *Managing to Discriminate*. London:
      Routledge.
6.   Miles, S. (1998) *Consumerism*. London: Sage.
7.   Abercrombie, N. (1991) The privilege of the producer. In Keat, R. and Abercrombie, N. (eds) *Enter-
      prise Culture*. London: Routledge, 43–57.
8.   Fournier, V. and Grey, C. (1999) Too much, too little and too often: A critique of du Gay's analysis
      of enterprise, *Organization*, 6 (1), 107–22.
9.   Du Gay, P. (1996) *Consumption and Identity at Work*. London: Sage.
10.   Korczynski, M. (2002) *Human Resource Management in Service Work*. Basingstoke:
      Palgrave/Macmillan.
11.   Korczynski, M. and Ott, U. (2004) When production and consumption meet, *Journal of Management
      Studies*, 41 (4), 575–99.
12.   Korczynski, M. (2005) Service work and skills: An overview, *Human Resource Management Journal*,
      15 (2), 1–12.
13.   Edwards, T. (2000) *Contradictions of Consumption*. Milton Keynes: Open University Press.
14.   Leidner, R. (1993) *Fast Food, Fast Talk*. Berkeley: University of California Press.
15.   Tyler, M. and Taylor, S. (2001) Juggling justice and care: gendered customer service in the contem-
      porary airline industry. In Sturdy, A., Grugulis, I., and Willmott, H. (eds) *Customer Service*.
      Basingstoke: Palgrave.
16.   Bishop, V., Korczynski, M., and Cohen, L. (2005) The invisibility of violence: Constructing violence
      out of the job center workplace in the UK, *Work, Employment and Society*, 19 (3), 583–602.
17.   Bishop, V. (2006) Violence on the Frontline. PhD thesis, Loughborough University.
18.   Hubert, A. B. (2003) To prevent and overcome undesirable interactions: A systematic approach
      model. In Einarsen, S., Hoel, H., Zapf, D., and Cooper, C. L. (eds) *Bullying and Emotional Abuse in
      the Workplace: International Perspectives in Research and Practice*. London/New York: Taylor and
      Francis, 299–311.

19. Rayner, C., Hoel, H., and Cooper, C. L. (2002) *Workplace Bullying: What we Know, Who is to Blame, and What Can we Do*. London: Taylor and Francis.
20. Lewis, D. (2000) Workplace bullying – a case of moral panic? In Sheehan, M., Ramsay, S., and Patrick, J. (eds) *Transcending Boundaries: Integrating People, Processes and Systems* (conference proceedings), Brisbane, Queensland, Australia: Griffith University.
21. Liefooghe, A. P. D. (2003) Employee accounts of bullying at work, *International Journal of Management and Decision Making*, 4 (1), 24–34.
22. Bishop, V. and Hoel, H. (2006) Customer bullying in job centers, Working paper.

CHAPTER 7

THE CALL CENTER

Enactments of Class and Nationality in Transnational Call Centers

Kiran Mirchandani

Organizational analyses of emotion work have documented the feeling work provided by caregivers, healthcare professionals, flight attendants, lawyers, bill collectors or customer service representatives.[1-8] The term "emotion work" has been used to describe the often invisible dimensions of the feeling work that people do as part of caring for their families or performing their paid jobs. Daniels notes that emotion work involves four interrelated behaviours: "(1) attending carefully to how a setting affects others in it . . . ; (2) focusing attention through ruminating about the past and planning for the future; (3) assessing the reasonableness of preliminary judgements . . . ; and (4) creating a comfortable ambiance."[9] Emotion work includes monitoring one's own reactions to situations, caring for others, and establishing links between people and events.

More recently, theorists have noted that emotion work often goes hand in hand with another form of work termed *aesthetic labor*. This is the "mobilization, development and commodification of embodied 'dispositions' [which] are possessed by workers at the point of entry into employment."[10:37] Witz and her colleagues note that, "as aesthetic labour, employees are *part of* the materialization of the corporate idea, along with the architecture and interior design."[10:45] Through recruitment and training, ideal workers are identified as those who not only correctly perform emotion work, but who also look good and sound right to customers.

Much of the reflection on aesthetic labor and emotion work to date has focused on workers in face-to-face service occupations. Individuals in these occupations are required to continually interact with others and be responsive to the needs of their clients and customers. However, in recent years, there has been a dramatic shift in the nature of service work as global processes have facilitated the exchange of services across national boundaries. Van den Broek estimates that the service sector now constitutes 20 percent of world trade and with the growth of telecommunications technology, the service economy no longer requires the co-location of customer and worker. As a result, service has become "tradable across international borders"[11:59] and emotion work has become a transnational phenomenon.

This chapter documents the nature of emotion work done by transnational service sector workers and, in particular, the ways in which the work they do problematizes issues of class and nationality. I consider the ways in which call center employees perform the aesthetic labor of *sounding right* when workers and customers occupy different national landscapes. I explore the ways in which workers enact their class positions vis-à-vis their customers and each other in the context of their location and colonial heritage. I argue that organizational analysis of aesthetic labor and emotion work, considered transnationally, raises issues of class, subservience, and national boundaries. This chapter draws on 25 in-depth interviews conducted with transnational call center workers in Pune and New Delhi, India.

Methods

The primary purpose of this project was to explore the nature of call center work within the context of global economy relations. The call center industry has been identified as India's "new sunshine sector."[12] The dot.com bust and the recession in the West led to the increased subcontracting of back office and service work to low-wage countries. Interviews were conducted in 2002 and 2006 with workers in New Delhi and Pune. Although customers were not interviewed, workers provided detailed descriptions of their interactions with customers and these are included in the analysis. All respondents were with organizations serving American, British, Australian, or Canadian clients.

Twenty-five workers (13 men and 12 women) were interviewed. Respondents were, on average, 26 years of age. Only four respondents were married; the remainder were single. All respondents had bachelors' degrees, and several had masters' degrees or additional diplomas as well. Workers interviewed in 2002 earned between Rs 5,500 and Rs 10,000 (US$125–225) per month with the exception of one male worker who had seven years of work experience and earned Rs 30,000 (US$670). For respondents interviewed in 2006 salaries ranged from Rs 10,000 to Rs 25,000 (US$225–560) with an average salary of Rs 16,000 (US$360). A significant portion of salaries was tied to performance incentives. Although extremely low in comparison to comparable salaries in the West, these salaries are considerably higher than those in local service industries.[11] In addition to good salaries, call center jobs are attractive to workers because of the clean work spaces and the fact that these organizations are marketed as fun places to work. Employees also receive perks such as free transportation, free dinners, free gifts for good performance, onsite cafeterias, pool/snooker tables, table tennis facilities, and bank machines. These are not usually available in other workplaces in India.[13–16]

Racism, Nationalism, and the "Theft" of Jobs

There are two forms of emotion work that workers see as key to call center work: first, the ability to deal with abuse and racism with acceptance and subservience; and, second, the need to fashion their customer service work as professional, white collar employment. While in some ways these are forms of emotion work that most call center workers perform, in the case of transnational service work, ethnic stereotypes merge with nationalism to produce unique configurations of racism, which forms the backdrop against which work occurs.

Racism and subservience

Emotion work in the context of call centers involves learning to not take the rude behavior of customers personally, maintaining self-worth in the face of abusive customers, and handling rejection. Call center workers note that strategies for managing abusive customers are taught during training programs and through on-the-job learning. One woman, for example, shared her training notes which were interspersed with visual depictions of the expectations that abuse was part of the job. One was a cartoon of a frazzled worker with the caption, "Hi, I'm an idiot! My name is Kumar Varum Verma. Thank you. Please kick me!" Other workers noted:

> We do come across people who do abuse us a lot. For us if people do abuse us, we have to give them warning, and then we can actually drop the call. That is one thing we can do. Okay, we are working in call centers, and means somebody just abuses you, otherwise we can't drop the call, we have to deal with it. But yes, if the person gets into an argument or he starts abusing, because they do abuse a lot. Girls they cry, they cry on the floor, and we have to tell them, don't take it so personally. It's like it's just like you calling up your mobile company and you are not happy. Something was supposed to be done which they didn't do, naturally you are not happy, and are screaming at them. It's just that in India we don't abuse but for them they do.

> Sometimes they're really pissed off. They really start, like, using four-letter words and you have to listen patiently. You have to listen to the customer, and after he finishes, try to cool him down and try to solve the problem. But you have to listen to the customer, whatever he is saying.

> We don't argue back. Arguing back is a strict no no. We can't say anything to the customer . . . We have been told so many times during our training that you have to keep cool, you have to keep cool, that it actually tends to brainwash your brain, drill your brain with that sentence. So we have to keep cool, and we have to understand that they are just our customers, the people who don't know anything. We are programmed to function in such a way; during the whole training period everyone will say that you have to keep cool, and that they are not abusing you, they are just abusing the company, things like that.

The types of abuse workers most frequently report, however, relate to the fact that many customers express an overt desire to deal with a Western rather than an Indian customer service representative. Customers feel free to express racist views that would have been grounds for legal discrimination or harassment suits if they had occurred face to face within North America or Europe. In fact, with the anonymity which customers enjoy, many feel entirely comfortable making overt racial slurs over the phone:

> Many of the times the customer used to, like, I don't want to talk to an Indian, he used to hang up.

We do get a lot of angry customers. I felt very bad when I had a drunk guy, who'd just called up for no reason . . . When he found out it was a call center in India, and started abusing for no reason, and just kept the phone down. I was shocked. It was one of my first 10 calls.

I know you guys are Indian, you took my application. So why didn't you process it? So you have to tell them that maybe there was a technical problem, it's not my fault.

Many of the customers when they call, and you say the welcome phrase, they just ask one single question – am I calling India? If you say yes, they just ask: I want to talk to someone in the US, I don't want to talk to Indians, and at that point of time we have to tolerate and we cannot say anything because it is our job responsibility as well as it comes under our customer satisfaction . . . parameters.

One day a person went, you know, I don't want to speak to you. You have broken English. Please give me someone American.

Sproull and Kiesler note that organizations often establish hierarchies through the use of physical space (office size or decorating schemes). They argue that reminders of these sources of inclusion or exclusion disappear or fade in virtual organizations.[17:43] In contrast, the quotes above reveal that hierarchies between workers and customers are extremely entrenched in virtual organizations such as transnational call centers. For customers calling in, there is little accountability; their responses remain largely anonymous and free from the normative requirements of public interactions as they are often calling from the privacy of their homes. Workers, however, are closely monitored and easily identified through the technologies such as the telephone and computer. In fact, their words are more closely and easily monitored than those of other workers in face-to-face service settings. Workers are aware of the fact that they can be easily traced by customers, and that supervisors frequently listen to their calls. This inequity between workers and customers is further complicated by the fact that some companies ask call center workers to mask the fact that they are located in India. Maintaining the illusion of being situated somewhere else exposes workers further to abuse:

"Where are you?" So we try to just come out of it, just say this is Warranty Service. I know what he's asking about, but still I need to say this. "No, I want to know where you are located." This is the warranty service centre and we are not allowed to disclose our location. We need to say very frankly. "Why: some secret is happening over there? I know you are in Bangalore, I know you are in Mumbai" – things like that they used to say. Sometimes you need to give false statements. Once a customer called over here he said in Hindi "shukriya," I was not very used to it, I was still very new to the phone. So I said okay "thank you." He said, "Yea, you know Hindi man; I said shukriya and you said thank you. Are you in India?" So again I have to say, "No sir, I've never been to India."

Much of the racism expressed by customers is directed towards their dissatisfaction with global subcontracting regimes. Workers said they were continually accused of personally "stealing" American jobs.

Americans are not really happy outsourcing the job to India. Because I still remember a call from a very old guy, and after doing all the things possible to satisfy his needs, he made one statement, "You know V—, you did a great job, however I hate you, because I hate all Indians. And my son is unemployed because of you, because the jobs are being outsourced to India.

Then you get a lady . . . she used to work in a call center. She just called up just to say that you people are just so scripted and I hate you people and I hate you Indians just because of that.

If they come to know that you are in India, then they get wild, because they don't want people from India taking calls for them; they ask you to transfer the calls to the US.

Maintaining dignity

Workers are not allowed to respond to such comments by naming it as racism. Indeed, the only condition under which workers are allowed to disconnect a call is if a customer raises his or her voice in an abusive manner. Even in this circumstance, workers are required to provide three warnings:

We cannot disconnect the call saying something. We have to provide techincal support or whatever support irrespective of what he/she is telling. We can disconnect the call only if a customer is using a slang, and that too after warning him three times, and even after three times he continues to use a slang word or especially the swearing type, we can disconnect the call after warning him.

In case you find a customer who is very difficult, even then you cannot disconnect the call. The customer was warning me, if you disconnect the call I will surely go and complain to [the American company] . . .

The behavior of abusive callers is implicitly sanctioned, given that workers must provide three warnings before disconnecting a call. It is only repeated abusers who can be challenged. Under these circumstances, workers are left to develop individual strategies to get their jobs done and to interrupt the repetition of abuse. Given that an integral part of their work involves building customer trust and rapport, workers develop individual strategies for dealing with nationalistic racism.

I don't know how to convince people and tell them that I'm not going to harm you even if I tried. And some or them are so skeptical about giving information, I say okay if you don't trust me, here's my name, here's my employee ID, here's where I work, so if anything goes wrong please feel free to catch me. That's the only way I can tell them.

You know, trust me, there's no other way. I want to tell them what is it you have to lose? We end up losing the job. We end up losing so many more things. I feel integrity is very important. . . . I don't know how to help such people, but the only way I can help them is here's what you need, if you feel that you've been cheated this is enough for you to get me into trouble. I tell them that I'll even give them my supervisor's name.

I used to say sorry about all the inconvenience that is happening with you, however I am trying to serve you to the best I could. Well in case you have any personal grudge with me, you could always hang up the call and call back. If you want me to assist me, I would be very happy to. It was a very simple and blunt statement, I understand that it could be very insulting for that particular person who is calling in, but I need to maintain my dignity, my Indian dignity as well.

The work of maintaining *dignity* in the face of customer racism and abuse constitutes a large part of workers' emotion work. Workers feel attacked not only due to the nature of their jobs as service providers and telemarketers, but also as a direct result of their ethnicity, national origin, and geographical location. In response to these attacks, workers create geographically specific scripts through which their self-worth as "Indian" can be manifest. For example, some workers construct themselves as professional therapists and carers. Others emphasize the very different class positions of the average customer, who may have little or no education and a poor standard of living, and the average Indian call center worker who is a university graduate:

There are a lot of old people also that are hard of hearing, and you have to talk to them like you're explaining to a little child, because a lot of them are not very good with mobile phone, and they don't even know what a SIM card is, and people say *gosh!* Are Americans so dumb, they don't even know what a SIM card is? Probably when mobile phones came to India, Indians were the same; a lot of people don't understand that they don't have patience to understand that. You have to explain to them like little children how to put the phone, how to put the SIM card together.

This one time I was on a call, and there was this lady, and I couldn't pronounce her surname. She was American and she said, you know, what difference does it make, I'm getting divorced. I said I'm very sorry, you know, because I didn't know what to say. She said, oh don't be sorry, I've had 12 years of a disastrous marriage, and I don't know what to do. I've to start from scratch, all over again. And you know I told her there are so many things you can do, move on with your life, get a job, get a post, so you know. So then I just made a little joke – you want to know what, you're speaking to somebody who is miles away, and it's 2 a.m. in the morning and I'm still talking to you. So then she started laughing. So at the end of the day, she did put the phone down but she was really happy . . . by the time she was done with me she was actually giggling.

Despite these strategies, workers embody extremely contradictory class relations and managing these class ambivalences requires considerable emotion work. For example, workers are encouraged to view their jobs as professional, white collar employment – they work in clean offices, are required to dress professionally, and receive extensive training in well-equipped board rooms. Yet, as noted earlier, much of their jobs involves dealing with customer abuse and racism, with servitude and deference, which are antithetical to their understandings of professional, white collar work. One worker talks about the frequent assumption made by her partner, friends, and family about her work in a call center. She says:

It's not even a job. It's like you're in school. You're monitored. You can't laugh loudly.
You can't talk loudly. You have to get up at this time. You have to sleep at this time. You
have no life. You have to be in a certain way at a certain time. If you exceed your break
by one minute a warning letter is issued.

She responds to this view by emphasizing the professional nature of her work:

It's that serious, believe me. Where I work I have to be in trousers and in a shirt every
single day . . . you always have to be prim and proper. You have to be your best, you have
to look your best when you go to work . . . I told my boyfriend, in fact you'll be surprised
the girl who owns A— Towers [a huge mall] works with me. You'll be surprised about
the kind of girls that work with me. Some of them are so decent I can't tell you . . . come
see the code of conduct. Come see the kind of people there are. Come see the kind of
discipline – you won't find it in any other organization.

However, workers do recognize that much of their jobs involve repetitive and
scripted processes akin to factory work. Many point to the misfit between their abilities
and educational levels and the actual nature of their jobs. As one man notes:

Work is quite smooth, it is quite simple also, but one thing that I fail to understand is
the particular job which I am doing, I don't think that the graduate person is required
for that particular job, especially after he gets training. So I think it would be better if
only a person of 12th standard would be. Because I have nothing to type, I have nothing
to talk because everything is ready made. For this particular thing I don't think a graduate
is required.

Professionalizing call center employment

Despite the actual work tasks involved, employing only workers who are "graduates"
is a central component of the transnational call center industry. Indeed, Indian workers
are discursively "marketed" by local media and business advocates in terms of the high
levels of education and skill that workers possess. As noted in a report by the National
Association of Software and Service Companies:

Instead of those hordes of young ladies, think for a moment about call center manning
by some very different kind of people. Think of doctors and pharmacists for medical
services, architects and structural engineers for construction materials, chemists and
agriculturalists for pesticide formulations, and automotive mechanics and driving
instructors for automobile after-sales service. . . . India has a vast reservoir of domain
expertise across industries and businesses. Our educational institutions turn out millions
of qualified people in a large number of disciplines.[18]

Such marketing is accompanied by sophisticated recruitment procedures, which
many call centers have adopted, including multiple interviews and tests for prospective
candidates. The construction of call center work as a privileged occupation is created
through this extensive screening process in place at the recruitment stage. Workers

(all university graduates) describe being selected from hundreds of applicants, and interviewed for hours before being offered the job:

> I was interviewed for six rounds with [the career consultant], then with [the call center] I interviewed for three rounds. Then I cleared the final interview, then I got the call.

> Around 200 people were shortlisted. And out of that 17 people were selected.

> [The interview took] seven or eight hours . . . one was the TOEFL test, and then they gave me a small objective type technical test, after that I was also given a one-to-one round, and then she gave me something to read out, maybe to see my accent, to see how I speak. Then I have a detailed questionnaire . . . I had again a one-to-one round with the technical people. Once I cleared that one, then I had a HR interview. After that HR interview in our company we get to be interviewed by a vice-president or the CEO of the company . . . maybe a hundred people apply and only seven or eight, or maximum ten, are accepted.

The emphasis on recruitment points to the fact that employers search not only for workers who can perform the emotion work of managing racism and abuse while maintaining the aura of their jobs as professional white collar work, but are also able to do the aesthetic labor of *sounding right*.

Accent and Class: Performing the Aesthetic Labor of Sounding Right

There is little clarity on the professional or technical qualifications workers need to "sound right" in transnational call centers. Indeed, beyond the stipulation that workers should possess a university degree and customer service skills, there are no other universal selection criteria in terms of subject of study or prior training. As Van den Broek notes, "given that around 90% of Indian call centres service English-speaking countries and companies, personality, attitudes and social skills roughly translate to proficiency in English diction."[11:63]

As a result, call center workers receive extensive training on "Voice and Accent," which involves detailed information on pronunciation, grammar, rate of speech and emphasis. As Witz and her colleagues note, "through the embodied performance of interactive service work, the physical capital of employees is valorized and converted into economic capital by and for organizations."[10:41] Training programs are used to eliminate employees unable to achieve the correct embodied performance required:

> They are spending too much on training on us. Because they are just filching you like anything that you are able to communicate with the people who are sitting 7 hours apart of you. They are very particular that if you are not able to score that 85+ you are kicked out of the company in C-SAT (Customer Satisfaction) . . . so after the 6 weeks of training, there is one week of transition, that is the customers are calling you and you are sitting live on calls. And you need to clear that as well for a week, if you're through you're ready to go ahead, if you're not through you are out of the company.

The process of learning to speak to foreign clients is termed *accent neutralization* and *correcting rate of speech*. Training programs serve to correct the ways in which trainees speak:

> The training is basically divided into two parts, one is communication skills training, and the other is process training. Communication skills: basically it means that you have to develop . . . it is basically getting the American accent, because we, as Indians, we have to have a neutral accent. If somebody has an MTI [mother tongue influence], it is getting out of that to a neutral accent, and then into an American accent. It's basically to get, you know . . . if you are talking with your customers, the customers should not feel that they are talking to an Indian, that's why we change our names also. We use names like John and Jack.

> For rate of speech we are given a pamphlet and we are asked to read from the pamphlet. Now within one minute wherever we stop we are given a rating. If it is within 90–120 words a minute it is considered ideal. If it is more then they told me to read more and more things and they told me to record my voice. I had an [American brand] cell phone, and I used to call their customer service and speak like an American. If they used to understand me then I was very happy. If not I used to think of another problem and call them again. So that way I used to get practice with that. If they say "sorry sir I cannot understand you, can you please repeat," I used to get a hint that okay my rate of speech is high.

Accent and rate of speech are said to need correction so that customers can communicate easily with workers. Implicit, however, is the construction of appropriate and inappropriate Indian accents – those that can be easily "neutralized" and those that cannot. As Witz et al. note, "the kinds of embodied dispositions that acquire an exchange value are not equally distributed socially, but fractured by class, gender, age and racialized positions or locations."[10:41] Within this context, it is South Indian and rural accents that are consistently constructed as problematic:

> There were people who were coming from the local medium, like Marathi medium schools and all; they couldn't speak, and they couldn't handle the process at the same point of time. For them it was even worse, because if they tried to get the pronunciation right, they messed up on the process; they forget what they are supposed to do next.

> Voice and accent training is mainly about removing people's South Indian accents.

Accent is not just a signifier of education or geographical location but, most importantly, it is also a signifier of class. This is evident in the ways in which accent differences are expressed by workers in terms of class hierarchies:

> (You said that you were surprised to be working with people from different stratas. What do you mean by that?) Educated, uneducated, your language is the main problem. This girl I was putting up with lived in a place that was like a slum. There were times that I felt like telling her that some maid servants I've had are far more attractive than you are. And they have more manners than you; they are more soft spoken than you are.

Accent also relates to the colonial heritage of educational hierarchies set up during British rule in India, where English-medium convent schools were established to train the local elite. "Convent school" graduates are normatively preferred for call center work:

> When you're a convent-educated girl, and you show relevant experience, they hire you.

Ideal call center workers possess neutral accents and Western outlooks as a result of their education, geographical location, and class position. Language serves as a stratification device through which class as well as regional hierarchies between workers are enacted. Accordingly, two discourses seemed to prevail in workers' discussions of their language: discourses of language as embodied knowledge and discourses of language as acquired skill. Workers who are convent educated and from urban areas talk about English language abilities as embodied traits while others construct language as a skill:

> Like, no matter how much you train somebody . . . Now some of the people, I'm not lying to you, and I mean it literally when I say they have grammar issues. You have to teach them how to speak proper English first . . . forget an accent or forget pronunciation. You need to get your the's and a's in position to speak well. And that I thought was a major issue that nobody really dealt with. If I was really recruiting somebody, I'd first pick somebody who knew how to speak good English . . . to speak good English, that is something that you have to teach somebody while in school, not over 6 weeks of training. You can't rectify grammar issues or mother tongue influence. This is a very common problem I've seen with most Mahrashtran people I've seen work in BPOs [Business Process Outsourcing companies]. No matter how much they say, that thing is always there in their pronunciations.

> What they think is that they can train you on voice and accent. They can train you on process, re-process, but they can't train you on grammar because [after] 15 years of studying to get it right, you won't get it right in 15 days.

Other workers, often themselves from rural backgrounds or with local language schooling, constructed Indians as malleable, trainable resources and noted that language skills could be easily acquired through successful training programs. Training successes are widely celebrated and success stories form a part of motivational material used in training programs.

> I didn't have a neutral accent. I had a mother tongue influence in my accent earlier because we weren't so conscious about our accent and all earlier . . . I never made it a point when I was in school to improve the accent or neutralize it. I didn't know that the accent has to be neutralized. I thought whatever I'm speaking is correct as far as my grammar is correct. But later on when I moved here I knew a lot of things that I should have been saying.

> There was a workshop on speaking abilities. There was one female who came from some remote part of India and she was not very good in speaking English, so she was put in

the back office work – the non-voice part. She was doing very well there because she was intelligent, but she was not really able to confidently speak. So there was a workshop designed for her and some more people like her, and after that she had shown a lot of improvement and she was taken for a voice process, which was a big achievement for her, and for the company.

To "sound right," workers have to therefore learn to perform aesthetic as well as emotional labor. While Witz and her colleagues note that the focus on aesthetic labor allows for an analysis of the embodied nature of service work, these embodied characteristics are far from stagnant. Indeed, the very construction of aesthetics as skill or trait requires emotion work, which workers do in order to make sense of the changes to their way of speaking required for their work. In fact, not only do training programs encourage workers to sound a particular way on the telephone but workers also report needing to become particular kinds of people to work in call centers:

I was very shy when I just joined my new organization . . . and saw how people didn't agree with people who were shy – how they make you nervous, and, you know, when you speak you were asked to do projects, and you were asked to stand in front of so many people and everybody is judging you. . . . So I did see that you have to be a certain way . . . somebody who comes across to be very bold. I don't know what to say – wouldn't say provocative behavior, but I did see a lot of girls who were that and they'd manage to.

I had to change. I realized that if I was going to be shy, people are just going to eat me raw. They are going to have fun at my expense, and I had to . . . I was left with no choice but to change. It was kind of realizing, about what people are all about. You're respected if you're a certain way, you're not respected if you're a certain way. People always thought that I was this dumb girl who had everything but it's not like that. People think I don't have problems at work. Even today where I work, what problems can you have? You wear good clothes, you look good, you come live in a good society. But they don't realize ever since I've come here, I'm a totally different person. Ever since I've come to this industry I'm a totally different person.

In the context of transnational call center work, becoming a totally "different" person involves emulating the traits, outlooks, and ways of being of Western clients. Stuart Hall and his colleagues have explored the ways in which the notion of the "West" functions as a mechanism through which societies can be classified and, more importantly, ranked. He notes that, "West is a historical not a geographical construct . . . [and refers to] a society that is developed, industrialized, urbanized, capitalist, secular and modern."[19:196] Part of the aesthetic labor of working in transnational call centers therefore involves becoming Westernized and defining local cultures, languages, and customs as backward and incorrect.

Conclusions

Analysis of emotion and aesthetic work have added enormous depth to discussions of the labor involved in maintaining organizations and identities. The data in this chapter demonstrate that this labor occurs not only in face-to-face service work, but is also an integral part of global work regimes. Recent literature has emphasized the need to highlight the ways in which globalization is actually "achieved." Critiquing the construction of globalization as an inevitable and irreversible process by which capitalism dominates nations, labor markets, and households, Bergeron, for example, focuses on the " 'gaps and margins' of the processes of global capitalism."[20:999] Sassen, in a similar vein, notes the need to "shift emphasis to the *practices* that constitute what we call economic globalization and global control."[21:196] These theorists argue that grand theories that characterize globalization as a "meta-myth,"[22] a "rape script," or "a narrative of eviction,"[21] do not sufficiently allow for an exploration of the incomplete and contested nature of the movements of capital and labor. Instead, the way in which workforces are neither homogeneous, nor passive in relation to globalized work relations needs to be highlighted. The analysis in this chapter suggests that globalization requires the continual maintenance of relations between organizations, customers, and workers across national boundaries. These relations exist on the basis of the emotion and aesthetic labor that workers do as part of their jobs in order to "feel right" and "sound right."

Aesthetic and emotion work occurs within the context of power and hierarchies. These are structured not only by intra-organizational processes and individual traits of workers, but also the broader contexts of colonial histories and inequities between nations. As DeVault has noted, despite the attention paid to emotion work in the past twenty years, there have been a number of relatively neglected kinds of emotion work, such as the work involved in "adjusting to inequality."[23:55] In earlier writing,[24] I argued that while there has been reflection on the gender and class differences in emotion work, these have provided only partial understandings of the work that individuals do in racially and nationally diverse contexts. Emotion work depends not only on the gender and ethnicity of the worker, and the occupation within which they are employed, but most significantly on their social location vis-à-vis the stratification within the environment in which they live. Indeed, colonial histories, subcontracting relationships, and racialized stereotypes combine with workers' racial backgrounds and class resources to give rise to complex power structures which determine the nature of the emotion work that women and men do as part of their paid work.

There are several ways in which power is manifest in transnational call centers. First, micro-politics infuse work norms, surveillance regimes, and training curricula. Workers are asked to deal with customer abuse and racism as part of the requirements of their jobs and to accept the power of faraway, anonymous clients whom they serve. Their work is also heavily monitored by supervisors and trainers who use technologies such as satisfaction scores and computers to determine their salaries and job tenure. At the same time, workers exercise considerable power over customers by performing the roles of therapist or knowledge-holder. They construct the Western preoccupation with protecting jobs as unreasonable in light of neo-liberal agendas.

Power is also manifest in the creation of workers' class positions. As Skeggs argues, respectability is one of the "most ubiquitous signifiers of class" and seen to be the property of middle-class individuals.[25:3] The creation of call center work as professional, and workers as middle class occurs through a continual power struggle amongst workers as well as between workers and customers. Through these forms of emotion work, call center workers attempt to "live with industrial systems without losing [their] human dignity."[26:296]

There is an interactive effect between these micro-politics and the discourses of neocolonialism which underlie the very subcontracting of work from capital rich to labor rich countries. Workers are deeply cognizant of power relations between the Indian organizations for which they work and their Western clients who hold the power to shift the location of work at any time. Workers themselves perform a form of nationalism in their attempts to define Indians as most appropriate for call center work. This is in light of continual media reports that India is in competition with China, Southeast Asia, or the Caribbean for call center jobs. As Indians, workers see themselves either as already possessing the correct traits to perform the aesthetic labor of sounding right, or as being highly trainable to learn to perform this labor. In sounding right, however, the already established hierarchy between those who are serviced (normative Western subjects) and those who serve (immigrants, people of colour, those in the Third World) is further entrenched.

Overall, this study of transnational call center work suggests that the consideration of emotion and aesthetic labor as transnational phenomena allows for the explorations of the ways in which organizations are embedded within nations and manifest historical and societal stratification systems.

Acknowledgments

This project was funded by the Social Sciences and Humanities Research Council of Canada. The author would like to thank the interview participants for their enthusiastic and generous involvement with the project.

References

1. Aronson, J. and Neysmith, S. M. (1996) "You're not just in there to do the work": Depersonalizing policies and the exploitation of home care workers' labor, *Gender & Society*, 10, 56–77.
2. DeVault, M. L. (1991) *Feeding the Family: The Social Organization of Caring as Gendered Work.* Chicago: University of Chicago Press.
3. Gubrium, J. F. (1989) Emotion work and emotive discourse in the Alzheimer's disease experience, *Current Perspectives on Aging and the Life Cycle*, 3, 243–68.
4. Heimer, C. A. and Stevens, L. (1997) Caring for the organization: Social workers as frontline risk managers in neonatal intensive care units, *Work and Occupations*, 24, 133–63.
5. Hochschild, A. (1983) *The Managed Heart.* Berkeley: University of California Press.
6. Pierce, J. (1995) *Gender Trials: Emotional Lives in Contemporary Law Firms.* Berkeley: University of California Press.
7. Rafaeli, A. and Sutton, R. J. (1991) Emotional contrast strategies as means of social influence: Lessons from criminal interrogators and bill collectors, *Academy of Management Journal*, 34 (4), 749–75.
8. Van Maanen, J. and Kunda, G. (1989) Real feelings: Emotional expression and organizational culture, *Research in Organizational Behaviour*, 11, 43–103.
9. Daniels, A. K. (1987) Invisible work, *Social Problems*, 34, 109.

10. Witz, A., Warhurst, C., and Nickson, D. (2003) The labour of aesthetics and the aesthetics of organization, *Organization*, 10 (1).

11. Van den Broek, D. (2004) We have values: Customers, control and corporate ideology in call centre operations, *New Technology, Work and Employment*, 19 (1), 59.

12. *India Today*, November 18, 2002.

13. Mirchandani, K. (2004) Practices of global capital: Gaps, cracks and ironies in transnational call centres in India, *Global Networks*, 4 (4), 355–74.

14. Mirchandani, K. (2004) Webs of resistance in transnational call centres: Strategic agents, service providers and customers. In Thomas, R., Mills, A. J., and Mills, J. H. (eds) *Identity Politics at Work: Resisting Gender, Gendering Resistance*. London: Routledge.

15. Mirchandani, K. (2006) Gender eclipsed? Racial hierarchies in transnational call centre work, *Social Justice*, 32 (4), 105–19.

16. Mirchandani, K. and Maitra, S. (2007) Learning imperialism through training in transnational call centers. In Farrell, L. and Fenwick, T. (eds) *Educating the Global Workplace: Knowledge, Knowledge Work, and Knowledge Workers*. London and New York: Routledge, 154–64.

17. Sproull, L. S. and Kiesler, S. B. (1994) *Connections: New Ways of Working in the Networked Organization*. Cambridge, MA: MIT Press.

18. National Association of Software and Service Companies (2001) *IT Enabled Services: Background and Reference Resources*. New Delhi: NASSCOM, C28.

19. Hall, S., Held, D., Hubert, D., and Thompson, K. (eds) (1996) *Modernity: An Introduction to Modern Societies*. Oxford: Blackwell.

20. Bergeron, S. (2001) Political economy discourse of globalization, *Signs: Journal of Women in Culture and Society*, 26 (4).

21. Sassen, S. (2001) Cracked casings notes towards an analytics for studying transnational processes. In Pries, L. (ed.) *Transnational Social Spaces, International Migration and Transnational Companies in the Early 21st Century*. New York: Routledge.

22. Bradley, H. (2000) *Myths at Work*. Cambridge: Polity Press; Malden, MA: Blackwell.

23. DeVault, M. (1999) Comfort and struggle: emotion work in family life, *Annals of the American Academy of Political and Social Science*, 56 (1).

24. Mirchandani, K. (2003) Challenging racial silences in studies of emotion work: Contributions from anti-racist feminist theory, *Organization Studies*, 24 (5), 721–42.

25. Skeggs, B. (1997) *Formations of Class and Gender: Becoming Respectable*. London: Sage.

26. Ong, A. (1991) The gender and labor politics of postmodernity, *Annual Review of Anthropology*, 20.

CHAPTER 8

WEB WORK

The Gendering of Emotions and Perceived Work Time: Chicks and Geeks at I.com

Nicole L. Kangas and Debra E. Meyerson

Research has demonstrated the powerful emotional and cognitive effects of being personally engaged in work[1] and, at the extreme, reaching a state of "flow," in which "total involvement in the task at hand results in loss of self-consciousness and the sense of time."[2] This optimal state has been associated with a range of positive emotions, such as happiness, strength, and alertness, which do not divert attention to self, and therefore are conducive to complete absorption in work.[3] When people become engrossed enough in work tasks to experience flow, "the sense of time is distorted: hours seem to pass by in minutes."[3:31]

While much has been written about the relationship between deep engagement in an activity and perceived timelessness, we know little about how perceived time and workload are influenced by negative emotional experiences of work. Do certain negative emotions translate into consistent overestimations of work time and workload? If so, are certain groups of workers, particularly those lacking power and legitimacy, more vulnerable to these emotions, and therefore more likely to feel overworked?

This chapter theorizes that differences in workers' emotional responses to their in-role identities lead to divergent work time and workload perceptions. Following Ashford and Humphrey,[4] we define emotion as *a subjective feeling state*. We suggest that positive emotions like joy, pride, and happiness are associated with an underestimation of time and workload, while negative emotions like anxiety and unhappiness are linked to distortions in the opposite direction. We developed this theory in the course of a qualitative study of young professionals in two gender-segregated departments within an internet media company. Our data reveal how the legitimacy and power associated with workers' identities and the gendered construction of their roles differentially shaped women's and men's emotional experience of work, and thus their time and workload perceptions.

Literature Review

Over the past decade, organizational researchers have shown an increasing interest in time as a characteristic of work, and the perception of time as an important quality of the work experience.[5,6] Numerous studies in social psychology have demonstrated a relationship between individuals' time awareness and their perception of time duration.[7-9] Activities that heighten people's attention to time consistently result in overestimations of time and workload, whereas activities that reduce people's attention to time produce the opposite tendency.[7,10] Consistent with these findings are reports of flow,[2,11] personal engagement,[1] and timelessness,[12] which describe a state of intense engrossment[13] in an activity such that one loses awareness of time and underestimates the time spent in that activity.

Studies of these deeply engrossed states suggest a link between people's salient work identities, or the identities that are prominent in the performance of work roles, and their work-time perceptions. Specifically, people's work roles may involve levels of cognitive and emotional absorption that cause people to become so focused on their work tasks that "time as an experience ceases to exist."[12:551] Positive emotions are an important component of this process. That is, only when role performances evoke positive feelings, such as joy, fulfillment, or exhilaration are people able to lose themselves in the activity at hand, and consequently lose awareness of self and time. This loss of self-awareness occurs because positive emotions allow us to channel our attention toward external tasks, like work. Conversely, negative emotions divert attention toward the self to restore an inner subjective order.[3,14]

Surprisingly, there has been little research on the relationship between negative emotions and people's time perceptions. Generally, we know that the more central an identity[i] is to an individual's self-definition, the stronger the associated emotions. When central identities spawn strong negative emotions, heightened self-awareness prevents engrossment in external tasks.[15,16] Accordingly, exaggerations of work time should emerge under these conditions.

To understand the link between emotions and perceived time, it is instructive to consider the role of preferred and non-preferred identities. Engagement and the associated positive emotions are possible when role performances demand expression of preferred identities, or the dimensions of self that people would like to use and express in the course of a role performance.[1] A business executive's identity as a professional, for example, is a preferred identity that is conducive to full engagement in work tasks and a feeling of timelessness at work.

Sometimes, however, role performances call up non-preferred identities, or identities that, in a particular context, evoke negative emotions, like anxiety, shame, or sadness. In the course of employment, for example, the business executive's identity as a mother may be a non-preferred identity that conflicts with her professional identity. Thus, when her mother identity is evoked at work, we would expect her to experience anxiety or other negative emotions. Because these emotions divert attention toward the self, they limit opportunities for engrossment in work tasks and lead to overestimations of work time and workload.

Importantly, role performances may require the deployment of core dimensions of self, but nonetheless stir negative or mixed feelings. When made salient, central identities that feel threatened will evoke feelings of anxiety or fear. For example, a feminist journalist might feel anxious if the publication she works for solicits advertising and partnership opportunities from mainstream companies that disapprove of feminist values. Similarly, identities that are associated with negative stereotypes or stigmas will spawn feelings of anxiety, shame, or defensiveness, sometimes simultaneously with feelings of pride.[17,18] The feminist journalist, for instance, may feel self-conscious and worry that her pro-woman slant is confirming the negative stereotype of feminists as "male bashers" while at the same time she derives pride and satisfaction from engaging in work that calls on a central self-dimension.[19]

When identities associated with negative stereotypes are made salient by role performances, individuals become hyper-conscious of those negative images. This hyper-consciousness is associated with anxiety and decreased performance.[19] Research has shown, for example, that African-Americans perform worse on standardized exams when they are faced with the threat of confirming a negative stereotype about their groups' intellectual ability than when they are told exams do not measure intelligence.[19] Applying this idea to the work context, role performances that are associated with negative stereotypes or stigma are more likely to result in hyper-consciousness, which prevents full absorption in work tasks and leads to perceptions of being overworked.

Power also influences emotions. Research in social psychology has demonstrated the relationships between elevated power and positive emotional responses, and reduced power and negative emotions.[20,21] Consequently, work roles that employ or make salient identities that are associated with reduced power in a particular context will tend to evoke negative emotions. As stated above, the more central and salient the identity, the stronger should be the emotional response.

As a status condition and identity, gender may differentially stir emotions for men and women, particularly when gender is highly salient in the context of men and women's role performances. For example, role performances that require men to perform masculinity – where masculinity is a source of power – would evoke positive feelings, such as confidence and exhilaration, unless role occupants felt personally misaligned with the role requirements. Conversely, role performances that involve women performing femininity – when femininity is devalued and associated with powerlessness[22] – would evoke negative emotions like insecurity, guilt, fear, and anxiety among women, even when women feel aligned with the role requirements.[23,24] This would be the case, for example, in work settings where women assume nurturing and care-taking roles that are viewed by the organization and society as less valuable than aggressive leadership and rainmaker roles. Here, the negative emotions stem not from misalignment with care-taking roles but from role devaluation.

This suggests that the subjective experience of time may be gendered. That is, differential time perceptions may be a consequence of the different emotional experiences of work associated with gendered status conditions. The research presented here explores this issue and formulates theory about the relationship between role performances, the emotional experience of work, and perceived work time and workload.

Data and Methods

The theory developed in this chapter is grounded in a qualitative study of young professionals in a San Francisco-based internet media company called I.com. The company operated a group of websites targeted to 13- to 30-year-olds who consider the internet an integral part of their lives. Founded in January, 1997, I.com employed 390 people at the time of our study.

The company was organized around network groups, which published original content on entertainment, dating, and other topics relevant to the young target audience. While formally part of the same organization, each network functioned as an autonomous business with its own managers, editors (writers), and artists. The networks were individually housed in separate suites within the I.com floor of an office complex. They had independent letterheads, business cards, and promotional items, such as brightly colored "Girls Rule" t-shirts or graphic video game posters, which reflected the style and mission of the particular network. Accordingly, network employees identified primarily as members of their networks rather than as I.com employees.

We studied participants in two networks – Girls Chat and Boys Club. Girls Chat employed 20 editors, artists, and managers, all of whom were women in their mid-twenties to early thirties. The network targeted girls between the ages of 13 and 30 and focused on issues pertaining to health, sex and fitness, careers and education, news, politics, entertainment, beauty, and relationships. Girls Chat members shared a mission to empower and entertain young women through the production of "edgy" content and the sale of fun, hip products on the website. None of the members were married or had children.

The Boys Club network was a highly successful cluster of website "channels" that focused on video games, science fiction, relationships and women, news, and movies and music, aimed at boys aged 17 to 30. During our study, Boys Club consisted of 22 editors, artists, and managers responsible for creating the content for Boys Club websites, which entailed researching and writing about these topics and creating art to accompany their text. Employees were men in their mid-twenties to early thirties. One man was married and had a child. Boys Club is the only network within I.com that survived the dot.com bust.

Data collection

We spent 24 days observing Girls Chat participants working, interacting, attending meetings, eating, and socializing. We shadowed them while they met with members of other departments, participated in on-site parties, and joined them in restaurants for employee gatherings. Observations did not follow a formal protocol. Initially, we looked for indications of how people thought and felt about their time, their workload, and the boundaries between work and non-work. Eventually, we sought clues about how they thought and felt about themselves in their role performances. Our observations followed the same pattern at Boys Club, where we spent 14 days observing. In both networks, we kept detailed field notes of our observations and, when possible, recorded dialogue verbatim.

To track employees' arrival and departure times, we timed our data collection so that one of the co-authors was on site at the beginning and end of each day. This was important for comparing their reported work time perceptions to actual working hours. We triangulated our estimates with information gleaned from formal interviews.

Our interviews were semi-structured. We posed broad "grand tour" questions (e.g., "Tell me about a work day") and asked follow-up questions to clarify points of interest.[25] We also asked each informant to provide details about when they typically arrived at and departed from work. These queries were asked in the context of their narrative to probe further into the particulars of their description, not as discrete questions about their start and end times. We believe that this mitigated social desirability effects.

We stopped interviewing when additional interviews strengthened the consensus within department and yielded no new information relevant to our emerging theory.[26] Ultimately, we interviewed 17 Girls Chat members and 13 Boys Club members. Interviews lasted between 60 and 90 minutes, and all were tape recorded and transcribed.

Data analysis

Data analysis followed an inductive process aimed at developing grounded theory.[26,27] Although our analysis was ongoing and iterative, it occurred in three stages: during data collection, first round of thematic analysis following data collection, and detailed analysis.

While we were still collecting data at Girls Chat, we examined the field notes for themes that surrounded employees' time perspectives and other topics. We realized early on that Girls Chat employees regularly talked about being overworked and appeared to hold exaggerated views of how much time they spent working relative to our observations. We also took note of how employees expressed themselves in the course of their everyday behaviors. For example, we were struck by the employees' vocal and persistent calls for "independence" and "self-reliance" while at the same time they worried about looking pretty and finding "rich husbands" so they wouldn't have to work. We became interested in a possible association between members' self-expressions and time perceptions, but we did not have a theory about how these two themes might be connected.

The second stage of analysis occurred following our formal data collection process. Here, we iterated between dissecting the data and reviewing pertinent literature. We compared emerging themes, various data sources, and the literature on subjective time, identity, and flow to guide our analysis and refine our concepts.

Because we were particularly struck by the shared perceptions of time and workload within each network, and the sharp variation between the networks, we decided to focus our third stage of analysis on workload and time perceptions, themes related to people's work identities, and a set of factors that we thought may contribute to these. To assess employees' work time we began by comparing employees' self reports with our observations of when they came and went. With a few exceptions, employees' descriptions in our interviews were consistent with the times we observed them arriving and departing each day from the office. We also calibrated our observations by asking at the beginning of each interview if the days we observed were typical.

Both authors independently analyzed transcripts and field notes to assess employees' time and workload perceptions. Words and phrases such as "not working ridiculous internet hours," "well balanced," "time for friends," and "manageable work schedule" are examples of the types of comments we coded as indicating reasonable work times and workloads. Conversely, comments like "too much to do," "completely overbooked," "trying to be super human," "shackled to my computer," and "spending all my time at work" indicated perceptions that work time and workload were unreasonable.

Analysis of these perceptions highlighted patterns, with Boys Club employees consistently reporting relatively light workloads, and Girls Chat employees reporting that they were overworked. Similarly, Boys Club members tended to report that work time "sped by," while Girls Chat employees often commented that time dragged on and work consumed far too much of their time.

Member Identities, Emotions, and Perceived Time and Workload

Our data point to a set of conditions that color people's experience of self and shape their time and workload perceptions. Before addressing these conditions, we set forth the data that motivated the investigation – our observations about actual and perceived work time – and we describe the comparable task environments of the two networks.

Patterns in time perceptions

Table 8.1 displays actual mean workday estimates in each group as compared with members' perceptions of their typical workload or work time. As shown, Girls Chat members, with a few exceptions, reported that time dragged on, that they worked long hours, and that they were overworked. Participants at Boys Club tended to underestimate time and workload, and many described experiences analogous to a flow state in which they had no sense of time passing.

These patterns cannot be attributed to the nature of the task, conditions of the task environment, or role demands outside of work given the comparability of these conditions across the two networks. Moreover, all participants in both networks were intrinsically interested in and motivated by their work. Below, we describe their task environments and develop our theory about the way gender shaped members' cognitive and emotional experiences at work and their work time and workload perceptions.

Table 8.1 Observed work time and perceived workload

	Mean work time	*Perceived work time and workload*
Girls Chat	9.0	Long; demanding
Boys Club	9.8	Reasonable; easy

Girls Chat and Boys Club: comparable task environments

Girls Chat and Boys Club operated similar businesses, and employees of both departments engaged in virtually identical tasks (i.e., writing, research, design) with comparable time pressures, daily posting deadlines, and similar support structures. To the researchers, the cultures of the two settings were equivalently loud, frenzied, and social. Members of both departments were stationed in cubicles, but at all times there were employees moving around and huddling over each other's computer screens. The task environments were similarly characterized by constant interrupts, multitasking, and looming deadlines. Virtually all informants claimed that their role requirements were well aligned with their personal interests and identities.

Employees of both groups were expected to mirror their target audiences' interests, attitudes, and behaviors. In other words, as part of their role performances, members were expected to employ and express culturally sanctioned versions of their gender identities. At Boys Chat, employees were expected to mirror the behaviors, thoughts, and feelings of their target male audience – geeky, hormonal young men in their teens and early twenties. Girls Chat members were similarly expected to embrace the image of womanhood they advocated in their writings as hip, independent, and sexual young women.

Within Boys Club, members focused either on video games or entertainment. The former group of employees provided information on new video and personal computing games, while the latter focused on researching and writing about movies, television, music, and science fiction comics as well as producing a section on "babes," cars, dating, and audio equipment. More generally, role performances at Boys Club entailed interacting with one another to uphold culturally sanctioned images of masculinity: acting out violence in the video games they wrote about, talking about the latest video games, and sexualizing all relations with women. The work of several entertainment editors involved discussing, researching, and writing about "hot chicks" in films. The "Babes Editor," for example, spent several hours each day selecting women to highlight on the site. Boys Club members were regularly seen peering over this employee's shoulder to observe and rank the contenders. In an astounding array of displays, including a centrally placed life-size blow-up doll of a scantily dressed woman, office décor reinforced the centrality of this aspect of the member role.

Boys Club employees regularly told us how lucky they felt to have a job that enabled them to do what they wanted to do and, importantly, be who they wanted to be. As one member put it, "We are not here because we are making lots of money. We're here because we love it. There's something special about Boys Club and the pride that everybody feels about what we are creating."

At Girls Chat, being in role involved modeling a particular image of self as young woman. The topics the women wrote about, the products they sold, and their expressions of self reinforced their hip, "go-girl," sexually progressive definition of womanhood. Girls Chat employees self-consciously displayed this image through their clothes, make-up, and hair. Members constantly evaluated one another's attire, and complemented co-workers on their "sweet get ups" and "fabulous ensembles." Several editors dyed their hair bright colors, providing endless subject for commentary. Hiring decisions also reflected their collective self-conception of being hip and progressive young women. When they selected a disc jockey for their new radio program, members described the new recruit as "so Girl Chattish – totally like us . . . cool, smart, and a little sassy."

Importantly, members also expressed their values and identities as feminists in how they interacted and what they wrote. For example, the women spoke proudly with one another about the need to look out for themselves in relationships, work, and personal matters. One editor explained: "No one else is going to make sure I get the promotion. I have to look out for number one." The editors similarly advised their readers to remain independent. In a dating feature, for instance, one editor wrote: "Giving up your bachelorette pad doesn't mean you have to sacrifice your identity. Make sure you don't lose sight of what's important to you. Part of maintaining independence is not altering the things you enjoy doing just because your partner doesn't . . ."

Finally, Girls Chat employees emphasized sexuality as a defining feature of their identities as women. The women openly talked about their own sex lives, focusing interactions around dates and cute guys, and covering their cubes with pictures of "hot" male actors. Expressing their own sexuality and acting on their sexual desires without censor was part and parcel of defining themselves as hip and independent young women.

In sum, Boys Club and Girls Chat members held comparable roles and spoke of the alignment between their valued selves and their roles when describing why they joined I.com. They worked under comparable conditions, yet, as shown below, while Boys Club members seemed psychologically engaged in their work, Girls Chat employees complained about how much work they had and how burdened they were by their workloads. This cannot be attributed to actual hours worked or to familial commitments outside of work since these conditions were comparable across networks.

Rather, our observations suggest that at Girls Chat, members' awareness and relative exaggeration of their time and workload were linked to two important factors that differentiate and speak to the gendered nature of their experiences: 1) the tenuous legitimacy of their gender identity and 2) the cultural ambivalence surrounding their gender roles. As we will show, Boys Club members enjoyed unchallenged legitimacy and social status, while the status of Girls Chat within the organization and the legitimacy of its message within society were precarious at best. In addition, Boys Club members also occupied roles with clear expectations for how twenty-something geeky boys should behave. The Girls Chat women, on the other hand, faced substantial ambiguity about what it means to be a young woman. We suggest that both of these conditions fueled feelings of anxiety among Girls Chat members, which contributed to exaggerations of work time and workload.

Legitimacy

Although Girls Chat's stated mission was to empower young women and to reflect the voice of this generation of hip, independent women, the larger I.com organization sent mixed messages about the legitimacy of this mission, and, by association, the women's current definitions of self. For example, during a meeting with the corporate sales team responsible for selling advertisements on the websites, the Girls Chat editors were cautioned to tone down the language about sex because "we need to be sensitive to those who are not comfortable with sex coverage." While the editors believed that "we are Girls Chat and we need to get behind the sex and relationships topic honestly," those who reflected market concerns about "racy content" questioned their focus and encouraged Girls Chat to abolish sexually explicit language to avoid offending potential advertisers.

Similarly, I.com executives and the corporate sales team wanted Girls Chat to partner with a large cosmetics company and a traditional clothing line. While Girls Chat members felt the association with "old school" makeup and clothing companies was contrary to the network's mission of empowering independent, edgy women, those outside of the network argued that it would "pump a lot of cash into I.com" and that Girls Chat would "need to widen its strategy to make the partnerships work." Specifically, the women were instructed to attract a wider audience by "becoming more mainstream" and "considering young women from more vanilla backgrounds."

In sum, despite the consensus among Girls Chat members about the progressive images of womanhood they expressed on their website and enacted in their offices, and the centrality of these images to the Girls Chat "brand," colleagues outside of the network were less sanguine about the legitimacy of these self-conceptions. The valued selves deployed in role were therefore, at some level, socially stigmatized, and, as such, members were bound to feel negative emotions, such as anxiety, fear, embarrassment, and self-doubt about their role-defined selves.[28]

Boys Club employees were, in contrast, the corporate heroes. The legitimacy and identity of members within the organization, and the market-at-large, was sound. Advertisers expressed no concern about Boys Club's sexually explicit content. One executive explained the obvious hypocrisy: "It's different for girls. [Girls Chat] is too far ahead of the cultural curve." Moreover, I.com benefited directly from members' capacity to identify with and cater to the young male audience who affirmed their masculinity through simulated violence and sex. Because Boys Club accounted for more than 50% of I.com's revenues and virtually all of its potential growth, the young Boys Club geeks were encouraged to express uncensored even the most vulgar and racy displays of self.

With the legitimacy of Boys Club firmly entrenched, members of this network enjoyed substantial power compared with Girls Chat members, whose version of womanhood constantly was called into question. In other words, although the work tasks themselves were similar at the two networks, the tasks made salient identities that were associated with reduced power for Girls Chat and increased power for Boys Club. This power differential did not go unnoticed by Girls Chat members. They were well aware of Boys Club's place as "one of the top sites for men." One Girls Chat editor articulated: "Their numbers are much bigger than ours. Everyone loves Boys Club. We need to increase Girls Chat stock within the company without losing sight of our message." Because reduced power tends to evoke negative emotions while powerfulness spawns positive emotions, it is not surprising that the expressions of anxiety and ambivalence we witnessed at Girls Chat were not apparent at Boys Club.

Gender roles

For many Girls Chat members, the work role activated not only members' current definitions of themselves as young women, but also readily accessible images of their future possible selves.[16] Possible selves include "individuals' ideas about what they might become, what they want to become, and what they are afraid of becoming."[16:954] These images operate as filters through which people interpret their current selves. In other words, salient future selves can shape how we perceive and feel about our selves in the present.

Possible selves are particularly salient during transitional life stages and life events.[29–31] The young adults in this study had all recently entered the workforce and were in the midst of developing new professional and personal personas. As part of this transitional period, some were discovering and considering a range of different hypothetical versions of themselves.[31]

At Girls Chat, for example, many women shared elaborate and readily accessible images of themselves as stay-at-home wives and mothers. Some had visions of themselves marrying wealthy men and staying home or scaling back paid work to raise children. One member explained, "I don't see myself as capable of doing both [work and family] and you can't sacrifice your family." Another commented, "I wish my boyfriend would get rich so I wouldn't have to work." One employee explained, "I want kids so staying in this environment would be difficult. I want to be able to spend the majority of time with my kids and I don't want to cart them off to a nanny." Another woman worried aloud about not having the time to "make homemade chicken soup." These were the same women who emphatically displayed their progressiveness and independence.

Taken together, our data suggest that although the discharging of their member role was expressive and affirming of their current conceptions of their gender identity, the salience of this central identity simultaneously evoked readily accessible conceptions of their selves as women in the future. That is, members experienced their expressions of self as hip, independent, sexually progressive women in the context of their images as future stay-at-home mothers and devoted wives. For these women, the discrepancy between their current and salient future identities – identities that were central to them – surfaced in their displays of self and leaked out in their self-consciousness and displayed self-absorption. The question of "who will I be?" was felt in the present as "who am I?"

In stark contrast, Boys Club members revealed no indication that they thought beyond the present. Notably, few members were able to access future self-conceptions even when we explicitly asked about their future roles and plans. Whether it was due to a reported psychological tendency of men to focus on the present time period[32] or due to departmental or childhood socialization, theirs was a world strictly in the here and now, and they collectively reinforced this mindset in the games they played and the articles they wrote. Their unfettered focus on the present meant that members were not worried about or distracted by future self-conceptions, which enabled them to engage fully – emotionally and cognitively – in their present role.

Gender, engagement, and subjective time

We know from existing research that individuals tend to respond to negative emotions by trying to resolve their source through self-regulatory and other defensive reactions.[14,33,34] Self-regulation involves directing attention toward oneself, which deflects attention from the present activity or task.[14] Accordingly, as negative emotions increase, one's attention shifts from activity to self,[9] resulting in an overestimation of time and workload.

Boys Club members, unencumbered by worries about the future or about the legitimacy of the selves they expressed at work, were not distracted away from the activities before them. Despite the similarities to Girls Chat in the nature of the tasks, task environments, and intrinsic motivation, their emotional experiences of self, attention to self and time, and time and workload perceptions could not have been further from their counterparts'.

In their self reports and in our observations, it was evident that Boys Club employees took joy in their work. Members reported that they regularly lost themselves in their activities and lost track of time. Their descriptions of their work experiences were, in many ways, reminiscent of descriptions of a flow state[11] and intense personal engagement.[1]

For example, one editor apologized for being late to a meeting after he "got sucked into" a "rad" comic book that he was reviewing. "It's so good. My day has been made." Another editor who was supposed to leave the office early one night explained "I got so into this new kick-ass game that I forgot [to leave]." Similarly, on numerous occasions, we observed Boys Club members trying to rally co-workers to go off-site for lunch. This often proved difficult since members were wrapped up in their writing. Indeed, rather than leaving to eat, the person who was looking for colleagues to dine with often ended up staying and participating in conversations about the gaming or entertainment content or observing their co-workers' activities on their computers.

In general, the Boys Club office was full of positive creative energy. There was a real sense that members did not want to be elsewhere, or doing other things. It was rare to hear members complaining or talking about non-work matters. Instead, they were focused on the tasks at hand, regularly commenting on how "dope," "cool," and "awesome" their work was.

Even when they weren't officially at work, they often became engrossed in work-related tasks. For example, an entertainment editor explained, "I have a really hard time going to a movie, even for my own enjoyment, without a notepad and pen . . . I don't know anyone else [at Boys Club] who doesn't think that way. I start jotting down a few notes and boom, by the end of the film, I have a story. The opportunity to write, and get my milage paid for, is really cool." Overall, the Boys Club members expressed a real joy about their work. The network head reflected this sentiment when he declared: "It's just the most amazing site. I am like *wow*, it is the greatest."

Like their Boys Club colleagues, Girls Chat members appeared to enjoy their work and took pride in their empowerment mission. However, unlike their counterparts, they appeared anxious and highly self-conscious about the identities they enacted and presented on their website. For example, during a meeting, members debated whether to use the words "love, dating, and sex" or "family, friends, and loves" as the subheading for the new "relating" portion of the site. Even if advertisers would allow them to use the word "sex," they saw some merit to focusing on family and friends instead of "limiting [them]selves to condoms, hook ups, and hotties." As one editor articulated, "We need to decide what we mean by 'relating.' I think we should define it broadly. It isn't all about sex. It's about children, grandparents, friends."

In contrast to the unfettered work of the Boys Club entertainment writers, the Girls Chat entertainment editors faced disagreement and ambiguity about, for example, whether to allow users to comment on or merely rate celebrities. Members acknowledged that allowing commentary could get "dirty" and "nasty," and there was debate about whether they should "have an authoritative voice" or allow the site to be a "sounding board." One entertainment editor explained that the decision was important because it "reflects who we think we are – how much ego we want to exert, and how much we want to support diverse opinions." Agreeing with this point, another editor said this issue was "totally stressing her out."

Stress and anxiety were common topics of discussion at Girls Chat. One editor told us that she was worried about whether to send out an email announcing her promotion. "I don't want it to seem like I am bragging, but I need people to understand my new role." Another member told us: "I get totally wound up and dream about work. The other day, work was the first thing I thought of when I woke up and it was Sunday. My friend had to talk me down. I don't know where this comes from, but it's tiring."

As this last example shows, some Girls Chat members, like their Boys Club co-workers, mentally brought their work home with them. However, unlike the Boys Club members, who seemed to enjoy and take pride in this arrangement, the Girls Club editors expressed negative feelings about work spillover. They also complained about their work and schedules while in the office.

As researchers, we found the overall emotional mood in the Girls Chat office to be noticeably different than at Boys Club. While the atmosphere in the Girls Chat office was far from doom and gloom (i.e. there were periods of laughter, singing, happiness, and pride), there was a good deal of negative emotion expressed, particularly in terms of stress, worry, indecision, and self-doubt.

In this network, we suggest that it was the immediacy and meaning of members' gender identity that contributed to their emotional experiences. To members of Girls Chat, salient self-definitions based on future conceptions directly conflicted with their current identities. For some of the women, this discrepancy coupled with the tenuous legitimacy of their current and core identities triggered feelings of ambivalence and anxiety.

In contrast to experiences of role engagement apparent in Boys Club, the women's tendency to attend to themselves as a response to the negative emotions they experienced diverted them away from their immediate activities. The women's heightened attention to self distracted and thus prevented these employees from becoming fully engrossed in work tasks in the manner of their Boys Club counterparts. This made flow or timelessness impossible[2,11,12] and instead contributed to their persistent exaggeration of work time and workload.

Discussion

This study explored the relationship between people's gendered experience of self in role and their work time perceptions. Based on a comparison of two gender-segregated network groups, the qualitative study points to the relationship between gendered conditions, members' emotional responses to these conditions, their patterns of attention to self and time, and ultimately their perceptions of work time and workload.

The member self and subjective time

Boys Club members faced role conditions conducive to experiences previously described as flow,[11] personal engagement,[1] and timelessness,[12] all characterized by intense absorption in an activity such that one loses awareness of self and time. Boys Club was the flagship network of I.com. Corporate executives, the sales team, and outside advertisers fully supported the network's mission and style. Thus, members did not have to worry about the legitimacy of the selves they expressed at work. Rather, in the course of discharging their roles, members expressed preferred aspects of their identities, and generally associated positive feelings with their member selves. As would be predicted, Boys Club employees lost themselves in their work and perceived that their work time passed quickly. Most members did not feel burdened by their work.

Girls Chat employees expressed and employed core aspects of their identities and were also emotionally connected to their work. Yet they did not derive the same unmitigated joy and fulfillment from their role performances as their Boys Club colleagues. Contrary to the situation at Boys Club, the Girls Chat members' in-role-selves had tenuous status and legitimacy – executives, advertisers, and colleagues outside of Girls Chat explicitly questioned aspects of the hip, independent image of young womanhood Girls Chat put forth. Accordingly, members were prone to feel negative emotions, such as anxiety, fear, embarrassment, and self-doubt about their role-defined selves. These negative emotions prevented members from losing awareness of self. Instead, members appeared highly self-conscious and tended to overestimate their work time. Time passed slowly and work was seen as taxing by these members. Despite their comparable hours, they reported being overloaded by the amount of time they spent at work.

In sum, our research points to the potential significance of people's emotional response to the selves they employ at work in shaping their work time and workload perceptions. Prior research on engagement and flow has suggested a relationship between loss of self-awareness and time. Our study suggests a more generalized relationship between the emotional experience of self-in-role, attention to self and time, and time and workload perceptions. It highlights how power, legitimacy, and status, which are organizationally and socially ascribed to people's identities at work, condition this process.

Specifically, we showed how individuals' emotional experiences of work, and thus their corresponding time and workload perceptions, may by gendered or more generally shaped by power differentials that play out in the context of organizations. Building on prior research on stereotypes and social stigma[18,28] and the psychology of power,[21] our investigation reveals the relevance of social legitimacy in shaping members' emotional and cognitive experience of self-in-role. As Goffman[28] suggests, when a role's legitimacy is not fully sanctioned by the organization or social context, members may feel ambivalent about themselves and their identification with the role. Role performances that call attention to people's ambivalence and confront them with such fundamental questions as "who am I?" can extract a significant emotional toll, even when the role is organizationally prescribed. These negative emotions, in turn, prevent full absorption in work tasks and contribute to people's tendency to exaggerate their perceptions of work time.

We observed this dynamic among Girls Chat members, but it is not an experience unique to this group in particular, or to women in general. Individuals are often assigned to roles based on a presumed match between their cultural identity and a marginalized target audience to increase legitimacy in and access to those markets.[35] African-Americans, for example, are often assigned to bank branches located in African-American communities or to product marketing groups aimed at African-American consumers that are outside of the mainstream market. Minority group members may, on the one hand, identify strongly with this work and enjoy expressing a core dimension of self. On the other hand, the salience of an identity associated with marginality, cultural stereotypes, and social stigma may also lead to heightened anxiety, ambivalence, and self-consciousness.[28,36] Research on stereotype threat has shown, for example, that the salience of a social identity associated with negative stereotypes can produce anxiety because of the looming threat of behaving in a way that corroborates the stereotype.[19] In such cases, the expression of a dimension of self-in-role may be identity affirming, insofar as the identity is important to an individual, but its salience can trigger negative emotions.

This emotional burden is likely to be exaggerated in roles that require members to express identities associated with negative stereotypes or stigmas. More research is needed to explore directly how individuals emotionally and cognitively experience roles that make salient core identities that are not socially legitimated or are associated with stereotypes, and the related consequences of these experiences.

We point to the importance of examining emotional responses to future roles and imagined possible selves, and the compatibility of these roles with present selves-in-roles.[16,31] Future selves act as filters through which individuals experience their current selves. Girls Chat members were expected to express their current identities as young women. While their enactment of this identity was affirming, it also evoked easily accessible images of themselves as women in the future that collided, in many cases, with their current self-conceptions. This reflects the conflicting, socially constructed definitions of womanhood that existed at I.com and that persist in society at large. Boys Club members were not faced with divergent definitions of manhood, and they expressed their identities as young men without invoking images of their future selves, even when explicitly asked about their futures.

With the exception of studies that explicitly consider future possible selves, research on the self-in-role relation is void of a time subscript and limited in the assumption of a one-to-one relationship between role and identity.[37-39] Our study supports the possibility that people's experience of their present self-in-role, and their associated organizational experiences, are often shaped by a two-dimensional sense of self that is stamped by time. That is, under certain conditions, people bring in their past or possible future selves as interpretive and emotional filters through which they make sense of who they are, what they are doing, and how they perceive their work and work time. Future research may benefit from considering how past and future conceptions shape individuals' present experiences of self, particularly when the legitimacy and power associated with current self-conceptions are undermined.

Related to this implication is the notion that perceived conflict or inconsistency between identities need not be rooted in competing role requirements. Existing research on identity conflict tends to assume that conflict stems from competing role demands, such as the demands of parents and professionals.[40,41] Our research points to another possibility – single roles can activate multiple identities or self-concepts. As we showed, for many Girls Chat women, the work role called up both progressive, independent selves, and traditional stay-at-home mom selves. Activation of conflicting identities can produce negative emotions[40,42,43] but the felt tensions are not rooted in conflicts between formal role demands. Single adults without children may therefore experience a level of stress and anxiety comparable to what is felt by working parents. Here, however, the negative emotions and tensions do not stem from the competing requirements of current roles. Rather, they arise from the conflict between current and anticipated selves, and the power and legitimacy associated with these selves.

Research on perceived time, work/nonwork conflict, and workload would benefit from a broader consideration of factors that shape people's subjective experience in-role beyond the actual amount of time they work or their competing role requirements. Persistent reports of overworking tend to rely on self-reports or diary studies that do not attempt to differentiate between perceived and actual time. As others have argued,[44] people's reports of excessive time may be due to a variety of factors that influence their subjective experience. Our study suggests the potential significance of people's in-role emotional experiences in shaping their time and workload perceptions.

It is important to note that we are not suggesting that the gender differences we observed are due to any essential difference between the men and women, but instead to the ways in which their definitions and experiences of gender were socially and organizationally constructed, and the differential legitimacy ascribed to each in this context.[45] The concurrent salience of conflicting present and future definitions of what it means to be a woman reflects the persistence of deeply entrenched, conflicting cultural constructions of womanhood in society and within the organization we studied. Women and men in Girls Chat and Boys Club were selected and socialized to mirror the exaggerated profiles of their gender-segregated audiences. They were expected in their roles to *be* independent and progressive women and geeky hormonal men respectively. Yet the women were embedded in a context that was itself ambivalent about its own definition of womanhood, reflecting broader and deeply entrenched social norms about women's roles that did not escape the experiences of these young women.

Limitations

Our study was intended to generate theory and, as such, the theory we describe is speculative and requires additional research designed to isolate and test the proposed mechanisms. For example, we assessed actual work time by triangulating our observations of when people came and went with self-reports of start and end times. The consistency between these two measures gives us some confidence that our assessments were reasonable, and we avoided the pitfalls of previous research that relied exclusively on self-report data. However, subsequent research aimed at testing the relationships should develop more precise instruments to capture more accurately actual and perceived time.

Furthermore, while we believe that the natural comparisons in our sample were particularly rich and allowed us to discount some alternative explanations for the variations in time perceptions we observed, we could not, in a qualitative study, isolate the variables. We therefore cannot claim that other variables, including individual differences such as time perspectives or time preferences, were not also in play. Studies with large random samples are needed to test the strength and conditions of the relationships suggested here.

An additional limitation of the study may be the generalizability of our theory to other settings that are less "exotic." With its youthful employee base, gender-segregated departments, and "colorful" culture, I.com is hardly a typical organization. Yet, as Weick and colleagues have highlighted, it is useful to study unusual organizations such as those that operate under very trying conditions but have fewer than their fair share of accidents because they "provide a window on a distinctive set of processes that foster effectiveness under trying conditions."[46:82] In a similar way, I.com provided a setting that magnified a set of identity-driven mechanisms that extend beyond this setting. Moreover, some of the components of the theoretical relationships we observed are supported by previous research.

Conclusion

This study demonstrates that role performances can make salient and require individuals to express core aspects of their identities. Consistent with work on identities and power, we show that the expression of these identities is not always associated with positive emotions. Rather, role performances that draw attention to discrepancies between present and future self-conceptions, or that bring the legitimacy of current and core identities into question, may be associated with negative feelings, such as ambivalence and anxiety.

We theorize that differences in people's emotional responses to the deployment of a central dimension of self lead to distinct time and workload perceptions. Specifically, we draw on literature about engagement, timelessness, and flow to suggest that positive emotions are associated with losing track of and underestimating time, and we suggest that the opposite association – between negative emotions and the overestimation of time and workload – also exists. We encourage future research to test the theory proposed, to determine the extent to which emotions influence time perceptions in the workplace and in other contexts, to investigate the impact of legitimacy and power on emotions, and to explore factors that interact with emotions to influence perceived time.

Note

i. The notion of central aspects of self does suggest that people's self-concepts or identities are stable. Identities are actively constructed, affirmed, and renegotiated in the course of social interactions[47] that in turn reflect, modify, and challenge existing membership definitions, role expectations, and group boundaries.[48] We acknowledge that while some aspects of identity are more fluid and contingent, other dimensions of self are more stable and central,[49] even if the salience of a particular identity may vary across situation and time.

References

1. Kahn, W. A. (1990) Psychological conditions of personal engagement and disengagement at work, *Academy of Management Journal*, 33 (4), 692–724.
2. Csikszentmihalyi, M. (1990) *Flow: The Psychology of Optimal Experience.* New York: Harper & Row.
3. Csikszentmihalyi, M. (1997) *Finding Flow: The Psychology of Engagement with Everyday Life.* New York: Basic Books.
4. Ashford, B. E. and Humphrey, R. H. (1995) Emotion in the workplace: A reappraisal, *Human Relations*, 48, 97–125.
5. Ancona, D. G., Goodman, P. S., Lawrence, B. S., and Tushman, M. L. (2001) Time: a new research lens, *Academy of Management Review*, 26 (4), 645–63.
6. Orlikowski, W. J. and Yates, J. (2002) It's about time: Temporal structuring in organizations, *Organization Science*, 13 (6), 684–700.
7. Bloc, R. A. and Zakay, D. (1997) Prospective and retrospective duration judgments: A meta-analytic review, *Psychonomic Bulletin and Review*, 4, 184–97.
8. Boltz, M. G. (1998) The processing of temporal and nontemporal information in the remembering of event durations and musical structure, *Journal of Experimental Psychology: Human Perception and Performance*, 24, 1087–104.
9. Vohs, K. D. and Schmeichel, B. J. (2003) Self-regulation and the extended now: Controlling the self alters the subjective experience of time, *Journal of Personality and Social Psychology*, 85 (2), 217–30.
10. Conti, R. (2001) Time flies: Investigating the connection between intrinsic motivation and the experience of time, *Journal of Personality*, 69, 1–23.
11. Csikszentmihalyi, M. (1975) Play and intrinsic rewards, *Journal of Humanistic Psychology*, 15 (3), 41–63.
12. Mainemelis, C. (2001) When the muse takes it all: A model for the experience of timelessness in organizations, *Academy of Management Review*, 26, 548–65.

13. Goffman, E. (1961) *Encounters: Two Studies in the Sociology of Interaction*. Indianapolis: Bobbs-Merrill Company.

14. Baumeister, R. F. and Vohs, K. D. (2003) Self-regulation and the executive function of the self. In Leary, M. R. and Tangney, J. P. (eds) *Handbook of Self and Identity*. New York: Guilford Press, 197–217.

15. Gordon, C. (1968) Self-conceptions: Configurations of content. In Gordon, C. and Gergen, K. (eds) *The Self in Social Interaction*. New York: Springer-Verlag, 115–32.

16. Markus, H. and Nurius, P. (1986) Possible selves, *American Psychologist*, 41, 954–69.

17. Gould, D. B. (2001) Rock the boat, don't rock the boat, baby: Ambivalence and the emergence of militant AIDS activism. In Goodwin, J., Jasper, J., and Polletta, F. (eds) *Passionate Politics: Emotions and Social Movements*. Chicago, IL: University of Chicago Press, 135–57.

18. Park, L. E. and Crocker, J. (2005). The interpersonal cost of seeking self-esteem, *Personality and Social Psychology Bulletin*, 31, 1587–98.

19. Steele, C. M. and Aronson, J. (1995) Stereotype threat and the intellectual test performance of African Americans, *Journal of Personality and Social Psychology*, 69 (5), 797–811.

20. Tiedens, L. Z., Ellsworth, P. C., and Mesquita, B. (2000) Stereotypes about sentiments and status: Emotional expectations for high and low status group members, *Society for Personality and Social Psychology*, 26 (5), 560–74.

21. Keltner, D., Gruenfeld, D. H., and Anderson, C. (2003) Power, approach and inhibition, *Psychological Review*, 110, 265–84.

22. Ridgeway, C. L. and Smith-Lovin, L. (1999) The gender system and interaction, *Annual Review of Sociology*, 25, 191–216.

23. Kemper, T. D. (1991) Predicting emotions from social relations, *Social Psychology Quarterly*, 54, 330–42.

24. Sprecher, S. (1986) The relation between inequality and emotions in close personal relationships, *Social Psychology Quarterly*, 49, 309–21.

25. Spradley, J. P. (1979) *The Ethnographic Interview*. New York: Holt, Rinehart, and Winston.

26. Glaser, B. and Strauss, A. (1967) *The Discovery of Grounded Theory: Strategies for Qualitative Research*. London: Wiedenfeld and Nicholson.

27. Sutton, R. I. (1991) Maintaining norms about expressed emotions: The case of bill collectors, *Administrative Science Quarterly*, 36, 245–68.

28. Goffman, E. (1963) *Stigma: Notes on the Management of Spoiled Identity*. New York: Simon and Schuster.

29. Strauss, R. and Goldberg, W. A. (1999) Self and possible selves during the transition to fatherhood, *Journal of Family Psychology*, 13, 244–59.

30. Knox, M., Funk, J., Elliot, R., and Bush, E. G. (2000) Gender differences in adolescents' possible selves, *Youth and Society*, 31 (3), 287–309.

31. Ibarra, H. (1999) Provisional selves: Experimenting with image and identity in professional adaptation, *Administrative Science Quarterly*, 44, 764–91.

32. Zimbardo, P. G. and Boyd, J. N. (1999) Putting time in perspective: A valid, reliable individual-differences metric, *Journal of Personality and Social Psychology*, 77 (6), 1271–88.

33. Greenberg, J. and Pyszcsynski, T. (1986) Persistent high self-focus after failure and low self-focus after success: The depressive self-focusing style, *Journal of Personality and Social Psychology*, 50, 1039–44.

34. Rothbard, N. P. (2001) Enriching or depleting? The dynamics of engagement in work and family roles, *Administrative Science Quarterly*, 46, 655–84.

35. Ely, R. J. and Thomas, D. A. (2001) Cultural diversity at work: The effects of diversity perspectives on work group processes and outcomes, *Administrative Science Quarterly*, 46, 22–273.

36. Crocker, J. and Park, L. E. (2004) The costly pursuit of self-esteem, *Psychological Bulletin*, 130 (3), 392–414.

37. Stryker, S. and Serpe, R. T. (1982) Commitment, identity salience, and role behavior: Theory and research example. In Ickes, W. and Kidd, R. (eds) *Personality, Roles, and Social Behavior*. New York: Springer-Verlag, 199–218.

38. Kunda, G. (1992) *Engineering Culture*. Philadelphia, PA: Temple University Press.

39. Dutton, J. E., Dukerich, J. M., and Harquail, C. V. (1994) Organizational images and member identification, *Administrative Science Quarterly*, 39, 239–63.
40. Lobel, S. A. (1991) Allocation of investment in work and family roles: Alternative theories and implications for research, *Academy of Management Review*, 16, 507–21.
41. Kossek, E. and Ozeki, C. (1998) Work–family conflict, policies, and the job–life satisfaction relationship: A review and directions for organizational behavior–human resources research, *Journal of Applied Psychology*, 83, 139–49.
42. Higgins, E. T. (1987) Self-discrepancy: A theory relating self and affect, *Psychological Review*, 94, 319–40.
43. Meyerson, D. and Scully, M. (1995) Tempered radicalism and the politics of ambivalence and change, *Organic Science*, 6 (5), 585–601.
44. Jacobs J. A. and Gerson, K. (2004) *The Time Divide: Work, Family, and Gender Inequality*. Cambridge, MA: Harvard University Press.
45. Ely, R. J. and Meyerson, D. (2000) Theories of gender in organizations: A new approach to organizational analysis and change. In Staw, B. and Sutton, R. (eds) *Research in Organizational Behavior, 22*. New York: JAI Press, 103–51.
46. Weick, K., Sutcliffe, K. M., and Obstfeld, D. (1999) Organizing for high reliability. In Staw, B. and Sutton, R. (eds) *Research in Organizational Behavior, 21*. New York: JAI Press, 81–123.
47. Goffman, E. (1959) *The Presentation of Self in Everyday Life*. New York: Doubleday.
48. Meyerson, D. E. (2001) *Tempered Radicals: How People Use Difference to Inspire Change at Work*. Boston, MA: Harvard Business School Press.
49. Alderfer, C. P. (1985) An intergroup perspective on group dynamics. In Lorsch, J. (ed.) *Handbook of Organizational Behavior*. Englewood Cliffs, NJ: Prentice Hall, 190–222.

CHAPTER 9

HOMEWORKING

Managing the Emotional Boundaries of Telework

Gill Musson and Katy Marsh

Home-based telework is a unique arena in which to examine both the performance of emotion and the construction of identity, cultural aspects of human activity that are closely related. Through our research, we consider how men and women construct and enact the roles and identities of professional and parent in this ambiguous environment, where both may be culturally appropriate.

Common wisdom suggests that women will privilege their nurturing roles as mothers and men will privilege their breadwinning career roles when home-based telework and parenting co-exist in close temporal and spatial proximity. In the main, this has been supported by our data, yet, through our research, we also found examples of women who chose not to represent and construct themselves as domestic beings, wives, and mothers and instead articulated narratives of professional ambition and success; and of men who chose to articulate narratives of being "family guys," who were not firmly entrenched within their organizational roles but instead expressed desires to be more hands-on and loving parents. This, we propose, must require substantial emotional work, particularly in reconciling constructions of what it is to be female/male and mothers/fathers with the social and cultural expectations attached to these roles. This led us to consider how men and women cope emotionally and rhetorically with what might be seen as a challenge to the gendered order of society.

In this chapter, we examine how identities are constructed, through narratives, using discourse as the building blocks in this process. Discourses make certain ways of thinking and acting possible – and others impossible or costly[1] – and as such they are part of the "unspoken cultural rules" that dictate the boundaries of certain roles and reveal the behaviors and emotions that are permitted within them. What we seek to discover here is how, or indeed if, legitimacy is achieved when these rules are challenged because although these rules define the culturally and emotionally acceptable ways to talk and conduct one's self, it is always possible to resist these hegemonic tendencies, at least to some degree.[2] We begin by discussing the emotions involved in home-based telework, and make explicit the ways in which we consider emotion to play a key role in the construction of identities, as both a guiding discourse and performative resource.[3] We go on to discuss the gendered nature of emotion before presenting two *atypical* case studies. Our subsequent commentary serves to reveal the theoretical implications of these cases. In our final section we conclude that home-based telework may reveal new contours of emotional practice, which may open up new avenues for both men and women in terms of how they understand and construct themselves as professionals and as parents.

Emotions and Home-Based Telework

Many studies of home-based telework allude to the importance of emotionality in this ambiguous context[4] yet few explicitly discuss the actual emotions that might be involved and why they may become more prominent in such settings. A crucial exception is the work of Mann et al.[5] and later Mann and Holdsworth[6] who sought to reveal the psychological impacts of teleworking in terms of stress, emotion, and health more generally. Mann et al. refer to the reduction of travel-related stress and stress caused by colleagues interrupting work in the traditional office setting as one of the emotional "upsides" of telework.[7] They also point out that working from home allows the rediscovery of the intrinsic enjoyment of the work. Mirchandani[8] – who focused solely on female teleworkers – concluded that this form of work allowed women "to care *for* as well as *about*" their families more effectively, particularly in enabling mothers to be present for significant moments in their children's lives, but also by allowing them to create these significant moments for themselves. As Hochschild[9] remarked, flexible work can foster new rituals of importance to the meaning of family life and in this way telework can be seen as reaffirming the notion of family. Taskin and Devos[10] describe telework as liberating, giving individuals greater control over their work and autonomy over scheduling this work hand in hand with family responsibilities. These positive emotional aspects of home-based telework are said to result in an increased feeling of loyalty to the employing organization.[10]

These beneficial aspects of home-based telework are counterbalanced in the literature by a heady list of emotional "downsides."[7] A frequently cited negative dimension to working remotely is the increased isolation of the teleworker, leading to feelings of separation and loneliness. This is said to happen because of lack of emotional support from co-workers[5] who, because of physical distance, are no longer aware when support is required. Rokach[11] goes so far as to describe these feelings in terms of alienation, abandonment, and rejection. Alongside these negative emotions run further negative feelings of frustration, often caused by the absence of technical support and/or the lack of control and influence over other people in the traditional office environment. Home-based teleworkers are also said to feel increased guilt when calling in sick[5] and resentment, or even anger, when work seems to dominate the home environment and family life. Frustration and resentment might also be experienced for different reasons, because of the intrusion of family members into work time, as the boundaries between work and family roles become increasingly blurred.[12] Female teleworkers in particular are said to experience guilt and worry about prioritizing work over family. These feelings appear to come to the fore when children are present in the home and being cared for by another adult while their mothers feel trapped in the home-office, able to hear and feel their offspring, yet unable to be with them. Women, it is suggested, may also feel unable to resist the guilt they feel when witnessing unwashed dishes or clothes.[13] On the other hand, men are, on the whole, reported to find working from home less stressful in this respect.[14]

In sum, telework commonly results in conflicting emotions, some positive and others negative. Alongside this, the blurring of boundaries between work and family life tends to create the conditions for emotional "spillover" of stressful work emotions into family settings, leading to generally heightened feelings of anxiety and fear.[15] The experience and expression of these emotions has a bearing on identity because emotion is one of the key routes through which identity is expressed and/or performed. Furthermore, emotional "effort"[7] or "work"[9] is demanded for the construction of identities. The latter is particularly the case in ambiguous settings such as home-based telework when, for example, frustration, guilt, relief, or joy may all be experienced in turn and even simultaneously. Emotion, then, can be seen as both an input during the process of identity construction, and also an output during the process of presentation and interaction with others – although we acknowledge that these meeting points of emotion and identity are without doubt less clearly distinguished in practice than in this theoretical framework. In the following section, we address the extent to which emotion can also be said to be gendered (another key aspect of identity construction), with certain emotional practices judged more appropriate for one gender than the other. We consider how this might have an impact on home-based teleworkers' presentations of self, as well as the process of their identity construction.

The Gendered Nature of Emotion

Historically, emotions belong in the private realm and are associated with women. The expression and influence of emotions are absent in most accounts of the rational, objective domain of work, except in those work environments where emotional labor is required for the work to be effectively accomplished. Even then, this emotional labor, done in the public sphere for a paid wage, is considered somehow different to the "real" emotion work involved in the home: for example, the emotions involved in managing and bringing up children. This unwaged work of the private sphere is, by definition, associated with women rather than men.[9] Although it might not be possible to separate the categories of emotional labor and emotion work quite so easily, women are considered better at "doing emotion" per se because, as part of their innate "feminine" makeup they possess "natural" emotional skills. Witness the plethora of articles promoting the "soft" human-focused skills supposedly enjoyed and employed by all women – regardless of talent or training – as a central aspect of effective "female" management styles.

A counterpoint to this view is that management is a "masculine" activity that takes place in a male dominated environment, and requires women to construct themselves in line with masculine stereotypes to be successful.[16] These arguments are commonly

based on dichotomous and essentialist ideas of what constitutes being female and male
– that is, that women and men are born with instinctive attributes and abilities that
determine their capacities and capabilities in a variety of activities and arenas. Writers
have shown how such ideas are social constructions that permeate social attitudes
about what makes a "universal" male or female and how these constructions influence
the way male and female behaviors are interpreted (Burr[17] gives a comprehensive
introduction to social constructionism.)

However, regardless of whether essentialist or constructivist views dominate, there
are clear historical differences in the public spaces and roles occupied by men and
women. Historically, men have primarily inhabited the public world of work, where
their skills and talents must be pitted against those of competitors. In contrast, women's
daily experience, typically rooted in the family, has traditionally been lived out in a
network of interconnected relationships, not based on competition but on mutual care
and cooperation. These very different societal conditions in which men and women
have been/are socially embedded give rise to the constructions of the female/male
"individual" inherent in Western capitalist society. Men are seen to be logical, objective, and value free, able to keep emotions out of the reasoning process, whereas
women are viewed as emotional and intuitive, and therefore prone to illogicality. Of
course, these distinct worlds of women and men have collided and collapsed to some
degree, largely because women have joined the ranks of the paid workforce rather than
vice versa. But this is a relatively recent phenomenon, and a quick scan of media and
popular culture texts, including academic texts, shows that the social conditions that
position and produce the male and the female are still rooted in these distinctions.
Emotion then, is still primarily a female issue and women are generally said to handle
emotions better than men in *all* contexts, but particularly in the private domains of
the home and family.

Alongside the gendering of emotion, the meaning and practice of parenting in the
modern Western world has also been profoundly gendered. Men still tend to occupy
the breadwinner roles as providers for their children, as distinct from the feminized
role of caring in the home.[18] Even in dual career households, this gendering of caring
still exists (if not the role of sole financial provider) and we do not dispute that this is
the reality experienced by most females and males, both as parents and as children.
Although working from home has the potential to shake up gender dichotomies,
including the gendering of emotion, the data from various studies that we, and others,
have conducted in different contexts show that most women and men continue to see
and experience the emotional management of the family as the domain of the woman.
However, there are exceptions in our data and it is to these that we now wish to turn.
In the tradition of Potter and Wetherell,[19] by examining variation in data and exploring
differences rather than similarities, we expose the "margin of play" that traditional
analytical methods focusing on consensus or collective experiences tend to mask.[20] It
is often through atypical examples that one can glimpse the wider implications of
changing social conditions and such instances can point to liberating potential because,
as Sartre notes, "freedom is that small movement which makes a totally conditioned
human being someone who does not render back completely what conditioning has
given him (sic)" (in Billig et al.[21]).

Background to the Study

The data we use here are taken from a larger study of home-based telework, which involved 14 men and women. We advertised both in management journals and parenting magazines to recruit a sample of men and women who both worked from home through electronic communication technologies, and were the parents of children aged 16 or under. The sample included a broad range of occupations, ranging from benefit claims processing and network engineering, to resource management and journalism.

Fineman[7] has stressed that "emotion's potential multifacetedness suggests that any one approach to understanding 'it' will be just that – one approach." Our method was informed by social constructionism. We conducted interviews in participants' homes and observed their homeworking spaces, which we recorded using a video camera. We invited participants to tell us about their experiences of teleworking and parenting. Initially the data were analyzed using discourse analysis: examining "certain legitimate ways of talking about subjects"[22] and how narratives are "built or manufactured out of pre-existing linguistic resources"[23] to explore how men and women accounted for the professional or parental facets of their identities. During this process, it became clear that emotion work was central to their accounts.

From the data collected, we were able to judge whether each participant generally favored a narrative with which they constructed themselves more strongly as parents or as professionals, or whether they attempted in their interviews with us to present themselves as somewhere between the two, appearing to perform neither identity more often or more clearly than the other. Yet, generally our participants did tend to favor one approach over the others, and the two case studies presented next are amongst the clearest examples of, in Kath's case, the performance of a professional narrative to define oneself and, in Dan's case, the favoring of a parental narrative to describe and define his experiences of life and the role of home-based teleworking as an integral part of this. In the following stories, italics are used to denote our participants' own words.

Teleworking Stories

Kath's story

Kath is 41 years old and married to Gary. They have two children, aged 5 and 8. Kath works as a European Resource Manager for a large international IT firm and has worked from home for six years. She spends around half of her working hours at home and the other half in her organization's regional office. Home-based work was something that Kath initiated herself, because it fitted in with her international client's operating hours, and also *because of the sheer volume of work, it began to become impossible to get anything done during office hours.* Her husband Gary also works from home for around 90 percent of his working hours.

A small downstairs box room is used as an office and houses a range of modern professional equipment. When we visited, there were three mobile phones on the granite coloured desk, a compact photocopier, fax, and the latest computing equipment, including a slim screen monitor, webcam, and scanner. One wall of the office was dominated by a large whiteboard and a black leather chair was the only seating. Kath and Gary are flexible about where in the home they base themselves to work, and they both separately stressed that *this is a wireless house*, and therefore each is free to take their laptop to any room and connect to office networks via wireless technology. An example of the multitasking this facilitated was expressed by Kath, who commented, *quite often if I'm just sitting down, going through emails and stuff, I can do that and listen to Andrew* [her 8-year-old son] *reading at the same time, so it makes him happy and also I'm clearing my mails out.* Kath remarks of the box room office: *it would be nice if it was bigger, frankly.*

Kath describes herself as *extremely driven, completely self-sufficient, very motivated, and very enthusiastic about my work.* She says *I love what I do and I'm lucky and fortunate that I'm actually very good at it and I'm recognized as being good across Europe, which makes me feel good . . . it gives me what I need.* She concludes, *if I didn't work, I'd be depressed and I'd be really upset, so it means everything to me.* Kath seemed to demonstrate her professionalism in terms of the autonomy she has over her work: *I think if you gave me a job where you had my boss sitting on my shoulder saying "Kath please do this . . ." I would have resigned*; and also, through her skills and worth to the business, describing herself as *a subject matter expert* in her organization.

Kath distances herself from *non-professional* people on several occasions in the interview, through comments such as: *if I just had a data entry job . . .* and *if you have, I don't know, people taking calls for a call center from home, I don't think that's going to make a difference to the world or to their families but I do think if you're looking at a professional person doing this type of role, I think it's fine; I think it makes a very positive impact on the family.* She also tells us of her fears that other home-based workers may *take the Mickey* by not working as hard as she frequently stressed she does, giving telework a bad reputation: *people use it as a reason not to work: "I'm working from home," and it actually just means mowing the lawn. Because of the nature of my personality, that wouldn't happen with me, but I can easily see it happening with other people.*

When asked if she sees herself more as a mother or as a professional she responds very quickly: *as a European Resource Manager* and when asked if working from home has changed how she sees herself, she remarks that she has always been focused on her career. She uses organizational jargon throughout her interview with us, and her professionalized talk spills over into her talk about her children: of work she states, *I'm given things that I have to deliver and it doesn't matter where I am or what I do as long as I deliver*; and of her children, she comments that they are given *deliverables* or *targets that they are expected to achieve.* She describes how her children benefit from seeing her work from home because *it's good for them to know that you have to work hard to make a living; it's not just going to come to them.* Kath talks about having children as being *a big responsibility: you have to be financially ok, as far as I'm concerned.* She tells us that her children are fortunate to have *an amazing lifestyle* and *travel extensively.* After-school childcare is provided by paid professionals and Kath comments, *I don't spend as much time with my children as people I pick my children up from school with.* Her son and daughter are used to seeing their mother taking work calls on her mobile phone at the school gates on the days that she does comes to collect them: *our daughter will say "Mum's on a call," or "she'll be late because she's on a conference call."*

Because her husband also works from home, Kath states that their relationship has improved, since he is able to be *more understanding of what actually takes place in family life,* which she describes as fortunate. She explains that between them they schedule collecting the children from school and organize various paid helpers to perform domestic duties. She also tells us that Gary is able to help with occasional tasks: *the grocery shopping on the whole has been done online and it's delivered when Gary is on a conference call, during the day, then he can be on a conference call on his mobile, and unpack the shopping.* Kath describes Gary's thoughts about her professional drive when we ask "What does your career mean to you?": *probably too much if you ask Gary; I think he would say that my career is probably the most important thing. I love my children dearly but they're going to grow up; my relationship with Gary is fine providing I'm working.* She concludes that working from home has *made me probably more of a workaholic than I was before – but more flexibly.*

Dan's story

Dan is 34 years old and is a single parent to his 4-year-old son, of whom he was awarded sole custody two years previously. Dan does not currently have a "significant other" in his life, although he employs a live-in au pair who shares the domestic work and *helps me with childcare.* Despite this, he stresses to us that he is very much a *hands on* parent. Dan works as an IT Network Security Consultant and has worked from home for two years, spending between 50 and 70 percent of his working hours at home, and the remainder in meetings with his team or with clients. Dan actively approached his organization about teleworking, specifically so that he could be more available to his son, despite there being a company office located 15 minutes away where he could work if he wished. He bases his work in the home in the communal dining room, on a small desk squeezed into a corner next to an ornamental dresser. He admits that occasionally his work does physically *spill over* into domestic areas. By working from home, he tells us, he can avoid travelling to meetings at his company's headquarters, which has caused some issues with colleagues: *one of the practical ways I work from home is to avoid going to London as frequently as I would if I wasn't being a dad, so one of the reactions would be that they're probably wondering where I am at a lot of meetings and why I'm always teleconferencing.*

Dan describes his role in terms of expertise: *To do this type of role you have to be an expert in your field; I'm highly technical in the knowledge field that I'm in.* He explains that he has always sought career success: *Since I was, maybe, 21, I was very ambitious, and wanted to be the top of the best. One of the qualifications I attained, around about the age of 23, was the highest you can get in the IT communications industry, and since then I've always aspired to stay at the top of my field.* Despite this he describes his career as a low priority compared to his family. He says of his role as a father, *it's the most important job that I'll ever do, whereas before being a parent, work was probably the biggest ambition I had. After having a child I wouldn't swap him for the world; obviously now I put family before work.* But by putting his parental role first, he seems sure there will be consequences for his career: *When you have child-caring needs, then that can impact your career progression – it can either slow it down, stop it, or set it back. I guess I'm at the point now where my career is still going forward but I can feel that it will either slow down because of my commitments to my child or it will have to take a step back and I'll have to do some downsizing.*

Dan describes the kind of parent he is as *loving, affectionate, you know; a mentor as well.* When asked if he sees himself as an IT professional or a parent, he replies: *definitely as a father.* When asked how working from home might have affected his relationship with his son, he responds: *hopefully Daddy won't be just someone who popped to work in the morning and came home at night, tucked you in bed.* He talks enthusiastically about the positive impact of telework on his home life, stating that it has allowed him to become *more of a father.* In his talk about fatherhood, he refers to the strong bond that exists between himself and his son (*As soon as you become a father and you get that bond with your child, then that's first and foremost*) and mentions both the physical and emotional care he provides for his child (*bringing up a son alone, you know he always wants his cuddles, he wants affection, and he gets it; he gets that off me in equal measure*).

With regard to the reaction of his son to having his father around, he comments: *he loves it because he's always got the opportunity to have his knee kissed better.* As if to confirm this, during our interview with Dan, his son ran in with a cut finger, which Dan did indeed kiss better and, upon sending his son back outside to play, commented *that's what you're able to do working from home.* When asked more specifically about how working from home has affected his family life, he responds, *I think it's just put everything into perspective, to know that there is a balance to be met. You can get too hung up on a job and a career, and you lose sight of what the important things are in life. I think that working from home has allowed that balance to become quite clear and set in mind, so you know that your family is important and work is important to feed and sustain that family, and that's why you do it.* He talks about telework as a privilege and an opportunity: *I know that I'm probably in a very privileged position to be in a job which allows me to have flexible working.* He also describes how it has enabled him to balance work and family life: *We always talk about work/life balance and obviously if you're spending most of that time in work, it's not much of a balance, so having a work/life balance working from home is a lot more do-able.*

Commentary and Implications

We stress that the cases presented in this chapter are *anomalies* in our data, though others in our sample provided less extreme examples of these findings. Still, the two stories presented do not fit with our general findings, or indeed our expectations for how men and women might account differently for the priorities taken in work and family life. But we believe that exploring these "out of the ordinary" examples, we are able to raise significant issues[19,20] that may not emerge from investigating the emotional paths more commonly expressed by working parents in teleworking contexts.

In her interview with us, Kath presents a compelling account of a mother who prioritizes her professional role over that of being a parent. She articulates her career as the most significant aspect of her life and the key factor defining her identity and she is not guarded in this respect. A career, Kath states, is something she *loves and needs* and it is *the most important thing* to her. Work demands, rather than those of the family, led her to work from home. In stressing just how busy she is, she articulates her value to the organization and offers us a story of both needing and being needed by the organization; an emotional connection that she does not articulate when discussing her family. The modern, professional workplace that she and Gary have constructed in their home expresses the financial and material commitment given to their work. When she mentions a desire for a *larger home-office* and pride in her *wireless house* where work can be done *anywhere and at any time*, we take this to mean that the prospect of work taking over the home environment is not experienced negatively. Rather, this, along with the technical paraphernalia and material status symbols such as the dominating black leather chair, suggest to us that being seen as highly successful in her professional role is a source of pride to her, even in the context of home life. Further examples of her desire to be seen as a successful career woman might be derived from her marking herself as a *professional* wherever and whenever possible in our conversations. This *professional* identity is reinforced when she continually emphasizes the investments she makes to her career in terms of time and commitment.

Kath repeatedly stresses the financial input that her work provides for her family, as well as the moral example she sets by demonstrating her strong work ethic. Interestingly, talk relating to provision of opportunities and material goods for children occurs in our overall data set with regard to being a "good father" and clearly reflects a discourse more commonly associated with fatherhood in the wider social and cultural milieu. Furthermore, Kath certainly does not present a sentimental story of motherhood, as might be more commonly associated with women. When she describes parenting she does so in terms of *managing and scheduling* reflecting a rationalized and organized approach and indicating the "professionalization" of her family life. What is absent in her talk is any guilt in relation to the lack of time she has available to spend with her children, an emotion that we have found common in the talk of working mothers. Rather, she is proud of her ability to *multitask* when she listens to her son read and reads her emails at the same time. Although she stresses that some of the domestic tasks and school runs are performed by her husband, Gary, she does not mention – and neither does he in his interview with us – that he engages in any of the emotional care of the children.

A key emotion that Kath clearly demonstrates throughout her narrative, then, is pride – but primarily in her professional life rather than in motherhood. She makes no apology for prioritizing her career over her role as a parent, presenting no feelings of guilt and apparently refusing to conform to the expected apologetic notions of working mothers. It is important to note, however, that her material circumstances (and the behavior and attitude of husband Gary) are factors that make this possible.

She presents herself as confident in her assertions that "good" parenting can result from mothers pursuing careers and growing as individuals, in order to set good moral examples and provide materially for their children. Home-based working has allowed her to maintain more of a presence in her home than she otherwise may have been able to, although her physical presence should not necessarily be seen to imply an emotional one. Kath clearly performs her identity for us through a masculine script of professionalism more commonly associated with the workplace. It may be relevant that, in the workplace, competence is generally associated with emotional detachment – the suppression of emotion is the hallmark of a true professional.[24] From this perspective, professional rules of conduct dictate her emotional performance in the home. In this sense, we can conclude that Kath's emotions in the home are performed according to the masculine emotional norms of the workplace – even though they are performed by a female in what is taken to be a traditionally female context, the masculine/professional discourse dominates.

In our second case, Dan presents himself as a father engaged in prioritizing family life over his career. In his interview with us, he expresses his desire to be emotionally and physically available to address his son's needs at all times. He stresses that this is facilitated by telework, which he sought to do specifically for this purpose. The material location of his work in a communal family room ensures that he is physically available but he also claims that working from home has acted as a catalyst in allowing him to take a step back from the daily grind of work and put his priorities into perspective. In his talk about parenting he uses emotional discourses more commonly associated with women – words such as love, affection, and tenderness pepper his narrative. Dan also openly engages in, and appears to relish, the giving of physical affection to his son. We see this as evidence of his desire to perform the feminized role of caring in the home.[15] Interestingly, Dan tells us of the overriding priority that his career once had in his life, as if to underline how much he now puts his son's emotional and physical welfare before success at work. We could, of course, read this as an emotional sacrifice, yet his drive and energy for his caring role belies that interpretation. As with Kath, pride features highly in Dan's narrative, but it is pride expressed in his desire to be a *good and modern father*, and that crucially entails engaging emotionally with his son, rather than confining himself to playing the breadwinner role.

Importantly though, Dan still performs a convincing professional identity in our interview – for example, when he highlights his achievements in terms of the qualifications he has gained, his reputation as an expert, and being *at the top* of his field. Yet, it seemed to us that the need to project a strong masculine/professional identity was not the central goal of Dan's narrative. Adopting the feminized caring discourses in this interview context did not appear to threaten his masculine identity or make him feel, to himself or to us, less of a man. We can explain this through Dan's fit with the "new man" identity, which is indeed potentially attractive and endearing.

Dan does acknowledge the potential cost to his career and professional reputation posed by working from home and refusing to travel to company meetings as often as his non-teleworking colleagues. But again he does not present any emotional costs to us, and expresses little regret at these potential effects on his career; instead, he enthuses over the many benefits of home-based work, such as gaining the love of his son and even the admiration of others in society. But, importantly, his material circumstances – the fact that he can hire an au pair to help in the household, for example – makes the fulfilling of his emotional desires through fatherhood possible. These same material circumstances also allow Kath to engage her professional self through paid (female) help. But Dan's material circumstances differ from those of Kath in what may be a significant way. His material circumstances as a lone father, able to hire female help, also open up the possibilities for Dan to emotionally engage with fatherhood because an au pair is unlikely to compete in the same way a mother might to be the main provider of emotional care for a child.

The absence of a significant female other – whose identity attracts the same social capital – means there is little challenge to Dan occupying this traditionally feminized role. In addition, we could speculate that Dan's use of feminized discourses will not threaten to subsume other aspects of his identity, as Kath's use of such discourses might. Perhaps Kath feels she has little choice but to adopt the traditional, masculine professional script more commonly associated with fatherhood, lest she be consumed by the feminized caring discourse of motherhood. And, yet, we might see Kath's adoption of such masculine discourses as compromising her emotional approach to motherhood, because our cultural expectation is that women will, and perhaps should, put their family first at all times.

Telework – New Contours of Emotion

We see Kath and Dan as real examples of home-based teleworkers struggling against the tensions and contradictions inherent in the discourses of emotion associated with the social and cultural stereotypes of working parents. These struggles are important indicators of the possibilities inherent in home-based telework for individual change, but equally significant for implications for wider social change. As such, we believe that Dan's struggle is probably made easier because the "new man" discourse facilitates this, and even rewards the performance of such an identity. Interestingly, though, Dan's struggle to achieve and maintain such an identity may also be made easier because of the absence of significant female others or "emotional competitors" in his and his son's everyday lived experience. Just as women often report that bringing up children as a single parent is made easier in some respects because of the absence of other points of view about what is the "right" way to control and discipline children, so it may be that single men are more able to engage with the emotional aspects of parenting in the absence of significant female others. Either way, Kath has no such positive "new woman" discourse on which to draw or with which to engage.

This raises the interesting issue of why such a discourse is not available to women, and leads us to ask what the emotional costs of this absence might be. For Kath, the professional armor that was so prevalent in her interview data leads to a gender atypical engagement with emotion work. To appear convincing as a professional, it seems necessary for her to reject wholeheartedly the typical female-oriented discourse of care, and the emotional struggles commonly associated with women in work contexts.

Whether there is a longer term emotional cost to Kath, or indeed to Dan, we cannot say, but we can conclude that in the realm of emotion and parenting, men might be said to occupy a win–win situation that women generally do not. If men become more emotionally involved parents, this new take on male identity is likely to be seen as commendable. If women prioritize their careers, they may be seen as *un*emotional, even heartless, and possibly less feminine – yet, if women prioritize the raising of children, they can be constructed as anachronistic and even indolent.

These stories suggest that home-based teleworking has the potential to reshape the contours of emotion work, and particularly the gendered emotions (and the concomitant power relationships) seen as "normal and natural" for men and women in relation to work and the family. Kath belies the emotional tensions commonly associated with working mothers, and Dan subverts the stereotypes of the emotionally detached male. Furthermore, these stories suggest that role/family boundaries are capable of blurring in much the same way as spatial and temporal boundaries blur when paid work comes into the home environment.

A potential consequence of this blurring – when fathers do caring and mothers do professionalism in the home environment – is that there is potential for the traditional power balances between the genders to shift, as indeed there is for change in traditional gender/identity constructions. These wider social implications are played out within a shifting landscape of technological change, in that the option to engage at all with identity plays such as these is made possible only through the advent of the technology. Alongside these technological advances, changing work practices make telework possible. So these shifts in work norms can lead to shifts in wider social norms – if indeed we can class Dan and Kath as exemplars of such. But these changes are only likely to occur through technological progress and the will and ability of organizations and individual employees to embrace this new mode of work. In this sense, the social change possible through home-based telework may be restricted to a select professional group.

The case studies presented here have raised important questions about the interplay of emotion and identity and how these may be researched. If we see Dan's and Kath's experiences as microcosms of social change, we may also reflect on the benefits of research that focuses on such lived experience. Exploring the notion of human agency is fundamental to an understanding of what changing work practices actually mean to the people that "live" them, as is exploring how emotion and identity are played out in that process. Too few studies focus in on these potential sites of social change. We may also reflect that such changes have emancipatory potential, but only in appropriately supportive social conditions, and often these conditions rely almost totally on social others (largely women) playing traditional supporting roles to sustain the smooth running of the family. We might conclude, then, that one person's emancipation from the emotional confines of traditional gender roles relies heavily on others being rather rigidly confined within them. Nevertheless, home-based telework is currently providing a site of opportunity to challenge and subvert traditional emotional stereotypes. By exploring this, we offer a challenge to the conceptualization of emotion as something that can be measured, and instead highlight the complex link between emotion and identity in lived experience.

Acknowledgment

Our thanks to the White Rose Scholarship Scheme SHE 5003, which funded the doctoral research on which this chapter is based.

References

1. Philips, N., Lawrence, T. B., and Hardy, C. (2004) Discourse and institutions, *Academy of Management Review*, 29 (4), 635–52.
2. Grant, D. and Hardy, C. (2003) Introduction: Struggles with organizational discourse, *Organization Studies*, 25 (2), 5–13.
3. Butler, J. (1990) *Gender Trouble: Feminism and the Subversion of Identity*. London: Routledge.
4. Hylmo, A. (2004) Women, men and changing organisations: An organisational culture examination of gendered experiences of telecommuting. In Buzzanell, P. M., Sterk, H., and Turner, L. H. (eds) *Gender in Applied Communication Contexts*. London: Sage.
5. Mann, S., Varey, R., and Button, W. (2000) An exploration of the emotional impact of teleworking, *Journal of Managerial Psychology*, 15 (7), 668–90.
6. Mann, S. and Holdsworth, L. (2003) The psychological impact of teleworking: stress, emotions and health, *New Technology, Work and Employment*, 18 (3), 196–211.
7. Fineman, S. (2003) *Understanding Emotion at Work*. London: Sage.
8. Mirchandani, K. (1998) Protecting the boundary: Teleworker insights on the expansive concept of "work," *Gender and Society*, 12 (2), 168–87.
9. Hochschild, A. R. (1983) *The Managed Heart*. Berkeley: University of California Press.
10. Taskin, L. and Devos, V. (2005) Paradoxes from the individualization of human resource management: The case of telework, *Journal of Business Ethics*, 62, 13–24.
11. Rokach, A. (1997) Relations of perceived causes and the experience of loneliness, *Psychological Reports*, 80, 1067–74.
12. Tietze, S. and Musson, G. (2005) Recasting the home–work relationship: A case of mutual adjustment? *Organization Studies*, 26 (9), 1331–52.
13. Bibby, A. (1999), in Mann, S. and Holdsworth, L. (2003) The psychological impact of teleworking: stress, emotions and health, *New Technology, Work and Employment*, 18 (3), 196–211.
14. Olson, M. H. and Primps, S. B. (1990) Working at home with computers, *Computers, Ethics and Society*, 189–281.
15. Halford, S. (2005) Hybrid workspace: re-spatialisations of work, organisation and management. *New Technology, Work and Employment*, 20 (1), 19–33.
16. Swan, E. (1994) Managing emotion. In Tanton, M. (ed.) *Women in Management*. London: Routledge.
17. Burr, V. (1995) *An Introduction to Social Constructionism*. London: Routledge.
18. Halford S. (2006) Collapsing the boundaries? Fatherhood, organizations and home-working, *Gender, Work and Organization*, 13 (4), 383–402.
19. Potter, J. and Wetherell, M. (1995) Discourse analysis. In Smith, J. A., Harre, R., and Van Langengrove, L. (eds) *Rethinking Methods in Psychology*. London: Sage.
20. Kilduff, M. and Mehra, A. (1997) Postmodernism and organizational research, *Academy of Management Review*, 22 (2), 453–81.
21. Billig, M., Condor, S., Edwards, D., and Gane, M. (1988) *Ideological Dilemmas: A Social Psychology of Everyday Thinking*. London: Sage.
22. Fairclough, N. (2003) *Analysing Discourse: Textual Analysis for Social Research*. London: Routledge.
23. Gill, R. (2000) Discourse analysis. In Bauer, M. and Gaskell, G. (eds) *Qualitative Researching with Text, Image and Sound: A Practical Handbook*. London: Sage.
24. Harris, L. C. (2002) The emotional labour of barristers: An exploration of emotional labour by status professionals, *Journal of Management Studies*, 39 (4), 553–84.

CHAPTER 10

CONSULTANCY

Management Consultancy and Humor in Action and Context

Andrew Sturdy, Timothy Clark, Robin Fincham, and Karen Handley

> *A shepherd was herding his flock when a huge BMW stormed up. A sharply dressed young woman stuck her head out of the window. "I can tell you how many sheep you have!" she declared. She parked, took out her BlackBerry and connected it to the NASA website where she called up a satellite navigation system, scanned the area, and opened up a spreadsheet. Finally, she printed out a lengthy report on her miniaturised printer. "You have 173 sheep," she declared. "Correct," said the shepherd. "You are obviously a management consultant.... You turned up here uninvited, and tried to impress me by using a lot of technology to tell me something I already knew."*[1]

Management consultancy has been one of the fastest growing occupational sectors since the mid-1960s and currently generates worldwide revenues of over £100 billion.[2] The huge expansion in consulting has meant that consultants have become key agents in the process of knowledge production. They act as conduits through which knowledge from a variety of sources is appropriated, transformed, and, sometimes, transferred into, and from, client organizations. They also legitimate or "rubber stamp" knowledge already held by their clients. Whether as employees or citizens, few of us can escape their influence.

Despite this apparent success – or, rather, because of it – the activities of consultants raise strong levels of ambivalence and occasionally outright hostility. Often, this is expressed not so much in direct criticism, but through jokes, such as the one above. Like lawyers, consultants are in one of those occupations that are the butt of many disparaging jokes. One of the oldest jokes, that has been doing the rounds since the 1960s, is that: "A management consultant is someone who will borrow your watch to tell you the time (when you didn't ask to know) and then sell it to someone else (who didn't know that they wanted to buy one)." You may well have heard this before or, if not, then others like it. Consulting jokes have become part of popular business discourse. It seems that their services have become indispensable while we love to hate them at the same time. Why is this and what does it reveal about work and organizations and their emotional texture? Providing some answers to these questions is the purpose of this chapter. In particular, we shall use humor as a window on some of the emotions of consultancy. We shall do this in two related contexts:

- broader humor discourses around consultancy, such as that reflected in popular jokes and criticisms, and
- how consultant-related humor is experienced and practiced in actual client–consultant interactions.

Our main focus is on the latter, where we draw on the findings from an in-depth investigation of four consultancy engagements.

In keeping with the approach of the book overall, our perspective is a critical one. But this does not mean simply reinforcing common criticisms of consultants. Rather, we are interested in locating the activities of consultants and their clients, including their emotions, within power relations, especially those of capitalism and hierarchies. For example, we set out the way in which tensions in client–consultant relations are expressed, interpreted, diluted, and/or deferred through "put down" humor from clients and tactical joking from consultants.

To a lesser extent, we also seek to be critical with regard to emotion in that we reject what Barbalet[3] calls the "conventional" opposition between rationality and emotion as well as the more open view where emotion is seen as an acceptable alternative approach to rationality. Rather, we see rationality and emotion as continuous, yet conceptually distinct. This is quite a complex idea in theory, but is less so in practice. For example, rational activities such as setting and addressing consulting project objectives are necessarily imbued with emotion, or at least feelings, such as a passion for objectivity or a felt desire for successful completion. Likewise, and following Burkitt, we reject other related oppositions such as those between mind–body and culture–nature. This means that although we see emotions as conceptually distinct from the feelings they represent or hide, they are not simply expressions of some inner and otherwise hidden processes (i.e. feelings), but multi-dimensional (thinking, feeling, moving) "modes of communication" which are both cultural *and* corporeal/embodied and arise in social structural relationships of power and interdependence.[4:37] Indeed, our emotion focus is based on such relations in the context of management consultancy. We hope to show how emotion lies at the heart of what frequently appear to be professional-rational, *emotionless* encounters in organizations – client–consultant meetings – and, at the same time, how these can be linked to broader, if muted, popular criticisms of capitalist employment relations.

The chapter is organized in the following way. Firstly, we selectively explore some of the literature on emotion and humor. We then briefly introduce some examples of general consultancy criticisms, on which popular discourse is based, and then examine specific instances of such humor in client–consultant interactions. We conclude with a short discussion that compares these contexts and the implications for emotion in the context of consultancy and more generally.

Emotion, Humor, and Consultancy

Structures of emotion

There are numerous approaches to emotion associated with a range of disciplines that are too broad and internally diverse to be covered in detail here.[5] For example, one might focus on specific emotions or particular perspectives – emotion as judgment, communication, sense, or as control, for example. Alternatively, attempts are made to span the multidimensional nature of emotion – behavioral, physiological, discursive, cultural, cognitive, and social structural. While acknowledging these different aspects, we shall focus on structural and related discursive, or language-based, aspects of emotion.

It should be uncontentious to assert that emotion is intimately linked to social structures (or other conceptions) of power and inequality. However, perhaps because of the long association of emotion with "inner selves" and/or individualistic psychology (cf. social psychology), the connection continues to be contested (for example, see Craib[6]). This critique can be readily dismissed by reference to a long history of sociological and critical psychological literature that points to emotional outcomes and conditions of social structures, even if "emotion" was not an explicit focus – alienation, suicide, "fear of freedom," anxiety, racism, etc.[7]

As well as linking emotion to patterns of power, incorporating structure into analysis is important because it goes some way to de-individualizing or collectivizing emotion. This can be explored in terms of broad class/status/gender patterns of feeling through the "civilizing" or training of emotion more generally.[8] For example, Gerth and Mills cite the case of the apparently accepted practice of fainting among nineteenth century middle-class women in the USA to show that the "chance to display emotional gestures, and even to feel them, varies with one's status and class position."[9:12] Similarly, they point to particular moods associated with economic conditions in particular periods and for particular groups such as the "anxiety and depressive fear" of small entrepreneurs under the structures of monopoly capitalism and state of the twentieth century.[9:15] Indeed, and more generally, the emotional relevance of capitalism extends well beyond working life in organizations, touching all cultural domains:

> . . . through how it makes us see relations, define experience and manage feeling, the culture of capitalism insinuates its way into the very core of our being.[10:11]

Such connections are not restricted to economic structures, but to a broader "psychology of social institutions."[9] For example, different social systems (e.g. economic, gender, race) or institutions can be associated with emotional rules and resources as well as those for behavior more generally.[11] These systems may be explored in terms of their interrelationships and, in particular, their tensions and how they relate to direct emotional experiences such as ambivalence.[12] Here, conflicts between feeling and display – a serious joke for example – might be conceived more socially as a tension between different structural pressures – acting as a man or as a manager for example – rather than simply in psychological or psychoanalytical terms as an "inner–

outer" tension.[4] Likewise, the power relations of management consultancy are fueled by feelings and, to a lesser extent, emotion – the emotions of controlling others rather than the typical focus on how we control our own emotions and feelings.[13]

Humor and emotion – the "put down"

As with emotion, there is an enormous, longstanding and classical literature on humor, and a range of different perspectives is evident, such as: cognitive approaches, where the emphasis is on in/congruity; psychoanalytic studies associated with the release from tensions and anxiety; and, our main concern, social perspectives where attention is focused on issues of power and status and disparagement in particular.[14] There are clear parallels or overlaps between humor and emotion which are reflected in the different perspectives.[15] But even at the commonsense level, the experience of finding something amusing (and/or insulting) can be seen as an emotional reaction. However, we are equally concerned with the affective conditions of humor and joking relations as with their consequences, especially those associated with the experience of tensions arising from power relations, cultural norms, and prevailing discourses. To an extent, this has been explored in a number of work contexts, especially those of the shopfloor and non-managerial groups more generally, although another parallel with emotion is the overall neglect of humor in studies of work – yet another separation of the emotional and rational. In particular, attention is typically focused on micro-level analysis of work groups and cultures in relation to group cohesion, communication, and leadership, for example.[16]

The literature on "put down" humor, where amusement occurs at the expense of someone else, is of particular relevance to our focus on disparaging jokes about consultants. Here, emphasis is placed almost exclusively on what is a dominant tradition in the field of humor – functionalism. In other words, such joking is seen as either serving to create (i.e. functional for) cohesion or the illusion of it or, less frequently, as disintegrative – as a bridge or wedge.[14] The former view is derived from Radcliffe-Brown's early anthropological work, in which humor or joking is seen as a "peculiar combination of friendliness and antagonism"[17:196] – "a relation between two persons in which one is by custom permitted, and in some instances required, to tease or make fun of the other, *who in turn is required to take no offence* [emphasis added]."[17:208] Humor therefore allows a relationship of "permitted disrespect."

Put downs, as with humorous episodes more generally, are expressed in a relatively non-threatening context which Bateson[18] terms the "play frame." In this way, participants should regard such comments as "not serious." But, as we all know, jokes often hide something more serious, or gloss over deeper meanings. Tensions remain, even if they are latent. Thus, an alternative functionalist view is that such joking serves to express and reinforce power and status relations. For example, and of clear relevance to jokes about consultants, put downs can be directed at outsiders (e.g. consultants) to differentiate, exclude, and elevate one's self or group in terms of status (e.g. men over women) – "the more intense the negative disposition toward the disparaged entity, the greater the magnitude of mirth . . ."[16:260] Likewise, self-put downs or self-disparagement can be seen as ways to anticipate such relations in order to save face.[19]

However, context is again important, not least because status can be highly contested. For example, some argue that there is a "joking monopoly" such that high-status people can make jokes at the expense of lower status groups, but the latter cannot joke back. But, the reverse can also occur. Here, humor may be directed at high-status actors by subordinate groups, and not reciprocated, as a safe way to express resistance to feelings of low status or autonomy. This has been observed in the context of workers' jokes directed at managers[20] and, as we shall see, client comments to consultants. The rule of *non-reciprocation* suggests a kind of gift exchange – put-down jokes are permitted in return for compliance or the maintenance of power-status relations. However, it is not only context that is important, but a consideration of time. The expression of feelings of tension through the safety of a play frame may create some sense of cohesion at the moment the laughter occurs but this may only be temporary, in that unexpressed underlying conflict may become pent-up and require open expression at a later date. However, as we shall see, whether put downs become cohesive or divisive in their consequences depends on their interpretation by actors in context.

Others too have been skeptical of the functionalist tradition in humor research (i.e. put downs as a wedge or bridge), although few escape it completely. Hatch[15] adopts a broadly poststructuralist view of humor, arguing that it constitutes meaning and, in the case of irony among managers, the contradictory nature of organizations and organizing. This provides important insights into how language is used in the construction of "contradictory experiences" in worlds of work. More structuralist accounts like ours, where language is seen to represent "a reality conceived as separate from those who experience and express it" (e.g. capitalist employment relations) are rejected by Hatch.[15:276] However, this micro-, workplace-level approach, which neglects related societal discourses of humor, means that the widespread or general nature of organizational contradiction remains unexplained. In other words, the fact that all business organizations contain some familiar employer–employee tensions is seen almost as a coincidence. By contrast, our position is that while humor, emotion, capitalism, etc. can be seen as discursively constituted, this is only partial, in that other "realities" exist, whether structural or physical, even if they are *mostly* expressed and experienced (e.g. felt) discursively. For example, what Marx described as the "dull compulsion of economic relations" – the feeling of having little choice but to work for others to make a living – is not solely a localized or discursive phenomenon. It is necessary therefore to explore humor at different levels and reveal the ways in which it is structured within broader contexts (e.g. patriarchy, capitalism), if only, as we shall argue, partially structured. In particular, regardless of one's ontological or philosophical view of what is real, there is a need to examine how wider discourses and social processes inform the particular humor and associated emotion that is experienced and expressed in the workplace.

Emotion and humor in consultancy

Both emotion and, in particular, humor have been almost entirely neglected in the wide and growing literature on consultancy. This might be seen as surprising in that, as we have suggested, popular business and societal discourse is replete with jokes about consultants. Also, the association of consultancy with expertise and with organizational change would suggest that consultancy is a highly charged emotional arena. Indeed, one of the few studies, if not the only study, to examine consultancy and emotion directly, focuses on how consultants can and should manage the emotional states of their clients.[21] These are seen as arising from various "negative" organizational situations (i.e. management problems) combined with the cultural business norm of prohibiting the expression of strong or negative emotions. Thus, throughout their interactions with clients, consultants are seen as helping clients emotionally by "the reduction or alleviation of those negative affective reactions and moods that impede appropriate client thinking and behavior."[21:536] This is seen to be achieved not only by addressing the organizational problem and providing an extra resource – the traditional role of consultancy – but through providing psychological support, enabling clients to express their emotions and helping them reframe problems.

While such a therapeutic focus is entirely legitimate, if unconventional in the largely rationalistic discourse of consulting prescription, it is problematic in other respects. Firstly, it follows rationalist traditions by suggesting that emotion impedes effective or "appropriate" client action rather than also informing it (e.g. commitment). Secondly, it reproduces the commonsense notion of consultants as experts who help their clients rather than the more complex and varied picture provided by more critical literature and that which sees consultants as also learning from their clients.[22,23] To a large extent, each helps the other but in different ways. Finally, it assumes that the sole emotional issue is that of the clients' experience of the "organizational" problem and the pressures to solve it. It does not consider explicitly emotion-related consulting such as that associated with emotional intelligence or personal effectiveness.[24] But, more importantly, it neglects the emotional issues associated with the use and presence of consultants themselves.

While emotion is largely absent in the more general literature on consultancy, it is actually implicit in all the main conceptions of the client–consultant relationship. For example, consider Werr and Styhre's[25] four framings of this relationship: helper–recipient (as above); manipulator–victim; a contingent view of power/dependency relations; and partnership. Each suggests different positive and negative emotional contexts, such as feelings of fear and anxiety, relief, confidence, personal attachment, shared goals and experiences, even friendship. Likewise, the often isolated or liminal spacing of consulting projects and teams, separated from the day-to-day activities of the organizations of both parties,[26] can create its own emotional climate. Furthermore, different theoretical perspectives and empirical foci in the consulting literature hint at the emotionality of consultancy. For example, and most directly, psychodynamic studies point to the anxiety or existential threat posed by consultants to clients' sense of confidence and expertise as well as the, albeit often fleeting, sense of security felt at having a trusted adviser or achieving a grasp of the latest valued management technique.[27]

Similarly, more critical perspectives point to the significant potential for conflict in terms of threats posed to clients' internal status – being shown up – and even to their jobs. Consultants are well aware of this and seek to underplay the threat they pose in dealings with clients by using techniques designed to leave the client feeling that they are in control and the "real" source of expertise.[22] Indeed, such techniques might supplement those described by Lundberg and Young[21] directed at minimizing the stress of organizational change. At the same time, however, and as implied in a more contingent view of client–consultant relations, consultants also experience anxiety from more powerful clients[28] and occasionally feel the brunt of anti-consultant sentiment. In addition, although it has not been researched, it is likely that they experience some of the same feelings and tensions as those documented among managers who implement redundancies, for example,[29] as well as from hierarchical pressures to suspend what they might see as professionalism and sell on business to clients regardless of need.[22] Finally, studies of consultancy as knowledge transfer or mediation point to different levels of closeness and distance between the parties and, in particular, to consultants' position as more or less an organizational outsider,[30] which has clear emotional connotations. However, it is also important to recognize that emotion is not simply concerned with underlying relations of conflict–harmony or anxiety–security. At the same time, and as we shall see, while expressed emotion may sometimes seem absent in the seemingly rational and polite pursuit of project objectives, this does not mean that feelings are too.

Layers of Humor in Management Consultancy

Our account of emotion in management consultancy through the lens of humor is based on a range of sources and methods. To show how humor in action is partly informed by broader consultancy humor discourses, we combine a short assessment of humor in the open spaces of the business and popular media with a longitudinal study of the relatively closed world of client–consultant relations in four different consulting projects. We also draw on our own prior research on different aspects of consultancy. Details of this research are outlined elsewhere[22;31–33] but it is important to emphasize that neither humor nor emotion were originally explicit research objectives. Rather, humor emerged as a theme from our observations of clients and consultants working together. In particular, we were struck by the fact that, for the most part, interactions were characterized by formality in terms of what might be described as rational or professional behavior combined with conformity and with more general norms of politeness. Beyond a sense of calm and occasional urgency, emotion was rarely evident. Aside from some either subtle or explicit expressions of conflict and frustration with technical difficulties or broken promises, emotion was expressed most visibly through occasional instances of humor. Indeed, its relative rarity made it all the more visible in the sterile "emotionlessness" of most encounters. This is not to suggest that feelings were absent. Rather, their expression was largely hidden from the observer.

Consultancy humor in popular discourse

There are, to our knowledge, no studies of humor and consultancy. To an extent, this is to be expected, for consultancy practice is dominated by "rationalist-professional" discourse. Also, almost all consultancy research is based on post hoc, one-sided "snap-shots" from surveys and, in particular, interviews rather than observation of consultancy in action. However, and as we have noted already, in other respects it is surprising because, in broader business and public consultancy discourses, jokes are common-place. This is evident in other related contexts too. For example, a recent study of the law in the USA analyzed hundreds of lawyer jokes in terms of broader representations of the law in the mass media, political discourse, and public opinion surveys. It iden-tified an underlying *ambivalence* associated with belief in the law and increasing reliance on lawyers.[34] A similar study could be conducted of consultancy and consul-tant jokes, perhaps pointing to an increasing use of, if not belief in, management ideas combined with concerns about consultancy such as its insidious power, lack of account-ability, or association with job losses. While our aims and scope are more modest here, this does show how humor has a social structural or cultural quality beyond particular interactional settings. Jokes can be funny largely because they are about consultants or, rather, a range of more widely perceived and sometimes exaggerated characteristics associated with them.

Although by no means exhaustive, the following sets out some of the common, widely disseminated criticisms or negative images of consultants from clients and more generally (see also the work of Sturdy[22]):

- Excessive cost or doubtful value for money;
- Seek business and long-term dependency above client needs;
- Cut jobs/replace people;
- Abstract and standardized models – jargon;
- Parasitic of client knowledge;
- Lack industry knowledge;
- Associated with management fads;
- Formulate, but don't implement (lack accountability and effectiveness);
- Insensitive to client employees – arrogant;
- "Comfort blanket" or scapegoat for senior management.

These themes form the basis of popular jokes such as the ones quoted earlier. However, the issue here is not so much whether or not consultants actually have these charac-teristics or to what extent – there are plenty of popular accounts on this issue[35–37] – but why do such criticisms become expressed as humor and what does this say about consultancy and feelings about it. As we have seen, "put downs" can be integrative or divisive, but in each case the play frame ensures that they are viewed as relatively safe or inoffensive (i.e. indirect) ways of expressing criticism. This is readily under-standable in the context of direct client–consultant interactions. It can be seen as both functional and polite. But in popular discourse, consultants are not necessarily present. While some direct criticism of consultants is evident in the media and policy forums, for example, this is much less visible than that contained in jokes. There are a number of possible ways of making sense of why such criticism manifests itself as humor.

Firstly, as a number of studies have shown, the relationship between consultancy inputs and outputs is ambiguous.[38] This, combined with the fact that consulting work is largely hidden from view, creates uncertainty and suspicion. Thus, jokes become equivalent to how the media use the term "allegedly" in relation to criminal activity. Secondly, and most importantly, joking in this context is about power, powerlessness, and particular power effects. As noted earlier, those perceived to be in positions of power and influence have long been the butt of jokes, but in this context and in the public sphere, joking is not about fear of retribution from those in power – a safety valve for resistance. Rather, it reflects a paradoxical assertion of superiority or, in effect, an unwillingness to admit powerlessness. For example, not everyone is critical of or makes jokes about consultants – as one senior manager quoted by Sturdy[22] said, "I like working with consultants, as long as they report to me and not my boss." To criticize consultants directly – "I am threatened by you; I resent you because you are the experts and have influence" – is to acknowledge their relative power and one's own powerlessness and is therefore unlikely.

But it is not solely a question of face saving. There is, perhaps, a moral element to the feelings around some consulting humor, albeit one based on ambivalence. Consultants are not the object of humor simply because of their perceived relative influence or status and wealth. If they were associated with bringing happiness, health, and prosperity to all, it is unlikely that the humor would be as prominent. Rather, humor reflects a concern that consultants are a negative force, responsible (or scapegoats) for cutting jobs and/or ineffectiveness – "they screw up everything for ever."[1] But why is this expressed as humor? Here, and as intimated above, Galanter's[34] study is useful to develop in the consulting context. If we take the most emotive case of job cutting, direct criticism might reflect a more or less implicit challenge to managerialism or capitalism, which produce the associated logic of redundancies. But for a whole host of reasons, this is difficult to sustain in many contemporary contexts, not least because most of us are intimately implicated in such systems. Thus, humor reflects ambivalence or a way of avoiding the embarrassment of holding contradictory concerns and feelings, if not fully articulated beliefs. It does, however, also reflect some degree of criticality or *political emotion*, in much the same way as stand-up and other political comedy represents a challenge, albeit a muted one.

Such political and structural analysis of humor is linked to, but an important extension of, the more microlevel of analysis common in studies of humor where the focus is on group processes. However, it is important to exercise some caution at all levels of analysis and interpretation. For example, making a joke about consultants by drawing on familiar humor discourse might simply reflect the speaker's use of a particular situation in an attempt to be funny or liked and have no connection with her or the recipients' particular political feelings about, say, consultants and redundancies. Nevertheless, and as the following section shows, there is often a two-way relation between popular and work-based humor in consulting. Popular jokes are drawn from the concerns and experiences of those working in client organizations and, as we shall argue, humorous criticisms of consultants in work contexts reflect popular themes as much as those specific to the immediate context. Indeed, this use of broader humor discourse can serve to dilute any critical intent even further – "I wasn't really criticizing you. It was just a (another) *consultant* joke."

Joking in meetings

Context, popular themes, and integration

In this section, we are primarily concerned with humor that is, or appeared to be, specific to the emotional texture of consulting engagements rather than everyday humor associated with organizational or other events in general. Nevertheless, it is important to highlight the importance of other contextual factors for the nature and occurrence of humor more generally. The inclination to initiate humor, and its accept-ability, will vary. For example, from our case study observations, it appeared that some individuals were more jovial and/or better at delivering witty remarks. Likewise, in one of the cases, humor was far more prevalent overall and this seemed to be linked to the fact that the parties were relatively close and/or familiar with each other. By the end of the project they had worked together for a substantial period of time (around two years), with frequent interactions, including partly informal activities such as attending sporting events. The culture of the client organization (a medium-size mutual savings bank) was also relatively informal and drew on a local, regional (north-ern England) culture, which, again, was quite informal. In addition, in all the cases, humor often occurred at the start or end of formal meetings and in breaks for coffee or lunch, for example. This is unsurprising in that such points can be those of height-ened anxiety or relief and represent or announce the liminal space between formal and informal activities with their associated norms.[32]

We have noted how, in general, put downs in the play frame of humor are recog-nized as less threatening – "not serious." We have also suggested that in the context of consultancy, such jokes may be even less of a threat because they are part of a broader business discourse and therefore not personal. However, specific put-down consulting jokes, such as the ones cited at the beginning of the chapter, were never observed. It is likely that they would be considered clichéd and/or insulting and felt as awkward, except perhaps in the closest or most familiar of relationships or most informal of contexts. For example, in the most distant relationships and formal con-texts, such as consultancy policy forums, consulting humor overall, let alone explicit consultant jokes, is largely absent. Both clients and consultants have a particular inter-est in protecting themselves and not giving offense, so politeness, professionalism, and the understatement of negative assessments or feelings are the norm. This seemingly emotionless world of rational action also seemed to fit many of the consulting project meetings we observed. However, there was some joking around the themes of the criticisms listed in the previous section (i.e. put-down humor), although less fre-quently in the case of the most senior consultants.[i]

In keeping with one of the most common characterizations of consultants as job cutters, three of the four projects had more or less direct implications for cuts in staff, albeit not in the short term. However, no joking references to this were observed. This might be a result of the indirect or emotive nature of the issue or because the project team members themselves were not under threat and, for the most part, shared the same efficiency goals. However, one can easily imagine humor around this subject among those outside of the project teams, but they were not observed and, in one case, the project was so sensitive that the consultants' presence was kept a secret from all but the most senior management. In terms of another popular theme, the cost/value for money of consultants, some joking references were made, in terms of both expenses (e.g. excessive claims for milage) and fees. For example, one client joked when handing a report to the consultant to review: "I don't want to pay for you to move commas!" Similarly, there were occasional comments about consulting (management) jargon, even if they did not always imply a rejection of it. For example, one junior client team member observed:

> . . . I mean, at the first meeting [with the consultant], terms were used that I'd never heard . . . Things like the Gantt chart . . . I mean, I've heard of a pie chart! [laughs] I mean a lot of techno-speak. And I don't mean that rudely . . . it's the way. I mean, I must say, I think Chris and I are now into that; we throw these terms in . . .

Likewise, her colleague teasingly asked the consultant: "Can we use any of the terminology about methodology that was in your . . . paper? Or is that just bollocks?" And, in another case study project meeting, the client CEO commented, with a broad smile, that he had initially been sent the consultants' report but had not understood it – "now I've got the English version!" [followed by much laughter]. Indeed, a related, although less direct, focus of humor was around the expert, modern, and rational image of consultants. For example, on discovering that his (public sector) organization had a more recent version of a project management software package than the consultant, the client said to his consultant: "Let's take a moment there, Mark [to enjoy the role reversal]!" Similarly, when reviewing the consultants' report page by page in a joint meeting, one client got ahead of the others present and was informed of this. He replied with irony: "And I haven't [even] had a coffee yet!! It [the report] is just too exciting!" And on the same theme, in response to the consultant's question about what the objectives of a formal workshop they were planning were, the client playfully replied: "To fill in an hour?!" [laughs]. To which the consultant replied: "That's very frank!" [joint laughter].

As noted above, the material threat posed by management consultants (i.e. job loss) is mainly experienced by those with whom they do not work with most closely or directly. To client employees working in the project team, the threat is mostly an existential one, the challenge to their identity as experts or as competent.[22] This is a source of considerable tension, resulting in the common criticism of consultants as arrogant or insensitive. It is also one that some consultants seek to diffuse through humor, including irony and self-deprecation. One of the consultants we observed was quite conscious of this and used it in his direct interactions with the senior clients as the following extracts demonstrate.

> *Consultant:*   [looking through client's workings in a report] OK.
> *Client:*   Enough? [said quickly to the consultant while showing him his workings]. Thank God he didn't look at the last pages! [ironic]
> [Laughter, followed by the consultant grabbing the papers as though pretending to inspect the last pages.]
> *Consultant:*   Just an observation – we're not being terribly focused this morning? [Clients respond: "No, no."] And I'm conscious I'm being a bit of a bully, but what does that

all mean? Practical action? . . . You need to delegate responsibility. . . . we seem to have got into the comfort zone of talking about nitty-gritty detail, because planning's too hard! [laughter] So . . .

Such practices can be seen as aiming to soften the "teacher–learner" relationship, which gives rise to particular tensions in a context where the client might consider him/herself as a fellow expert and/or a sovereign consumer, not a pupil, and therefore feel disempowered or threatened. It can also help achieve greater closeness with an "outsider" by providing a break from formality. Similarly, humor can be used by consultants with clients, with the effect of creating a sense of shared purpose or experience in relation to others, beyond the project team for example. For instance, the same consultant joked with his client about distributing a draft report to other client managers late in December:

> *Consultant:* Wrap it (the report) up for them. (Tell them to) stick it under the tree! Read it after your Christmas dinner.
> [Much joint laughter.]
> *Client:* I have to go with you there, mate.
> *Consultant:* . . . I know I said it in jest but a big part of me is saying you do give it to them and say Merry Christmas! But . . . no, no . . . OK.

However, consultants' instrumental efforts to develop closer, less threatening relations with their clients, through humor or otherwise, to become more like insiders, are not always successful. Indeed, clients use humor to mark out or reassert boundaries between themselves and their consultants. For example, in one of the projects, two client team members made a private joke and laughed together with the effect that the consultant, the only other person present (except the observer) was excluded. Similarly, in another project, the assertion of insider–outsider identities was vividly expressed by a client manager through a reference to the color of identity badges used by staff of the company (red) as opposed to visitors. Here, in a large project meeting discussion of increasing and urgent work demands, the consultant project manager talks as if he is a client, by asking for more of a particular client employee, Sarah's, time. The client manager's response was: "He's after his red badge!" [waves her own security badge] [much group laughter]. She's our Sarah, not your Sarah!" [sustained group laughter].

In this way, the consultant is put in his place, as an outsider, a supplier, subservient to the "sovereign" client, not part of it or of some pretence at shared interests. At the same time, this is, as in all the above cases, seemingly achieved in the safety of the play frame so that any criticism intended is softened and not felt as sharply as direct rebukes would be. But can we make such claims? Might the above cases of humorous put downs not still be felt? Indeed, they might be experienced even more severely because the norms associated with such humor – "it was just a joke" – largely prohibit addressing conflicts and tensions directly. Jokes can hurt. More generally, too, and as noted earlier, we need to be cautious about our interpretation of humor and its conditions and consequences, as we now briefly argue.

Microstructures

If the above extracts do not appear especially amusing to the reader, it is because they are presented in written form out of context. Particular comments are not necessarily, or even often, funny in themselves.[39] In particular, most laughter is initiated by speakers with various non-verbal, as well as verbal, cues to indicate that they are joking, such as laughter itself, comic gestures, facial expressions, and prosody.[40] In this way the speakers endow their remarks with affiliative potential or, at least, temper direct criticism. For example, in one of the cases, there was a disagreement over whether a piece of work required was included as part of the contract with the consulting firm – a familiar source of dispute given the uncertainty surrounding much consultancy and the feeling from clients that they are paying heavily for a service. The senior client manager and chair of the meeting intervened in the discussion, expressing surprise when the consultant suggested that the task would be extra. This initially appeared to come as a sharp rebuke and direct criticism of the consultants. However, after a pause he put out his hands and mimicked a set of scales going up and down. At the same time his face showed an incredulous expression as he rolled his lower lip over his top lip so that it protruded and emitted a raspberry. He also quickly surveyed the other participants. In response to these gestures they all laughed. Thus, a criticism became a humorous incident. Humor in this sense, then, is not so much integrative as a dilution and deferral of conflict and saving of embarrassment given a norm of avoiding open conflict and its associated "negative" emotions. Indeed, one can imagine that the comment was still felt as a criticism by the consultants and one which would have to be resolved.

However, even in situations where participants laugh collectively at a comment, it is important to recognize that multiple interpretations – and, therefore, feelings – are possible, even likely. For example, in the case cited earlier where the client CEO asked for an "English version" of the consultants' report and, with his accompanying smile, provoked group laughter, interviews immediately after the meeting revealed that the participants had very different takes on the incident (see below). These partly, but not wholly, relate to their particular structural position in the client–consultant system. In particular, a number of participants, especially the consultants, did not see it (*or admit to seeing it*) as a criticism of the consulting firm or as reproducing familiar jokes about consultant/technical jargon. Indeed, in one case, the joke was seen as self-deprecatory rather than a criticism of consultants:

> *Criticism of consulting firm:* "I felt Peter was criticizing XYZ and the way they can sometimes make things overly technical and complex." (*Client employee*)
>
> *Criticism of individual consultant:* "I agree with Peter. I saw that report and the guy just didn't produce a clear report." (*Client employee*)
>
> *Lack of clarity:* "We are all learning fast. Peter was commenting on our frustration at having to make decisions with incomplete information"; "It was about XYZ's communication with us." (*Both client employees*)
>
> *Individual client's preference for clear information:* "Peter's not technically-minded; I can just imagine his reaction to that report. He likes things in plain English. That's what should have been done." (*XYZ consultant*)

Incongruity: "They think of us as techies and often joke that we speak another language." (*XYZ consultant*)

Not funny: "I don't really remember the remark. I'm not sure if I laughed." (*Client employee*)

Similarly contrasting interpretations were evident in other cases, such as the "red badge" incident discussed earlier. Here, again, views were polarized between those of the clients and the consultants, with the former seeing the issue as one of the consultants "going native" while the consultants saw it as either a criticism of their commitment to the client or, less seriously, as a matter of being unable to provide adequate resources at the time of need.

Overall, then, we can see how comments are invested in humor through various cues, but how the occurrence of an expressed emotion displayed through communal laughter neither reflects an underlying unity in the group nor necessarily conflict. Indeed, expressed interpretations can vary largely in line with structural positions, particularly those of client and consultant.

Conclusion

In this chapter, we have sought to explore some features of the emotional nature of management consultancy through the lenses of both humor and a structural view of emotion. In particular, we have focused on critiques of consultancy or put-down humor and the efforts of consultants to diffuse relationship tensions through the use of humor with their clients. While much of the literature on humor, and put-down humor in particular, offers explanations at the level of the group in terms of cohesion, status, norms, and saving face, for example, we have sought to extend such analysis to broader structures and tensions such as those of capitalism. For example, we outlined a number of themes in popular humor discourse which point to an ambivalence over the success, status, and use of consultants in relation to their management role in helping to effect outcomes that are felt to be negative, even morally troubling. In this way, put-down humor of consultants can be seen to reflect an, albeit muted, critique of the system and/or outcomes of contemporary economic relations.

Such humor discourse was presented as both a condition and consequence of that which is produced in direct client–consultant relations, although the two are by no means identical. Consultancy jokes are informed by practice, and joking relations in face-to-face situations draw on similar themes, but are less confrontational or emotive (e.g. cost, jargon, rationality). However, our analysis of joking within consulting projects suggested the need for some caution in broad structural analysis on its own. Rather, more specific contextual factors were shown to be important, not least the relative closeness of felt relations and formality of activities. Indeed, in general, observation of clients and consultants working together in formal meetings revealed a largely predictable drama of politeness and professionalism – one free of expressed emotion if not feelings. But the humor that both occurred at and constructed the margins of rational interactions revealed something of the emotional texture of the tensions inherent in client–consultant relations. This was not restricted to put-down comments from clients, but to the joking by consultants to anticipate, deflate, or diffuse client concerns arising from the existential threat consultants posed to their identity as expert, autonomous, or powerful. Here, joking sometimes formed the weapons with which insider–outsider boundary battles or skirmishes were fought between the two parties. But we also saw how what might appear as structural conflict or negotiation to some, might be interpreted and felt differently by others or even go unnoticed. Here the methodological importance of combining observation with inter-views was revealed, although a broadly, if loosely, structured pattern remained with perceptions often in keeping with client and consultant positions.

Overall, our research confirms some of the claims of classic literature on humor in relation to how humor both reflects and dilutes or obscures tensions arising out of status and power difference. However, this literature is polarized in such a way that it does not allow for any other outcome – humor as neither wedge nor bridge. Moreover, attention is typically focused on the immediate situation rather than the way in which some aspects of humor are grounded both structurally and discursively in broader relations or how conflict may dissipate or grow over time. A similar criticism can also be directed at the emotion literature, although, here, the broader structural literature tends to neglect the micro-interactions and loose structuring which bring emotions and feelings into being often in subtly different ways for the various actors. Further-more, much of the emotion literature avoids what appear at first sight to be relatively emotion-free zones such as the professional-rational business meeting. And yet, in keeping with a view of rationality and emotion as continuous, these are the very spaces where emotion, if not feelings, is made most visible through contrast and focusing on the temporal and spatial margins such as interludes and asides.

Our analysis has, however, been necessarily selective and partial, which leaves much room for further research. In particular, and partly as a result of the data collection not having an emotion–humor focus at the outset, we did not explore the participants' feelings of being the agent or object of put-down humor, especially in the normative context where criticism should not be taken seriously or openly addressed. Further-more, our focus was not only limited to emotion associated with client–consultant specific relations (cf. organizational change and uncertainty), but also neglected more positive emotions associated with relations of harmony, trust, and shared purpose which are not always so evident through humor. Finally, our analysis could be extended to include consideration of, and research on, more practical and policy concerns, such as the implications for knowledge flow between the two parties and, more politically, for public preferences in terms of the nature and outcome of organizational reforms. Nevertheless, we hope to have drawn attention to the importance of a multilayered emotional understanding of the politics of management consultancy.

Acknowledgment

We acknowledge the financial support of the ESRC for the project titled "Knowledge Evolution in Action: Consultancy–Client Relationships" (RES-334-25-0004), under the auspices of the

Evolution of Business Knowledge Research Programme, without which this research could not have been undertaken.

Note

i. It is important to emphasize that put downs always came from clients. Consultants never initiated humorous comments about clients, although they may occasionally have joined in the laughter when other clients did so. It is also very likely that, in private, consultants would joke about and put down clients. Indeed, this "reciprocal denigration" has been reported elsewhere, including comments about their working pace and hours compared with clients. However, access to such back stage consultant activity is severely restricted to researchers.[41]

References

1. www.jokesmagazine.com
2. Greiner, L. and Poulfelt, F. (2005) *The Contemporary Consultant: Insights from the World Experts.* Mason, OH: Thomson South-Western.
3. Barbalet, J. M. (1998) *Emotion, Social Theory and Social Structure – A Macro-Sociological Approach.* Cambridge: Cambridge University Press.
4. Burkitt, I. (1997) Social relationships and emotions, *Sociology*, 31 (1), 37–55.
5. Williams, S. J. and Bendelow, G. A. (1996) Emotions and "sociological imperialism" – A rejoinder to Craib, *Sociology*, 30 (1), 145–53.
6. Craib, I. (1995) Some comments on the sociology of emotions, *Sociology*, 29 (1), 151–8.
7. Weiss, H. and Brief, T. (2001) Affect at work: An historical perspective. In Payne, R. and Cooper, C. L. (eds) *Emotions at Work*. Chichester: Wiley.
8. Elias, N. (1978) *The History of Manners – The Civilising Process*, Vol. 1. Oxford: Blackwell.
9. Gerth, H. and Mills, C. W. (1953) *Character and Social Structure – The Psychology of Social Institutions*. San Diego: Harvest/HBJ.
10. Hochschild, A. R. (1998) The sociology of emotion as a way of seeing. In Bendelow, G. and Williams, S. J. (eds) *Emotions and Social Life – Critical Themes and Contemporary Issues*. London: Routledge.
11. Whittington, R. (1992) Putting Giddens into action: Social systems and managerial agency, *Journal of Management Studies*, 29 (4), 693–712.
12. Pratt, M. G. and Doucet, L. (2000) Ambivalent feelings in organizational relationships. In Fineman, S. (ed.) *Emotion in Organizations*, 2nd edn. London: Sage.
13. Fineman, S. and Sturdy, A. J. (1999) The emotions of control, *Human Relations*, 52 (5), 631–63.
14. Terrion, J. L. and Ashforth, B. E. (2002) From "I" to "we": The role of putdown humor and identity in the development of a temporary group, *Human Relations*, 55 (1), 55–88.
15. Hatch, M. J. (1997) Irony and the social construction of contradiction in the humor of a management team, *Organization Science*, 8 (3), 275–88.
16. Duncan, W. J., Smeltzer, L. R., and Leap, T. L. (1990) Humor and work: applications of joking behavior to management, *Journal of Management*, 16 (2), 255–78.
17. Radcliffe-Brown, A. R. (1940) On joking relationships, *Africa*, 13, 195–210 (cited in Duncan et al. (1990) and Terrion and Ashforth (2002), op. cit.).
18. Bateson, G. (1955) A theory of play and fantasy, *Psychiatric Research Reports*, 2, 39–51.
19. Sturdy, A. J. (2002) Front-line diffusion: The production and negotiation of knowledge through training interactions. In Clark, T. and Fincham, R. (eds) *Critical Consulting – Perspectives on the Management Advice Industry*. Oxford: Blackwell.

20. Ullian, J. A. (1976) Joking at work, *Journal of Communication*, 26, 129–33.

21. Lundberg, C. C. and Young, C. A. (2001) A note on emotions and consultancy, *Journal of Organizational Change Management*, 14 (6), 530–38.

22. Sturdy, A. J. (1997) The consultancy process – an insecure business? *Journal of Management Studies*, 34 (3), 389–413.

23. Fosstenlokken, S. M., Lowendahl, B. R., and Revang, O. (2003) Knowledge development through client interaction: A comparative study, *Organizational Studies*, 24 (6), 859–80.

24. Wellington, C. A. and Bryson, J. R. (2001) At face value? Image consultancy, emotional labour and professional work, *Sociology*, 35, 933–46.

25. Werr, A. and Styhre, A. (2003) Management consultants – friend or foe? Understanding the ambiguous client–consultant relationship, *International Studies of Management and Organization*, 32 (4), 43–66.

26. Czarniawska, B. and Mazza, C. (2003) Consulting as liminal space, *Human Relations*, 56 (3), 267–90.

27. Jackall, R. (1988) *Moral Mazes – The World of Corporate Managers*. Oxford: Oxford University Press.

28. Fincham, R. (1999) The consultant–client relationship: Critical perspectives on the management of organizational change, *Journal of Management Studies*, 36 (3), 335–51.

29. Kets de Vries, M. F. R. and Balazs, K. (1997) The downside of downsizing, *Human Relations*, 50 (1), 11–50.

30. Kipping, M. and Armbrüster, T. (2002) The burden of otherness: Limits of consultancy interventions in historical case studies. In Kipping, M. and Engwall, L. (eds) *Management Consulting – Emergence and Dynamics of a Knowledge Industry*. Oxford: Oxford University Press.

31. Clark, T. and Fincham, R. (2002) *Critical Consulting: New Perspectives on the Management Advice Industry*. Oxford: Blackwell.

32. Sturdy, A. J., Schwarz, M., and Spicer, A. (2006) Guess who's coming to dinner? Structures and uses of liminality in strategic management consultancy, *Human Relations*, 59 (7), 929–60.

33. Handley, K., Sturdy A. J., Clark, T., and Fincham, R. (2007) Researching situated learning: participation, identity and practices in client-management–consultant relationships, *Management Learning*, 38 (2), 173–91.

34. Galanter, M. (2006) *Lowering the Bar: Lawyer Jokes and Legal Culture*. Wisconsin: The University of Wisconsin Press.

35. Pinault, L. (2001) *Consulting Demons: Inside the Unscrupulous World of Global Corporate Consulting*. New York: Harper Business.

36. Craig, D. (2005) *Rip Off! The Scandalous Inside Story of the Management Consulting Money Machine*. London: The Original Book Company.

37. O'Shea, J. and Madigan, C. (1998) *Dangerous Company*. New York: Penguin.

38. Clark, T. (1995) *Managing Consultants – Consultancy as the Management of Impressions*. Buckingham: Open University Press.

39. Jefferson, G. (1979) A technique for inviting laughter and its subsequent acceptance declination. In Psathas, G. (ed.) *Everyday Language: Studies in Ethnomethodology*. New York: Irvington, 79–96.

40. Greatbatch, D. and Clark, T. (2003) Displaying group cohesiveness: Humour and laughter in the public lectures of management gurus, *Human Relations*, 56 (12), 1515–44.

41. Phills, J. A. (1996) Tensions in the Client–Consultant Relationship, Academy of Management Conference paper.

PART II

SHIFTING IDENTITIES

CHAPTER 11

Becoming a Successful Corporate Character and the Role Of Emotional Management

Caroline Hatcher

Open up any professional business magazine, peruse the list of any top 100 companies, or walk in to a boardroom anywhere in the world and almost certainly you can expect to see men in suits and a smattering of women. This division of labor seems so natural in corporate life that if one were to see the reverse, questions would be asked. Historically speaking, the credentials that have driven corporate life and allowed men to rise to the top have fitted well with a masculine identity and so the dominance of men in business is not really surprising. However, for contemporary managers, a new set of required credentials and competencies is emerging, and to ensure their career success, the performance of competencies around the "soft" skills of communication and passion are the new currency. Emotion has come center stage. Consequently, it might seem likely that the absence of women in the senior ranks of business will change.

Focusing on "being passionate," "speaking from the heart," and having "emotional intelligence competencies" is part and parcel of a whole series of self-help book titles (*Approaching the Corporate Heart*,[1] *Emotional Capital*,[2] and *Passion at Work*[3]), the subject of professional journals (e.g. *Management Today*[4-6] and *BizEd*[7]), the training initiatives of HR departments, and websites advertising consulting approaches, such as www.eiconsortium.org/. Emotional self-management and management of others are accepted as the mantra of effective workplaces. Indeed, having the capacity to deliver effective self-management of emotions and the management of the emotions of others now signals that a manager is a credible player in the contemporary landscape. This is different from those less "well developed" identities who peopled organizations in the past and those without emotional intelligence competencies in the present.

Performing this identity is thus as much about what is signaled as desirable as it is about being constrained to act in a particular way. In this sense, identity-making is about producing oneself as *a work of art*[8:351] that must meet certain "aesthetic values" and "stylistic criteria."[9:11] Identity-making is also about being disciplined and governed as a subject in organizational life. In other words, identity-making is about creating and projecting a particular sort of self to others as well as about avoiding other performances that are out of bounds. Identity-making is neither a matter of authenticity nor inauthenticity. It is a "creative activity"[8:351] achieved through daily practice. By exploring the prescriptions for the performance of a successful corporate character, the chapter argues that the knowledge produced about emotion, alongside other knowledge formations about gender, has played a significant part in the development of a new way of governing the workforce.

First, the chapter offers a way to conceptualize identity, drawing on the work of Foucault[8–12] and Rose.[13,14] This sets the frame for thinking about the rules for the formation of current managerial identity as the result of particular historically situated discourses. In the second section, a number of these discourses are used to explore the disciplinary practices that consultants, academics, and HR functions within organizations use to govern managers. The third section considers the role of the production of knowledge of feminists and in the women-in-management literature in establishing the "truth" of gender for business practice. The chapter then draws out the implications for managers of new forms of control that are indirect rather than direct, requiring self-regulation rather than regulation by others. This includes the role of embodied practice as a form of control, and the limits for change where female gender is still defined in terms of "softness," excess, and as the object of the male gaze. Taking a critical stance in relation to gender, I conclude that while the imperative to "value emotions" is made desirable in this new discourse, this operates alongside the traditional masculine/feminine hierarchy wherein the feminine is considered less desirable. Consequently, this new mantra about emotions will not necessarily automatically deliver the increased numbers of women leaders and managers that many hope for.

Conceptualizing the Ideal Corporate Character

Emotional labor is now a much valued resource in organizations[2,3] and has become so common in describing what constitutes the ideal corporate manager that to be without passion for one's work and to "lack" emotional responsiveness is be corporate-character-deficient (CCD). Self-development imperatives in organizations are translated into intensified processes of *emotionalization* and *aestheticization* that have become part of the work of (self-) management and managing others in a performance culture.[15] However, as Fineman[15] has suggested, emotions, until the last two decades, were largely regarded as feminine, private, and irrational, and outside the domain of the public, masculinized, rational world of work. This now seems to have changed.

All managers must become active in fashioning themselves in particular ways because their culture proposes, suggests, and imposes models of what appropriate ways to act are, in their circumstances, and this emerges as a particular inescapable sort of truth.[12:440] The observable increasing momentum to view emotion as critical to management excellence as a "truth" or common sense is one expression of this understanding and is applied to both men and women. However, there is no real truth, only "regimes of truth"[11:131] that are fashionable, that function as true, that have procedures and ways of describing that make them true, and become true according to who is charged with saying what counts as true.[11]

The active fashioning of this corporate character is deeply entwined with the development of personal as well as professional identity and is simultaneously about similarity and difference. As Hetherington[16:15] suggests, identity is about how subjects see themselves in representation and how they construct the differences "within that representation and between it and the representation of others." Consequently, when a contemporary manager shapes their emotions and communication within a particular social and cultural terrain, it "is articulated through the relationship between belonging, recognition or identification, and difference."[16:15] Foucault's later work is helpful here to further unpack this process. He theorizes the way individuals constitute themselves as subjects of *moral* conduct[9] and the dynamic interplay of codes of conduct and practices of the self-involved. He also accounts for the idea of *embodied* conduct when he conceptualizes the creative act of bodily performance of this "moral conduct" "through long practice and daily work."[8:351] Applied to the topic of this chapter, bodies are written on by the various and differing discourses of academics, management gurus, and feminists. This leads to the performance of acceptable repertoires of emotional labor and the rejection of others as inappropriate performance. These desirable repertoires will now be explored.

The Ideal Capacities of the Contemporary Manager

Various discourses shape an identity to produce an individual as a "work of art" who mirrors the aesthetic values and performs in line with the stylistic criteria of a particular period. For the contemporary corporate character, one of these emotional and aesthetic values can be imagined as the desire and value of "lifelong learning," and another, as suggested earlier, as "being passionate" about work. Another is "being rational." This section considers these "types of work" to which the corporate individual is responding – both as constraint on what they must do and not do, and as what is desirable or ideal.

The call to lifelong learning

The prescriptions for becoming an effective manager require numerous responses. For example, a commitment to lifelong learning is a key feature of the approach managers are expected to take when shaping their style of managing and relating. There is an expectation that managers will seek to perfect their personal managerial style throughout their working life[17–19] and will conduct a continuous fashioning of themselves through training and reflection. Managers also now expect and must accept that others will continuously appraise them for the purposes of both reviewing what they have achieved and setting goals for the future.[20,21] The expectation of active and ongoing change sets the tone for the shifting demands of identity management.

The myth of rationality

A second trajectory that is shaping managers' thinking is one of the long-cherished myths about how managers should think and act. This myth or accepted cultural understanding of Western society is built around the belief in expertise, objectivity in making decisions, and the requirement that managers approach problem-solving objectively. A belief in "science," "rationality," and "objectivity" underlies the idea of the corporate character as committed to efficiency, instrumentality, and rationality.[22] This myth of rationality is deeply institutionalized in organizations.[23] As Berglund and Werr[22:640] suggest: "Management concepts give managers a feeling of rationality, and, perhaps more important, ways to express and present rationality to others." However, the postmodern turn,[24] with its recognition of the messy, fragmented, and multiple perspectives on how the world works, has unsettled this landscape.

The myth of emotion

While the myth of rationality has traditionally provided a sound and accepted basis for governing organizations, the truth of this idea sits alongside the myth of emotion. Since the emergence of the excellence literature in the 1980s, "guru-speak" writers such as Tom Peters have argued for a "balance" of the rational and the emotional, for as Peters and Waterman warned, "we have to stop overdoing things on the rational side."[25:54] In achieving this new antibureaucratic stance, managers have been induced to identify with what has been traditionally understood as the ir/rational and disordered side of human development. In this scenario, the "heroic" manager on an "heroic quest," as Cairnes[1] describes it in *Approaching the Corporate Heart,* is given an opportunity for renewal and reinvention. These seductive images of managers transforming themselves both depend on and partly achieve legitimacy through the discourse of lifelong learning discussed above.

In this action-oriented paradigm, excellent organizations take advantage of the "emotional, more primitive side (good and bad) of human nature."[25:60] The valorization of this emotional side is contained within the logic that it can still be managed: "All that stuff you have been dismissing for so long as intractable, irrational, intuitive, informal organization can be managed."[25:11] Indeed, it allows Peters and Waterman to claim that "soft is hard."[25:11] Traditionally, the "hard" and difficult processes of scientific reasoning are juxtaposed with the "softness" of emotional work. In their move to remake the meaning of emotional activity as a hard task, Peters and Waterman compare emotional work favourably with the rigor of intellectual work.

The legitimacy of the centrality of "soft skills" in organizations is supported by a well-established popular therapeutic discourse, based on the imperatives of humanistic psychology and created over more than 30 years.[13,26] During the 1990s and early 2000s, the latest of a number of new waves of thinking about emotion emerged and can be loosely categorized under the rubric of "emotional intelligence."[27-29] The term has particular leverage because it has been linked to two other powerful discourses that operate in contemporary society: *a discourse of the intelligence quotient (IQ)* and *the discourse of competence or competencies.*

The first, a measure of capacity, is the idea of an intellectual quotient and its link to an emotional quotient (EQ) being one of a series of multiple intelligences.[30] The capacity to measure has a seductive appeal because, in the natural sciences, "numbers are commonly taken as an indication of precision and truth."[31:725] This idea of the measurable nature of EQ, as part of a cluster of intelligences and linked with IQ, gives EQ added leverage because a person's IQ has always been considered to separate and differentiate them from those with lower IQ. A mythology has also grown about the importance of EQ, with it being variously suggested in the media as more important than IQ. This blurring of the argument about the significance of IQ versus EQ is an important part of this "regime of truth." For example, in a recent article co-authored by Emmerling and Goleman[32] on the EI Consortium website (www.eiconsortium. org/), they confirm that IQ is "also" an important differentiator of capability and likely managerial successful performance but nonetheless focus predominately on EQ.

The performance of the academic master here carefully applying "rationality" and objectivity to the issue of emotional intelligence is an important legitimating strategy of the academic expert for shoring up the truth of emotion. Emmerling and Goleman carefully conclude, nonetheless, that while generally IQ was found to be a better general predictor of successful work performance than EQ in various studies, EQ was a better predictor of the "star performer (in top 10% . . .)."[32:5] They further confirm that "cognitions and emotions are interwoven in mental life" but having done so, return to the salience of emotions in practical terms, and acknowledge that the popular media has often "overlooked or downplayed" that "IQ is a threshold competence."[32:8] Perhaps a reminder of the ease with which Goleman himself slips between the academic and guru is his interview in the same year in a popular professional journal, which quotes him as saying: "It's the skills in the professional domain of emotional intelligence that much more powerfully seem to predict which person will be chosen to head a team or a group or a division or be named president."[7:23]

Those generating knowledge about EQ walk a fine line, managing simultaneously the rational legitimized discourse drawn on the grounds of objective academic research and assessment and the "aspiring guru rhetoric"[15] that proselytizes emotional intelligence. The "commodification" of emotional intelligence, as Fineman[15] calls it, presents this new ideal as highly persuasive, attractive, and inherently desirable – a product to be acquired and acquirable. Reading the self-help books on EQ, one cannot help but be struck by the rhetorical structure of the texts or with the number of times the metaphor of an emotional quotient (a metaphor based on IQ and linked to numbers, rationality, and measurement) is used. As Goleman concludes in his professional journal interview, "soft skills have hard consequences."[7:23]

Unlike IQ, EQ can be learned, according to this new imperative. Not only does this new knowledge about EQ come in a way that allows managers to differentiate themselves from others as a "superior performer"[33] but it also comes in an attractive package as a learnable product.[34] This second powerful discourse to which EQ is linked is through the way emotion has been harnessed as "EQ competencies." The linking of emotion to competencies is important because it feeds into the discourse of the measurement[31] and lifelong learning truths so central to contemporary discourse.[15,33] The discourse of competencies has many critics, but Townley[33] and Rees and Garnsey,[34] amongst others, have pointed to the emphasis that the competencies framework has on denoting that "superior" performance has an emphasis on "dissociation from others" and context and the capacity to deliver the performance as an autonomous act.[33:298] Being able to measure emotion (here, read EQ) just as IQ can be measured allows both the fine-grained disciplining, dividing, ranking, and tracking of improvements, and "constitutes yet another kind of relationship to the self" or a form of government of the self.[34] Again, this new knowledge about emotion is legitimated as "truth," based on the rationality, objectivity and instrumentalism of its operation.

Targeted books for management and leadership development, such as *The New Leaders* by Daniel Goleman, Richard Boyatzis, and Annie McKee,[35] provide a formula for using the "appropriate" six leadership styles: visionary, coaching, affiliative, democratic, pacesetting, and commanding. Even more significantly for this chapter, the authors list the 18 leadership competencies that mark out an emotionally intelligent leader. Cherniss and Goleman's[29] comprehensive guide to "*The Emotionally Intelligent Workplace*" opens with a foreword by leadership expert Warren Bennis. This edited book on how to select for, measure, and improve emotional intelligence in individuals and organizations provides further confirmation of the centrality of emotions to leadership success, and the rational, academically rigorous processes of confirmation of this new knowledge. It also attests to the manageability of emotion. And Druskat, Sala, and Mount's[36] recent text, *Linking Emotional Intelligence and Performance at Work*, supports the legitimation of the field. As one reader/reviewer on the amazon.com site suggests, the book will be appreciated by both academics and HR practitioners "who want to probe into this critical topic more deeply than the plethora of books on EI spewing forth from a booming cottage industry."[37] The confirmation of the rational, rigorous, and enlightened approach taken to all this knowledge development reassures the manager as learner that this toying with emotion is controllable, measurable, and manageable after all. It is another management competence.

The transformation of emotion into a set of competencies is illustrated by an example from the EI Consortium website of EQ best practice training (www.eiconsortium. org/model_programs/emotional_competence_training.htm). The case study captures the ways in which the moral conduct and embodied practice of the manager is shaped to produce the idealized corporate character. In the section on the website entitled Models of Programs, the case study of Emotional Competence Training reports on the training program developed at the large corporate success story, American Express. The case study describes the process and activities of the program and details the "rigorous evaluation" that measured the outstanding financial results delivered following the program. The case study starts with training in mindfulness, self-monitoring of emotional experience, and the role of "self-talk," and proceeds through this to rehearse how to "use" self-disclosure to manage the emotion of others. It also focuses on how to deliver "hard messages."

We are reminded here of Townley's[33] analysis of the ethical implications of competencies. In particular, her analysis raises concerns in terms of the ways in which self-management of hard messages, such as dealing with poor performance or dismissal, is achieved by creating distance between self and the other in these competency models. This, of course, protects the manager from negative experiences while dealing out negative experiences for the other, all the while performing in what is framed as a professionally competent, emotionally managed way. The question to pose here is whether the distance achieved through separation of manager and managed and developed through competency performance management strategies (both at the level of the creation of appropriate emotional response and in terms of nearness to others) will "diffuse the responsibility" to others.[33]

The final section of the program focuses on disciplining the self and the role of stress management, nutrition, and exercise in the management of emotion. This is the final step towards developing an "action plan" to achieve the required modifications of the emotional self and transformations of identity. The emphasis here is clearly on the rational, controlled performance of the body, heart, and mind to achieve superior performance, expressed as a series of competencies. The American Express program demonstrates, in a very tangible way, in this final phase, the variety of incitements to be an appropriate corporate character who has developed and uses an emotional space to achieve superior performance. This involves responses to the dynamic interplay of codes of conduct about self-mastery and mastery of others. This also demonstrates the requirements of *embodied* conduct in the creative act of bodily performance of the emotional and expressive self "through long practice and daily work."[8:351]

The Corporate Character and Gender Performances

This next section poses the question: in this EQ competence environment, can women successfully shape themselves up as corporate characters? The case has been made, to this point, that managers are now called on to be "passionate"[25] in the workplace and in the performance of managerial practice. Indeed, Goleman has emphatically claimed that "a life without passion would be a dull wasteland of neutrality, cut off from the richness of life itself" but nonetheless maintains that the "goal is balance."[28:56] All this is framed within a model of control, rationality, autonomy, and instrumentalism.

However, an important part of these changing expectations could also potentially redraw the traditional masculine/feminine hierarchy of rationality/emotion. Can the binary oppositions of man/woman, control/excess, hard/soft, autonomy/connection, distance/separation, tamed/untamed, and learned/natural (nurture/nature) be unsettled to allow women to find their place in senior roles in organizations? In a practical sense, this new ideal corporate character would seem to finally open the boardroom doors for women. Women might even have some possible advantage here. This was the argument Helgeson made in the 1990s when she entitled her book about women in management *The Female Advantage: Women's Ways of Leadership*.[38] She argued that this was the era of the female ethos, and that the very qualities linked to emotion that had always marginalized women in public life were becoming the ethos of the new ways of leadership.

However, management has long been recognized as a masculine space.[39–41] As Sinclair suggests, "work accomplishes masculinity" and the two identities of manager and man "have fitted hand and glove."[39:84] Women-in-management writers and

feminists have equally insisted that women are good at emotion work and quite naturally know about emotional connection and care. Gilligan put the case for a different
moral development for males and females succinctly when she proclaimed:

> Male and female voices typically speak of the importance of different truths, the former
> of the role of separation that defines the self, the latter of the on-going process of attach-
> ment that creates and sustains the human community.[42:156]

Building on Gilligan's work, various researchers have identified the ways in which
the differing patterns of moral development lead to different modes of cognition. In
the paradigmatic or categorical model, cognition is viewed as information processing
in which concepts are coded to make sense of the world. This paradigmatic model is
the dominant way to think of cognition. This is linked to a male gendered pattern and
is, of course, the model closely aligned with a model of scientific reasoning, rationality,
and instrumental behaviour. The other model of cognition identified by researchers,
linked to female gender, is described as "narrative," and is formulated around cognitions that are "less distant and impersonal."[34,43] In this mode, events are "selected and
populated with actors with their own histories and motivations. . . . the narrator more
often uses their own voice."[34:560]

Whether as expressions of essentialist claims about women's "natural" capacity to
connect and care or as expressions of their recognition of the socialization of women
into helping roles,[34,44] the truth of women's competence in emotion has considerable
legitimacy and commonsense appeal. The production of knowledge about the inherent
strengths of women and their rightful identification as the "keepers of the keys" to the
heart can be seen in the popular press and in academic analysis, and the focus on "difference" in the leadership styles of men and women further supports such a claim.[39,44]

Nonetheless, women still remain *other* to the masculine world of work. It is clear
that this knowledge regime of truth about the capacities for nurturing, connection,
and "soft" skill is not synonymous with the emotional competencies discussed earlier.
In this space of women's emotions, they are neither managed nor "hard" to master;
they are apparently not disciplined and controlled, and require connection rather than
autonomy, and closeness rather than distance or separation. Indeed, women's knowledge of emotions has always been expressed as freely given and an excess of emotion
rather than controlled: untamed and untrained, and, ultimately, unmanageable[45] and
intuitive.

Embodying Corporate Character

To further illustrate this *otherness*, it is useful to consider another dimension of the
control aspects of emotional competence training used at American Express. This
relates to the embodied corporate character and how emotion is expressed bodily.
Bodily performance is an important part of any professional identity. The American
Express training discussed earlier in the chapter focused initially on mindfulness and
self-reflection and then moved to the performance of appropriate emotions. However,

it also focused on nutrition and exercise. It is important to recognize here that being passionate or being emotionally competent is understood as a "controlled" production of the heart. But this also flows to how to express this emotion as controlled performance bodily. The challenge for women, then, is to recognize how to perform emotion in a way that matches the constraints of the emotional competency framework.

Bordo reminds us that women's bodies are "trained, shaped and impressed with the stamp of prevailing historical forms of selfhood, desire and femininity."[46:14] Consequently, for women, there are always the historical tensions between learned behaviors in early socialization periods and the fashionable corporate "look" of the moment. Can the female gendered corporeal regime, with its idealized ways of walking, dressing, talking, and interacting and feeling, be subsumed in the contemporary corporate character successfully?

One study of professional identity-making for women alerts us to the possible challenges that women face. These include how to perform their bodily work appropriately, to discipline and simultaneously display their sexual embodiment, and to successfully express their emotions both professionally and in line with expectations about femininity. Trethewey[41] explored the various ways in which professional women experienced their bodies as texts to be read by those in their organizations in a series of interviews on women's understanding of their embodied professional identity. The strongest theme that emerged was that, as corporeal selves, the professional body is "fit." As one interviewee suggested:

> I think the new standard is fit. With our young people it is. In fact, at the last training session I was at, the major focus is non-fat . . . And I've seen more pressure to be fit in the workplace than I've ever seen before.[41:430]

Several of the interviewees discussed the organizational focus on "body types," the incitement for a "look of youth and vitality," and the links that corporations make between fitness, endurance, and control. Comments were made by interviewees about the problems of "breasts," being on the "stocky side" and fitness as a signifier of "having . . . her life under control."[41:430] Naomi Wolf's analysis of how women "feel" about their bodies expresses this even more emphatically: "When they discuss [their bodies], women lean forward, their voices lower. They tell their terrible secret. 'It's my breasts,' they say. 'My hips. It's my thighs.'"[47:150]

Trethewey[41] also makes it clear that women themselves were contributors to this pressure to succeed corporeally and also that it was just as dangerous to look *too* fit, as the bodily self could be misrecognized as too athletic and perhaps lesbian. The female body needs to be androgynous enough to demonstrate signals of femaleness under control but the "almost masculine" body of the lesbian is too dangerous. While the unfit body might signal the excesses of the heart to male managers, the too fit body signals otherness to women as well as men. The masculine/feminine binary hierarchy is simultaneously reasserted and troubled by these constraints.

The interviewees compared their options for performing and expressing themselves with the wider range of embodied identities available to men. The women commented on the ways in which men's clothes allowed more variation of weight and shape by their design. They suggested that mediated messages about what successful men look like are less narrowly prescribed because we are constantly seeing successful men of all shapes and sizes but, mostly, the successful women we see are young, often computer-generated, thin, and frequently on the cover of *Cosmo*.[41] Even those images generated in business magazines show the fit body. An example of this exposure to gendered bodies is provided by a full colour cover (both front and back), entitled *Reinventing Leadership*, featuring seven men and one woman.[48] Another, with cover page and an article entitled "Passion for business," shows the smiling, attractive, blonde, fit-looking Katie Lahey, CEO of the Business Council of Australia.[5] Expressing their corporate character is fundamentally about delivering performance within a closely prescribed and narrow emotional self which must "fit" the mold of the business body.

In addition, the women in the study highlighted that they needed to discipline their bodies to "look professional" *for* their mostly male colleagues at the senior level. The analysis suggests, as both Trethewey[41] and Bartky[49] conclude, that "[f]eminine movement and posture must exhibit not only constriction, but grace and a certain eroticism restrained by modesty: all three."[49:67] Fitting the mold of the corporate character in the performance of emotional competence is a balancing act for women, where running the race with endurance and control must be finely balanced against the eroticized but graceful self.

Whereas the women defined their corporeal performance mostly in terms of "lack," they also pointed to its excessively sexual self with a tendency to overflow.[41:437] This includes pregnancy, emotional displays, and dress. The consequence for failing to dress appropriately, for example, is to be considered "a sexual rather than professional being."[41:443] Achieving this balance between lack and excess is the challenge reported in the study. Equally, emotions that overflow through tears or emotional outbursts jar with the idealized corporate character. Mythologies built around menstruation and the overflow of both fluids and emotions contribute to this excess. This constant evaluation of the "excessively female" emotional performance[40,41] makes the journey to "superior performance" a high risk one, across a terrain filled with pitfalls and surprises.

In another text on the body, voice coach Rodenburg[50] draws attention to the shifts in training demands that she is experiencing in the UK as women resist or react to the "adoption of male habits" that had got them to powerful positions. They claimed that something had been lost, and that they felt "hollow and empty." As one woman said, "I'm in danger of losing my grace."[50:107] Nonetheless, the women in both studies recognized the tensions between feminine emotionality and masculine professionalism.[41:441] This constant tension over the experience and expression of emotion as they shift between constraint and desire and between lack and excess adds an additional burden for women as they seek to embrace the corporate character.

Conclusion: Mapping Desire and Constraint for the Corporate Character

On the surface, it would seem that the pathways are opening for women to take their place at the tables of boardrooms, in senior executive positions, and across organizations more generally. The shift to the centrality of emotions potentially signals the opening of the doorways to success. The ideal corporate character has a balance of rationality and emotion in the new formulas for success presented in professional journals, training courses, and academic analysis. EQ and IQ competencies are taking their rightful place at center stage in the selection of staff, according to a whole movement of academics and a booming consultancy industry.

This new image of the manager offers both constraints on performance and creates desire to achieve this new identity. This new identity operates, supposedly, in an ungendered space. Typically, tests for EQ, conducted by consultants, are reported as overall measures of a vast range of complex qualities. However, as Fineman has proposed, the measurement of EQ "is no neutral act . . . and has become heavily impregnated with a value stance . . . [such that] the mapmaker and the map are complicit in shaping the direction of the field."[31:729] Authors of analysis of large-scale studies using Bar-On, for example, one EQ test, claim that there are no significant differences in performance on EQ tests overall for sex groups. This is largely the truth propagated by gurus in the field. "What" is measured remain remarkably opaque when this emerging truth is discussed in all but the rarest of analyses.

Not only does a complex, nuanced, and tantalizingly unknowable object, emotion, become "knowable" in researcher-led categories through tests such as these, but the male/female hierarchy remains untouched as the subscales are unpacked. So, for example, according to the claims of the Bar-On test, there are differences in some subscales, with women scoring higher on interpersonal skills and men scoring higher on stress management and adaptability.[51] In other words, the mapmakers claim, on average, men and women perform in similar ways overall, but women don't do so well at the "hard" end of the scale.

However, because EQ, as a knowledge object, is increasingly being used as a signifier of the place of emotion in organizational discourse and translated into a competency, the broad term, EQ, decreases the transparency of the delineation of what is actually required to achieve superior performance and, at the same time, reinforces women's failure to meet the full range of qualities required of the contemporary corporate character.

The knowledge of women's capacity to connect and care, whether thought of from an essentialist perspective or recognized as learned, does not necessarily align with dimensions such as managing stress and adapting to the demands of economic imperatives. The "hard" decisions may well need "hard" skills of disconnection, "hard" messages, and the use of emotion in such ways as to separate the interests of the individual from that of the organization. Judging who can deliver superior performances relies on the human hand, a hand that is shaped by the social values of the organization and recognizes the salience of specific dimensions of this complex concept. It is likely that those qualities at the "masculine end" of the continuum may well still retain their salience.

Equally, will women succeed at delivering this particular brand of "emotion," drawn as it is around issues of control, rationality, objectivity, and measurement? As one research consulting agency suggested, commenting on employee engagement: "Employees learn to give a better score each time [on surveys] because that's good for their manager."[52] The question remains, though, whether the constraints of performing this particular form of the expressive emotional self are such that women may choose to do otherwise.

This question also turns around the pressures for bodily performance of endurance and control. I have argued that the majority of women's bodies are seen as excessively sexual, stamped with the marks of untamed femininity with its big breasts and thighs, and subject to the male gaze of the boardroom and the dominance of male numbers in senior executive positions. Can most women seamlessly and consistently fit the glamorous model of the corporate character, exuding constrained passion, high levels of vitality and endurance, and ultimately the signifiers of controlled and distanced care?

Learning to care in the new formulation requires that managers learn the skills of self-reflection, the performance of passion, and the ways that others think. The performance of EQ, then, becomes technically the management of the emotions of self and others. When considered through this lens, the new "emotion" valued in organizations is not so much about care and connection as it is about an objective determination about how to "perform" appropriate emotion and to express it in such a way as to deliver results: the competence of emotion.

The delivery of emotion as controlled, objective, and able to be measured sits at a considerable distance from the priorities of the truth of care and connection in which many women and men have been socialized and trained. There is a clear disjuncture between the discourses around which gendered rationalities or systems of logic have been developed and the establishment of the truth of the contemporary meaning of emotionally competent managers. The masculine/feminine hierarchy remains very stable in this new configuration of knowledge about emotion. There is little reason to be optimistic that this will change in the near future.

References

1. Cairnes, M. (1998) *Approaching the Corporate Heart*. Sydney: Simon & Schuster.
2. Thomson, K. (1998a) *Emotional Capital*. Oxford: Capstone.
3. Thomson, K. (1998b) *Passion at Work*. Oxford: Capstone.
4. Bathgate, M. (2001) What's all this passion business? *Management Today*, May, 14–19.
5. Thomsen-Moore, L. (2005) Passion for business, *Management Today*, July, 11–13.
6. Cooper, C. (2005) The challenges of management, *Management Today*, July, 18–23.
7. Shinn, S. (2003) Intelligence @ work, *BizEd*, September/October, 19–23.
8. Foucault, M. (1991) On the genealogy of ethics: An overview of work on progress. In Rabinow, P. (ed.) *The Foucault Reader: An Introduction to Foucault's Thought*. Ringwood, Victoria: Penguin, 340–72.
9. Foucault, M. (1992) *The Use of Pleasure*. London: Penguin.
10. Foucault, M. (1979) *Discipline and Punish*. (Trans. Sheridan, A.) London: Penguin.
11. Foucault, M. (1980) *Michel Foucault: Power/Knowledge. Selected Interviews and Other Writings 1972–77*. (Ed. Gordon, C.) London: Harvester Wheatsheaf.
12. Foucault, M. (1996) The ethics of the concern for the self as a practice of freedom. In Lotringer, S. (ed.) *Foucault Live*. New York: Semiotexte, 432–49.
13. Rose, N. (1991) *Governing the Soul*. London: Routledge.
14. Rose, N. (1996) Identity, genealogy, history. In Hall, S. and du Gay, P. (eds) *Questions of Cultural Identity*. London: Sage, 128–50.

15. Fineman, S. (2000) Commodifying the emotionally intelligent. In Fineman, S. (ed.) *Emotion in Organizations*, 2nd edn. London: Sage.

16. Hetherington, K. (1998) *Expressions of Identity: Space, Performance, Politics*. London: Sage.

17. Senge, P. (1992) *The Fifth Discipline: The Art and Practice of the Learning Organization*. Sydney: Random House.

18. Crossan, M., Lane, H., and White, R. E. (1999). An organizational learning framework: From intuition to institution, *Academy of Management Review*, 24, 522–37.

19. Sun, P. and Scott, J. (2003) Towards better qualitative performance measurement in organizations, *Learning Organization*, 10, 258–71.

20. Sun, P. and Scott, J. (2005) An investigation of barriers to knowledge transfer, *Journal of Management Knowledge*, 9, 75–90.

21. Townley, B. (1993) Performance appraisal and the emergence of management, *Journal of Management Studies*, 30 (2), 221–38.

22. Berglund, J. and Werr, A. (2000) The invincible character of management consulting rhetoric: How one blends incommensurate while keeping them apart. *Organization*, 7 (4), 633–56.

23. Meyer, J. W. and Rowan, B. (1977) Institutionalized organizations: Formal structure as myth and ceremony, *American Journal of Sociology*, 83, 340–63.

24. Featherstone, M. (1988) In pursuit of postmodernism: An introduction, *Theory, Culture and Society*, 5 (2–3), 195–216.

25. Peters, T. and Waterman, R. (1982) *In Search of Excellence*. Sydney: Harper & Row.

26. Connor, E. (1999) Minding the workers: The meaning of "Human" and "Human Relations" in Elton Mayo, *Organization*, 6 (2), 223–46.

27. Mayer, J. D. and Saveloy, P. (1997) What is emotional intelligence? In Saveloy, P. and Sluyter, D. (eds) *Emotional Development and Emotional Intelligence: Implication for Educators*. New York: Basic Books.

28. Goleman, D. (1996) *Emotional Intelligence. Why it Can Matter More Than IQ*. London: Bloomsbury.

29. Cherniss, C. and Goleman, D. (2001) *The Emotionally Intelligent Workplace: How to Select for, Measure, and Improve Emotional Intelligence in Individuals, Groups and Organization*. San Francisco: Jossey-Bass.

30. Gardner, H. (1993) *Multiple Intelligences: The Theory in Practice*. New York: Basic Books.

31. Fineman, S. (2004) Getting the measure of emotion – and the cautionary tale of emotional intelligence, *Human Relations*, 57 (6), 719–40.

32. Emmerling, R. J. and Goleman, D. (2003) Emotional intelligence: issues and common misunderstandings, *E-journal Issues and Recent Developments in Emotional Intelligence*, October, www.eiconsortium.org.

33. Townley, B. (1999) Nietzsche, competencies and ubermensch: Reflections on human and inhuman resource management, *Organization*, 6 (2), 285–305.

34. Rees, B. and Garnsey, E. (2003) Analysing competence: Gender and identity at work, *Gender, Work and Organization*, 10 (5), 551–78.

35. Goleman, D., Boyatzis, R., and McKee, A. (2002) *The New Leaders: Transforming the Art of Leadership into the Science of Results*. London: Little, Brown.

36. Druskat, V., Sala, F., and Mount, G. (2005). *Linking Emotional Intelligence and Performance at Work: Current Research Evidence with Individuals and Groups*. Mahwah: Lawrence Erlbaum Associates.

37. Anon. (2005) Review: *Linking Emotional Intelligence and Performance at Work: Current Research Evidence with Individuals and Groups*, www.amazon.com, accessed October 25, 2006.

38. Helgeson, S. (1990) *The Female Advantage: Women's Ways of Leadership*. New York: Doubleday.

39. Sinclair, A. (2000) Teaching managers about masculinity: are you kidding? *Management Learning*, 31 (1), 83–101.

40. Sinclair, A. (2005) Body and management pedagogy, *Gender, Work and Organization* 12 (1), 89–103.

41. Trethewey, A. (1999) Disciplined bodies: Women's embodied identities at work, *Organization Studies*, 20 (3), 423–50.

42. Gilligan, C. (1982) *In a Different Voice: Psychological Theory and Women's Development*. Cambridge, MA: Harvard University Press.

43. Boland, R. J. and Schultze, U. (1996) Narrating accountability. In Munroe, R. and Mouritsen, J. (eds) *Accountability, Power, and Ethos*. London: International Thomson Business Press.

44. Rosener, J. (2005) *Ways Women Lead:* Harvard Business Review *on Women in Business*. Boston, MA: Harvard Business School Publishing.

45. Hatcher, C. (2003) Refashioning a passionate manager: Gender at work, *Gender, Work and Organization*, 10 (4), 391–12.

46. Bordo, S. (1989) The body and the reproduction of femininity. In Jagger, A. and Bordo. S. (eds) *Gender, Body, Knowledge*. New Brunswick: Rutgers University Press, 13–33.

47. Wolf, N. (1991) *The Beauty Myth*. New York: William Morrow.

48. Australian Financial Review (2006, August). BOSS: *Reinventing Leadership*.

49. Bartky, S. (1988) Foucault, femininity, and the modernization of patriarchal power. In Diamond, I. and Quinby, L. (eds.) *Feminism and Foucault: Reflections on Resistance*. Boston, MA: Northeastern University Press, 61–8.

50. Rodenburg, P. (2000) Powerspeak: Women and their voices in the workplace. In Armstrong, F. and Pearson, J. (eds) *Well-tuned Voices*. London: The Women's Press, 96–109.

51. Gowing, M. (2001) Measurement of individual emotional competence. In Cherniss, C. and Goleman, D. (eds) *The Emotionally Intelligent Workplace: How to Select for, Measure, and Improve Emotional Intelligence in Individuals, Groups, and Organization*. San Francisco: Jossey-Bass.

52. Cherrington, J. (2005) Staff performance: Measure with care, *Management Today*, July, 14–16.

CHAPTER 12

Gender and the Emotion Politics of Emotional Intelligence

Stephanie A. Shields and Leah R. Warner

In the mid-nineteenth century, businessmen in Boston discovered the power of emotion. The Businessman's Revival, so nicknamed because of the unprecedented participation of young and middle-aged men, was one of numerous revivals held in Boston at mid-century. Revival-goers viewed the prayer meetings as sites for offering their emotional fervor to God, their emotions powering the vehicle of prayer for fulfillment of their requests. John Corrigan, in *Business of the Heart*, relates how revival-goers believed that prayer was "a platform for 'giving the heart to God' in exchange for certain favors" and that emotion "was like electricity moving through the telegraph line to God, who would respond to the sender upon receiving the message."[1:10] Corrigan describes how this objectification and commoditization of emotion in revivals, as elsewhere in commerce and interpersonal exchanges of all kinds, was accompanied by an understanding that emotional expression was both to be encouraged and highly regulated. Indeed, he argues, the creation of shared understanding of when and how strong emotion should be expressed or contained created the conditions for group membership, marking the group as distinct from and superior to excluded groups with their inferior emotional capacities. The businessmen's shared understanding of emotion validated their vigorous pursuit of economic goals and assured them that their prosperity was justified.

The themes of emotion as commodity and the basis for group inclusion or exclusion may be less visibly at the forefront of the current emotional intelligence movement, but with little probing, the politics of emotion are equally evident. In this chapter, we consider emotional intelligence (EI), generally conceived of as individuals' abilities to perceive, understand, and manage emotions – their own and others' – as it promises change in the workplace while it nevertheless maintains the status quo. We are concerned especially with how EI appears to open up the possibility of workplace transformation at the very same time that it covertly reassures that nothing will change. To be sure, emotional intelligence may be a valuable skill, but its analysis reveals the seemingly inevitable influence of the politics of emotion in everyday life. We ask who benefits and whose interests are served by incorporating EI into definitions of the good worker and good manager. More to the point, we consider how power relationships are maintained and reinforced.

Emotional Intelligence: The Lay of the Land

Interest in emotional intelligence has continued to grow internationally since the idea, which had been around in one form or another for decades, was popularized in the 1990s.[2,3] Emotional intelligence training programs have become widely advertised in the business world, touted as the key to excellence in business and professional leadership, since EI was famously declared by its first successful guru as accounting for "almost 90 percent of what sets stars apart from the mediocre."[4] Today it is easy to find books that apply the idea of emotional intelligence to childrearing, marriage, and self-help. Emotional intelligence's popularity and scope of application has grown despite a steady stream of criticism concerning the often unwieldy breadth of the construct, questions regarding the soundness of its measurement, and challenges to its actual utility to business and management.[5-9]

Main streams in EI

Drawing on Ashkanasy and Daus'[10] history of contemporary models of emotional intelligence, we can identify two broad streams of thinking on EI that currently dominate research and applications. The first derives from Salovey and Mayer's[2,11] four-branched abilities-based model and identifies EI as comprised of four distinct yet related abilities: *perceiving emotions*, which includes not only the ability to read one's own and others' emotions, but also to perceive emotion in cultural artifacts; *using emotions*, which entails using emotion in the service of various cognitive activities, such as identifying the optimal mood for completion of specific types of problem solving; *understanding emotions*, which involves understanding emotion labeling and the relation among emotions; and *managing emotions*, which is concerned with regulating one's own and others' emotions. Essentially, any emotion-relevant ability is encompassed by one of the four branches, making the construct's definition quite broad. The second model offers an even broader definition of emotional intelligence. It encompasses what some say is more accurately described as general social intelligence, rather than a uniquely emotional intelligence. Measurement using this model relies on self-reported personality attributes and behavioral preferences. This model is associated most closely with Bar-On's[12] multidimensional Emotional Quotient Inventory (EQ-i) and Goleman's Emotional Competency Index (ECI), and it is most widely represented in commercial ventures.

Emotional intelligence has been critiqued from many angles. Critiques have centered on how EI should be defined, measured, and applied in the workplace – and even whether it is a useful construct at all.[5,13] The proof of emotional intelligence's validity is circular: the most successful – those at the top of the organization or those who make the most money – are purportedly the ones more likely to have high EI; therefore, high EI is a major contributor to success. Defenders of the science of EI argue that EI research, unlike the management consultation EI programs that have proliferated, is both methodologically and theoretically sound and that it demonstrates EI is an important individual difference variable in organizational behavior.[14] Indeed, EI has appeal to the practical-minded: if a teachable skill enhances worker performance, it makes sense for businesses and managers to develop ways to teach and use it.

Our critical position

Our analysis of EI is influenced by our approach to emotion, which draws on two theoretical traditions. The first, *appraisal theory*, views emotional experience as arising from nonconscious evaluation of the situation's meaning for the individual.[15] The second is the *constructionist* approach, which takes the view that emotions and their meanings are created and maintained through social interaction.[16] Like many current emotions researchers, we view emotion as fundamentally embedded in actual or imagined social interactions.[17] Gender (and other intersecting dimensions of social identity) is, as we describe below, always a component of social situations; therefore emotion is inevitably linked to gender. We have specifically brought feminist theory into the mix in our analysis of EI because of its sophisticated and detailed treatment of power in everyday life.

We focus on the cultural conditions that make the topic of EI timely. In brief, we argue that EI, as conceptualized, studied, and applied, arises from a Zeitgeist that calls for negotiating the competing ideals of American individualism, and, to borrow a theme from journalist Thomas Friedman,[18] the new "flat world" of teams, globalization, and interdependence. The "new worker" of the twenty-first century must be connected to others to get the job done. Connections, whether virtual or face-to-face, require collaboration and people-skills that historically have been minimized and undervalued in the US. At the same time, there appears to have been a sea change in American attitudes toward emotional expression. We trace the beginnings to the era of Ronald Reagan's presidency, when the "Great Communicator" brought his actor's ability to express rational judgment *and* concern to public attention. His expressive style carried the message of an idealized emotion – emotion in the service of reason – that was much like idealized emotion of the late nineteenth century.[19] The Reagan era made monitored and controlled emotion an essential component of public life. More recently, norms in public emotional expression shifted again in response to the events of September 11, 2001. The attacks created an atmosphere in which public expression of intense emotion was an important part of coming to terms with the horror of the events. Having a deep, authentic sense of sorrow following September 11 separated the good from the terrorists. Public figures who cried on national television were applauded, and any individual who seemed unfazed was deemed a threat.[20,21] In the years that have followed, publicly shared emotion has given us a site in which to work toward collective understanding of world-changing events, whether terror attacks or natural disasters. "Owning" emotional authenticity – that is, having a right to experience and express particular emotions – marks the difference between the worthy and the unworthy. Intensity of feeling is prized, and at the same time the rules for when and how to regulate are aimed at putting controlled emotion to work.

The new value placed on emotion in public life would seem like it should benefit women, who are stereotypically associated with caregiving, concern, and emotional connection with others. Yet the rise of EI, we argue, has not benefitted women. The rise of EI corresponds to a period of increased presence and rising power of women in professions that had been for decades dominated by men. The proportion of women in middle and upper management has grown in the past three decades, but women remain grossly underrepresented in the corporate suite. *New York Times* reporter Julie Creswell[22] points out that it is not for a lack of women in the management pipeline. There may be the occasional female CEO in the media spotlight, but they gain attention in part because they are rarities. Citing data gathered by Catalyst (www.catalyst.org/), a nonprofit independent organization that studies women in the workplace, Creswell notes that "while top business schools are churning out an increasing number of female MBAs, only about 16 percent of corporate officers at Fortune 500 companies are women" and that "numbers are even sparer at the top of the pyramid: women fill only nine, or less than 2 percent, of the chief executive jobs at Fortune 500 companies." We can read the rise of EI as a subtle backlash against women's encroachment into male-dominated professional life. As in the Businessman's Revival, ideas about emotional competence draw the boundaries between the deserving and undeserving.

In this chapter we explore why and how the EI disadvantage to women occurs. We begin by examining the relation between the "hard" data on gender and its transformation into justifying business as usual. Second, we turn to the way in which EI's valuing of emotion in the workplace on the surface seems to support those who have been traditionally associated with emotion (i.e. women), but it ultimately serves the status quo through reconstruing the conventional line-management hierarchy into a softer "velvet glove of patriarchy"[23] hierarchy. Third, we look at the emotion politics that facilitate the maneuvers by which the maintenance of inequities is accomplished. We conclude with some thoughts on the future of EI, and possibilities for neutralizing or at least coping with the fact of gendered emotion politics. Throughout this chapter, we focus primarily on gender issues. We emphasize, however, that much of our analysis is also applicable to other groups that occupy the periphery of power.

Measuring EI: The "Hard" Data on Gender

How do we sort out what constitutes a good index of EI? If a person with high emotional intelligence understands the what, when, and how of emotion, how can we be sure that the measure of EI is something more than a general measure of cultural savvy? That is, we must consider whether a test of EI measures more than knowing the "right" answer about what is valued in emotional experience and expression. In this regard, the problems of measurement are much like those that plague the study of cognitive or general intelligence, especially the tricky relation between the construct and its measurement. The similarity does not end there. As with cognitive intelligence, we can ask how many kinds of intelligence there are, how independent they are from one another, and how important those different "intelligences" are across situations. As

Matthews et al. point out, there is no consensus as to whether the construct of EI "represents a cognitive aptitude for processing emotional stimuli, attributes of personality such as integrity and character, or some facility for adapting to challenging situations."[5:180] Indeed, Fineman[13:109] observes that "different authors offer different cocktails of attributes and competencies" in defining the phenomenon, which is reflected in the rather large menu of measurement.

Measuring EI – What counts and what doesn't?

People do vary in how well they are able to understand and manage their emotions, and these skills arguably contribute to success in all aspects of life that have a social component or that require self-management. That said, definitions of emotional intelligence are sufficiently vague to serve as a kind of catchall description of competence in understanding, controlling, and responding appropriately to one's own and others' emotions. For example, Goleman identifies five areas of emotional intelligence that cover a range of attributes and skills that extend well into general social competencies: self-awareness, self-regulation, motivation, empathy, and social skills.

Tests of emotional intelligence tend to rely heavily on items that measure the extent to which one has assimilated the culturally dominant views of appropriate emotion. Though the tests themselves may be objectively scored, items on emotional tests nevertheless constitute a catalog of dominant/majority emotion values. On subtests of the Mayer-Salovey-Caruso Emotional Intelligence Test (MSCEIT)[24] for example, the test-taker evaluates the efficacy of responses to particular emotion-evoking situations, names the emotion that results when other emotions are "combined," and identifies situations that can cause particular emotions. For example, one branch of the EI construct – using emotions – includes items for which participants identify emotions that would best facilitate a type of thinking, such as planning a birthday party.[25] Even though the test's developers acknowledge that there is no single factually verifiable and universally accepted true answer for most items, for scoring purposes, some set of responses *must* be defined as better or more preferable than others. The test-taker's score thus is based on the extent to which the test-taker's choices match those who should be most knowledgeable about emotion. In this case two different scoring methods can be used, either as the consensus of all previous respondents, or as the modal response of experts in emotion research.

Even though culturally specific knowledge about emotions and their management is widely known to well-socialized individuals (just as widely held negative and positive stereotypes are known and understood even by people who may not endorse them), the application of that knowledge is not an unquestionably equal opportunity occasion. An example from Salovey and Grewal's[14] overview of the four-branch model illustrates this point. One branch of the model, managing emotions, comprises the ability to regulate emotions in oneself and in others. As an example of managing others' emotions, they describe a situation in which "an emotionally intelligent politician might increase her own anger and use it to deliver a powerful speech in order to arouse righteous anger in others."[14:282] The emotionally intelligent male politician may be able to deploy his anger to effect change in the listeners without having to take into account other considerations that the female politician would ignore at her peril. And if that female politician were Latina or African-American, the "considerations" multiply. In other words, for the female politician, it is not solely about management of anger, but whether she is perceived to have a right to her position, as through external confirmation of her expertise and leadership status, that conveys her legitimacy to speak with anger.[26,27]

In sum, the same sort of criticisms that for years have been leveled against intelligence testing – that IQ tests are tests of acculturation, that they test what has already been learned and not the capacity for adaptive behavior – can be leveled against measurement of EI. Whether they rely on self-report or performance measures, EI tests favor those who are in the position to recognize privileged knowledge and deploy it. Recognizing knowledge is distinct from the ability or privilege to use it.

Yes, but

Inevitably a critique of the gender politics of EI is confronted with, "Yes, but what *are* the gender differences?" This seems like a simple enough question, but it is the wrong one. It is simple because it gives the appearance that tabulating differences and similarities across studies answers the question of how gender matters in EI. It is the wrong question because enumeration of similarities and differences is descriptive, not explanatory. Further, counting up differences and similarities paints EI measurement as a purely objective scientific endeavor, which is questionable. Fineman[13:109] cites Fairclough's[28] concept of "discourse technology," the use of scientific or quasi-scientific terminology to legitimize nonscientific constructs, in describing the contents of EI tests that "powerfully disseminate a particular creed about emotions." By totting up huge numbers of test-takers, developing test norms, and statistically comparing different groups' performance, the apparent legitimacy of the construct is solidified, even though it may rest on questionable psychometric assumptions. Comparison of women's and men's performance is ideally suited to this strategy as it involves testing groups that are assumed to be "natural" comparison groups and that have less political risk-attached comparisons than, say, racial, ethnic, or socioeconomic groups. (Some age and cross-national samples can also offer risk-free comparisons of "natural" groups, too.)

Each of the main streams of EI relies on different types of testing methods. Here we focus on the stream that tests people's beliefs about their own knowledge of emotion and capacity for emotion management because of its wider use in management consultation settings. Bar-On describes his self-report instrument, the EQ-i, as one that "measures *abilities* and the *potential for performance* rather than the performance itself; it is *process-oriented* rather than *outcome* oriented"[29:1110] (emphasis in original), and elsewhere as "a self-report measure of emotionally and socially competent behavior that provides an estimate of one's emotional and social intelligence."[30:364] The 133 items yield a composite score and 15 subscale scores, so there are plenty of opportunities to pick up differences.

Self-report is a valuable account of what people believe to be true about themselves.[31] That said, self-reports tend to mimic stereotypic gender differences the more general the questions are and the more the questions rely on retrospection. In fact, there is evidence that gender stereotypes can serve as a kind of heuristic, guiding respondents' answers when the task at hand contains ambiguity or generalities.[32] Given that the fundamental gender-emotion stereotype ("She's emotional; he's not.") is widely found and long enduring in Western cultures, it is interesting that few gender differences on Bar-On's and similar self-report measures are found. That tests focus on people's beliefs about their abilities is probably one good reason no differences are found: women and men alike are fairly persuaded of their emotion competence. It should be no surprise that the primary dimension along which differences emerge coincides with what each gender believes it excels in: women in emotional sensitivity, men in emotional self-control.

Bar-On summarizes his findings as showing no significant difference between adult males and females on the composite EQ-i score, with differences on "a few" subscales.[30] In summarizing his extensive findings in a posting to the primary listserv for discussion of emotions in organizational life, the main difference he reports is that women "appear to have the edge over men in being aware of that aspect of self-awareness that relates specifically to being aware of and identifying emotions" both in oneself and others. On the other hand, Bar-On concludes:

> . . . men are significantly better than women in managing and coping with emotions over time. Moreover, men seem to deal better with change, are more flexible and adaptive in coping with the immediate. They are better with immediately dealing with everyday types of environmental problems and coping with the pressure involved in these types of problems. An additional edge that men have over women in this regard is that they are more optimistic than women, which tends to facilitate emotionally and socially intelligent behaviour. [Bar-On posting to EMONET-L, May 31, 2001]

Bar-On further asserts that across the many thousands of cases that comprise the EQ-i database, "the same basic picture . . . reappears in country after country, especially regarding (1) women being significantly stronger than men in social awareness and interpersonal skills and (2) men managing emotions better than women." [Bar-On posting to EMONET-L, May 31, 2001.] Without dwelling on text, it is interesting that Bar-On describes women's advantage as a self-reported advantage, but summarizes men's self-reported emotion management skills as a bona fide EI advantage. Other investigators, however, using this or other self-report measures find no differences[33] or a difference that favors women.[34,35]

The point here is not to argue differences and similarities in actual emotion experience or behavior. Indeed, in this case, the similarities and differences in dispute concern what people believe to be true about themselves, not what they actually do with their self-narratives. We need to be cautious in interpreting the way that women and men represent their emotion expertise. In other emotion-relevant domains, there is a disconnect between beliefs and actual behavior. For example, women (as a group) fairly typically report greater empathy with others than do men, but behavioral gender differences in empathic behavior typically are not found.[36] In the case of self-reported anger experience, research typically reveals either no difference or men reporting greater anger frequency or intensity. In lab settings and naturalistic studies, however, differences tend to occur in anger-related aggression rather than anger per se.[37]

What Is Hidden, What Disappears?

The discourse on gender within the EI literature would suggest that EI should have a positive effect on perceptions of women in the workplace. It would seem that at last an emphasis on the importance of emotional skills might level the playing field for women; that expectations and training for nurturance, cooperation, and other emotion-related features that are prized in girls and women would show up as an advantage at work. On the surface it may seem that EI has debunked previous perceptions of women's emotions in favor of those that are more egalitarian. However, a deeper look at the discourse on gender within the EI literature reveals that the playing field is not as level as it seems. As Fineman[13:109] notes, the "moral dice are loaded when the very technique or concept creates distinctions that immediately relegate, with apparent force and authority, some people to a less worthy or 'competent' personal condition."

What does the work of "hiding" potential gender inequities within the EI literature? And what inequities lie beneath the surface? To answer these questions, we can take a look at when gender is discussed and how it is discussed. For example, when gender figures in discussions of EI, it is most likely to be in terms of gender differences and similarities. When gender differences are mentioned, they are typically framed in terms of a classic "equal-but-different" manner, such that one gender seems to make up for the other gender's weaknesses. Such arguments that say that women and men's differences are complementary have been used before to explain differences between men and women, and not without criticism.[38] The problem is that one side of the comparison is inevitably regarded as more valuable or better than the other side. The major criticism of complementarity explanations is that they fail to recognize the role that power and status play in determining which side of the coin is more socially valued. If we look at the way that "his" and "hers" types of EI are valued, we begin to see the inequities that exist. Specifically, one reason why the playing field is not level is that the types of EI that women are supposedly good at are not valued as much as the types of EI that men are supposedly good at. Thus, while women are prized for what they do, they still are seen as not as good *relative* to men.[i] Managing the emotions in interpersonal relations, strengths that women supposedly have, are not ultimately valued as much as managing one's own emotions, for the latter is ultimately associated with more competence in the workplace.

In *Disappearing Acts*, Joyce Fletcher[39] shows how qualities of the new worker – emotional intelligence and relational work – which are touted as essential to profound changes taking place in the workplace and needed for business success in the international context of the twenty-first century workplace are paradoxically valued in the abstract, but "disappeared" when women's engagement in these supposedly valued behaviors collides with persistent and powerful gender-linked preconceptions and expectations. Her study of female design engineers, women being a minority in both the industry and the firm, shows how the advantages that at least stereotypically ought to accrue to women actually are nowhere to be found. Fletcher argues that strengths in interpersonal relations (such as being supportive of others and creating relational connections) end up being ignored, "naturalized," or credited to others.

Another reason why the playing field is not level is that the types of EI that women are supposedly *not* good at are discussed in terms of individual capacities (such as an "inability" to handle stress), ignoring social structural interpretations. Self-report EI measures often include a component in which people report their ability to manage one's own socially antagonistic emotions, such as anger, anxiety, and frustration. Men report managing these emotions better than women report that they do. People who believe they can quell these feelings are assessed as more emotionally intelligent, in the sense that self-management increases productivity. However, anger, anxiety, and frustration are exactly the emotions that people feel on a consistent basis when they are being treated unfairly, such as in cases of gender discrimination.[40] Thus, those individuals who have a tendency to experience gender discrimination in the workplace might have more encounters that elicit the very emotions that they are supposed to suppress.

Specifically, how might acknowledging (as opposed to suppressing) these emotions help to better foster social change? Paying attention to these emotions helps make the signal clearer that something is wrong. Indeed, as Naomi Scheman observes about anger: "one's discovery of anger can often occur not from focusing on one's feelings but from a political redescription of one's situation."[41:25] She argues that when a person is told that she is not supposed to feel anger, her feelings that resemble anger will not be as well-defined as they would be for someone who is privileged to feel anger. If that person then fails to interpret her feelings as anger, those feelings may be experienced as odd or erratic, and thus less predictable than what is expected from someone whose right to anger is acknowledged. Scheman contends that sometimes the dis-validation of anger is sufficiently extreme that the individual is confused by the mismatch between what is felt and what the person believes should be felt. In these cases, others may step in to tell the person what she is feeling. The aspects of feeling that the individual pays attention to (and thus "feels") are, in part, dependent on who is instructing her to feel this way: "the interpretation of women's feelings and behavior is often appropriated by others, by husbands or lovers, or by various psychological 'experts.' Autonomy in this regard is less an individual achievement than a socially recognizable right, and, as such, people with social power tend to have more of it."[41:29] Therefore, Scheman argues, the right to have privileged access to one's emotions is unequally distributed.

Thus, perhaps women who pay attention to these emotions may also be more clearly sensing larger injustices that occur at work. If men are less likely to encounter injustices based on gender, they are less likely to be moved to feel emotions associated with injustices. By ignoring or downplaying the feeling and/or expression of these emotions, and thus weakening the signal, women may refrain from challenging the status quo. As a result, in valuing the individual's "management" of anger, anxiety, or frustration, instead of probing the context of these emotions' occurrence, the construct of EI privileges behavior that maintains the status quo.

EI and the Politics of Emotion

How is the disappearance of women's supposed advantaged abilities in emotion accomplished? What brings about the magical change – in appearance only – of power as usual into an apparently kinder, gentler version of itself? To explain this magic trick, we have to look at emotion in a different way – not as a skill set (as EI), nor as a natural and, therefore, unwieldy, untamable part of animal nature. Instead, we have to turn to the way in which the beliefs about and the representation of emotion in everyday life is itself a social construction, a commodity of the politics of emotion in everyday life.

By emotion politics, we mean the intentional or inadvertent use of one's own and others' emotions in asserting or challenging status and power.[42] We do not use the term "politics" lightly – the term is far from neutral. A common dictionary definition reveals how much so. Politics, *Webster's* explains, entail factional scheming for power and status within a group and sometimes involve deploying crafty or unprincipled methods to attain that power or status. Our emphasis is neither on "crafty or unprincipled" methods of politics nor on intentional jockeying for power. Instead, we consider subtle forms of emotion politics that occur underneath the radar. Perhaps the most obvious place that politics can come into play is in the labels applied to emotional behavior: My own "righteous indignation" is my opponent's "temper tantrum."

Emotions have a political dimension in that judgments regarding when and how emotion should be felt and shown are interpreted in the interests of regulating the organization and functioning of social groups.[42] In other words, the "right emotion," the socially appropriate emotion, the intelligent emotion is a partisan determination. Emotion meanings convey information about presumed responsibilities, rights, and privileges.[16,43,44]

The notion of emotion politics is partially informed by expectation states theory. Expectation states theory aims to explain how status beliefs operate to sustain social hierarchies. Specifically, expectation states theory begins with the premise that status beliefs, like stereotypes or norms, are widely shared cultural beliefs that express the status relationship between one social group and another within a given society.[45] These beliefs are consensual. That is, regardless of whether individuals are members of the advantaged or disadvantaged group, they endorse the reality of the status belief, even if not its legitimacy.

According to expectation states theory, shared status beliefs facilitate intergroup interactions, thereby creating conditions for reproducing status hierarchies. Shared status beliefs set up expectations regarding behavior within one's own group and between one's group and those higher and lower in the status hierarchy. Status beliefs thus can foster the reproduction of the groups' hierarchical organization in that people look for cues to define the situation, guide their own behavior, and anticipate and interpret how others behave. In this way, heterogeneous groups comprised of individuals who differ in status quickly sort themselves into reproducing the hierarchies reflected in status beliefs. When it comes to EI, status informs both what counts as "appropriate" emotion and also who is most able to be emotionally intelligent.

What counts as "appropriate emotion" and who is perceived to have it?

How does status within the organization interact with the appropriate use and expression of emotion? For whom is it risky to express emotion and what contexts define greater and lesser risk? When lower status individuals communicate their concerns, they run the risk of having that communication identified as inappropriately emotional, with larger consequences – or at least different consequences – than when higher status individuals express discontent. For example, when members of the dominant group discuss issues concerning groups with less power or status, the question of "Why are *they* always so angry?" almost invariably arises. The answer depends on who is in a position to write the rules as to what counts as a legitimate appraisal of unfairness. The assessment of anger, furthermore, is likely to include the judgment that, even if some anger is warranted, it is too much or wrongly directed.

Even though women have been traditionally stereotypically associated with emotion, nurturance, and social support, it is not a new phenomenon that men are still perceived to "do emotion better." In many emotion-related domains that are typed "female," men are still afforded the status over women. For example, Timmers, Fischer, and Manstead[46] found that their participants believed men are better than women in situations where sensitivity is required for competence (such as in nursing). Indeed, they conclude that where men are concerned, "emotions still seem to be more associated with ability, with good social and emotional skills." For women, on the other hand, "emotions remain linked to stereotypical femininity, that is, to their vulnerability, and thus to their loss of control and power."[46:58] Both men and women are held to competency standards, but apparently men are assumed to handle their emotions better than women, even in situations requiring sensitivity that are stereotypically associated with women's work.[47] Women are well aware of the power of gender-emotion stereotypes and the fact that these stereotypes up the ante in claiming emotional competence. Ellison,[48] for example, attempts to turn the stereotype of women's "natural" affinity with emotion to women's advantage. Her book, *The Mommy Brain: How Motherhood Makes Us Smarter*, designed to appeal to the working mothers who know all too well how maternal emotionality is routinely portrayed, attempts to turn the stereotype on its head. Ellison argues that the hormonal changes of motherhood and the demands of multitasking "can literally reshape the brain" – including a jump in emotional intelligence. It is a bold way to sell a new idea, but simply making a claim on emotional intelligence will not erode men's comparative advantage in being identified with expertise in emotion regulation.

One expressive style associated with manliness and coincidentally considered appropriate in the workplace,[20] is controlled expression that conveys deep and authentically felt emotion. This passionate restraint is celebrated in popular culture and exemplified in dramatic movie heroes, such as Russell Crowe in *Gladiator* or Vigo Mortensen in the *Lord of the Rings* trilogy. It conveys the individual's emotion as one of authentic feeling and self-control: "I can control my emotion (i.e., my self), and I can competently harness my emotion to control the situation." Shields has referred to this expressive style as "manly emotions," because even though this emotional style is expected of both men and women in contemporary American contexts, it derives its value from, and is defined by, a particular version of white, heterosexual masculinity.[20] Cultural value is placed on manly emotion through its connection to the expression of rationality and self-control. As an ideal, this style is elusive or only partially attainable for the individual in everyday life. Like other cultural standards, such as those for beauty, it may be completely and ideally expressed only in films and other works of fiction. It is important to emphasize here that manly emotion is not simply men's emotion. The passionate restraint of manly emotion is an ideal against which both women and men are measured. Indeed, research has demonstrated that gender informs the degree to which men's and women's displays of "manly emotion" are positively evaluated. Recently, Warner and Shields[49] demonstrated that male characters in a vignette that were portrayed as displaying a "moist eye" when sad about an upsetting event were evaluated more positively than women who were portrayed in exactly the same fashion, and more positively than men or women who displayed "visible tears." Even though in the "sad, moist eye" condition, both men and women displayed a socially appropriate expression, men were given an extra positive edge in the evaluation.

Emotion politics and disappearing acts in EI

The politics of emotion provide an explanation for how EI can seem so innocuous, but at the same time reinforce the status quo. Because EI is a teachable skill, it promises that anyone can advance. Success is in the hands of the individual who applies himself or herself to acquiring the skill. And it is not a skill that takes money or connections. So it is a very appealingly "American individualism" kind of promise. The "trainability" of emotional intelligence promises an earned meritocracy, one that prizes individualism in efforts to move ahead. Yet there is a double message in this apparent democratization. Anyone can do it, but only leaders (those deserving to lead) have it.

Moreover, advice that improving one's emotional intelligence can contribute to success in life seems harmless enough. In fact, it seems rather banal. But the message is that if you are successful, you already have this skill. So those who have the position of power are the ones, in effect, defined as already having emotional intelligence. In other words, the "right way" to do emotion (and think about it and understand it) becomes by definition the property of those with high EI. Since EI measures tend to focus on dominant culture emotion expression norms, "emotion outlaws" remain outlaws. The emotion skills that outlaws or others at the margins need are unlikely to figure in what counts as intelligence.

Conclusion – Is EI a fad about to fade?

As popular as EI continues to be, a number of critics have identified it as just one more fad in an area hungry for the next big thing that will transform organizational life.

Those critics argue that EI will inevitably go the way of former fads.[5] If that is the case, our concerns about continued marginalization of women and disappearing of their EI competence are misplaced, and we should move on. More likely, even though debates about the most appropriate conceptualization and measurement will continue, EI in some form is here to stay.

The positive side of the EI bandwagon is that it is part of a larger trend to acknowledge the significance of emotional events in the workplace. Research on emotion work, inspired by Hochschild's germinal *The Managed Heart*,[50] continues. Workplace bullying[51] and incivility[52] have more recently come to attention.[ii] Emotion is an important and significant addition to research on organizational environments. EI measurement has a certain utility, too, if only to reveal how much one's own understanding of emotion corresponds to those of majority culture. As an element of self-monitoring, this knowledge can be quite useful to individuals' occupational advancement. Knowing how to "do" majority culture is necessary if one hopes to fit in, understand, and advance in any organization, perhaps especially when one's appearance or background mark the individual as an outsider.

What, then, do we do about the disappearing of women's emotional/relational competencies at work? How do we change the gender bias in EI theory, research, and application? Making the hidden obvious, as we do, is a first step. But making the hidden obvious does not solve the problem by itself. If it could, there are enough women and men of good-will that the problem would be no problem by now; yet it persists. Considerable empirical data shows that gender discrimination in the workplace is more complex than acute incidents of harassment or blatantly unfair hiring practices. The vast majority of gender discrimination happens "under the radar." Valian[53] and others[54] have carefully detailed the power of implicit beliefs about gender of the sort that plague EI conceptualization, measurement, research, and application. While men may experience liabilities, the vast majority of gender discrimination in the workplace is experienced by women. Patterns of low-level gender bias have a cumulative effect on women's well-being, compensation, and professional development. First, they materially disadvantage women in terms of time sinks, lower pay, and lost opportunities.[53] Second, there is a measurable psychological and emotional toll of dealing with "everyday" stress associated with outgroup status.[55] Third, patterns of exclusion and bias feed back to institutional devaluation of women and women's performance with the result that women are less likely to be chosen for leadership positions and/or less likely to be able to take them. The accrual of disadvantage works similarly where emotion is concerned. Judgments about the presence and meaning of emotion are not made casually or lightly. Who is labeled "emotional" depends on who does the naming, who is named, and the circumstances in which emotion occurs. One example adapted from Valian shows how this works. Imagine that you are attending a small meeting. People around the table know each other, but you haven't met them before. You begin with the assumption that this is a group of peers, but you notice that some people's comments are listened to and taken more seriously than others'. Granted that you can evaluate the content of people's remarks yourself, but, nevertheless, you are influenced by the group's dynamics and you quickly sort who has higher status than others, whose passionate comments are listened to attentively, and whose reactions are dismissed as "emotional." Those whose emotional input is not valued now have less prestige and will be listened to less in the future, and "the gap between them and people who are gaining attention for their remarks will widen as their small initial failures accrue and make future failures more likely."[53:5]

The power and persistence of emotion stereotypes and biases calls for serious action on both research and applications sides of emotional intelligence. Basic consciousness-raising regarding the ways in which gender, race, and status are disappeared will help, but the effort needs to be continuous. We anticipate that any profound change would require scientific (empirical and theoretical) refinement of the EI construct. EI researchers will need to address what emotions researchers across disciplines have begun to incorporate into their thinking, namely, that emotions are interpersonal, contextualized events. Emotional experience, regulation, and understanding occur in relation to others within the organization and in relation to the organizational emotion culture itself. Thus, a truly gender-fair approach to EI can only be approximated if the interconnectedness of emotional intelligence is examined. That is, EI research may need to be less "psychological" (by which we mean focused on traits and knowledge), and more social structural (by which we mean focused on emotion structures and practices). Such research would address issues such as institutional regulation of EI – that is, policies or informal practices that enhance or hinder the emotional legitimacy of certain groups. For example, if office culture permits joking about sexual harassment litigation, it creates an environment in which expression of other emotional reactions to harassment is defined as outside the boundaries of ordinary discourse, and actual serious discussion of harassment is de facto made the exception rather than the rule.

Our hope for a scientific reframing of EI may be far too optimistic. The idea that EI is an easily measured, effortlessly learned skill, that is ostensibly open to everyone and that just might guarantee one's success in professional advancement, is too, too tempting. Arguments about the construct's scientific legitimacy ultimately are ineffective in the face of the promise of wide-ranging benefits to individuals and to society as a whole. The hard questions regarding who actually can and does benefit are not welcome questions. More important to EI's survival despite criticism, is EI's subtle effectiveness in ensuring that people can feel better about themselves and their emotion competence while leaving existing power structures unchallenged and unchanged.

Notes

i.   This construal of women's and men's comparative emotional strengths is reminiscent of the late nineteenth century, when the concept of complementarity was used to describe and affirm the comparative value of women's and men's emotional characters, which were assumed to be natural and normal.[17]

ii. See Jones[56] for a discussion of how gender issues risk disappearance as research on bullying and incivility continue to grow.

References

1. Corrigan, J. (2002) *Business of the Heart: Religion and Emotion in the Nineteenth Century*. Berkeley, CA: University of California Press.
2. Salovey, P. and Mayer, J. D. (1990) Emotional intelligence, *Imagination, Cognition, and Personality*, 9, 185–211.
3. Bar-On, R. and Parker, J. D. A. (eds) (2000) *The Handbook of Emotional Intelligence*. San Francisco: Jossey-Bass.
4. Goleman, D. (1998) *Working with Emotional Intelligence*. New York: Bantam Books.
5. Matthews, G., Roberts, R. D., and Zeidner, M. (2004) Seven myths about emotional intelligence, *Psychological Inquiry*, 15, 179–96.
6. Fineman, S. (2004) Getting the measure of emotion–And the cautionary tale of emotional intelligence, *Human Relations*, 57, 719–40.
7. Landy, F. J. (2006) The long, frustrating, and fruitless search for social intelligence: A cautionary tale. In Murphy, K. R. (ed.) *A Critique of Emotional Intelligence: What Are the Problems and How Can They Be Fixed?* Mahwah, NJ: Lawrence Erlbaum Associates, 81–123.
8. Locke, E. A. (2005) Why emotional intelligence is an invalid concept, *Journal of Organizational Behavior*, 26, 425–31.
9. Conte, J. M. (2005) A review and critique of emotional intelligence measures, *Journal of Organizational Behavior*, 26, 433–40.
10. Ashkanasy, N. M. and Daus, C. S. (2005) Rumors of the death of emotional intelligence in organizational behavior are vastly exaggerated, *Journal of Organizational Behavior*, 26, 441–52.
11. Mayer, J. D. and Salovey, P. (1997) What is emotional intelligence? In Salovey, P. and Sluyter, D. (eds) *Emotional Development and Emotional Intelligence: Educational Implications*. New York: Basic Books, 3–31.
12. Bar-On, R. (1997) *Bar-On Emotional Quotient Inventory (EQ-i) Technical Manual*. Toronto: Multi-Health Systems.
13. Fineman, S. (2000) Commodifying the emotionally intelligent. In Fineman, S. (ed.) *Emotion in Organizations*, 2nd edn. London: Sage, 101–15.
14. Salovey, P. and Grewal, D. (2005) The science of emotional intelligence, *Current Directions in Psychological Science*, 14, 281–5.
15. Kappas, A. (2006) Appraisals are direct, immediate, intuitive, and unwitting . . . and some are reflective, *Cognition & Emotion*, 20, 952–75.
16. Averill, J. R. (1991) Emotions as episodic dispositions, cognitive schemas, and transitory social roles: Steps toward an integrated theory of emotion. In Ozer, D., Healy, J. M., and Stewart, A. J. (eds) *Perspectives in Personality*, Vol. 3a. London: Jessica Kingsley, 137–65.
17. Parkinson, B., Fischer, A. H., and Manstead, A. S. R. (2005) *Emotion in Social Relations: Cultural, Group, and Interpersonal Processes*. New York: Psychology Press.
18. Friedman, T. (2006) *The World is Flat*. New York: Farrar, Straus and Giroux.
19. Shields, S. A. (2007) Passionate men, emotional women: Psychology constructs gender difference in the late 19th century, *Journal of the History of Psychology*, 10, 92–110.
20. Shields, S. A. (2002) *Speaking from the Heart: Gender and the Social Meaning of Emotion*. New York: Cambridge University Press.
21. Ahmed, S. (2004) *The Cultural Politics of Emotion*. New York: Routledge.
22. Creswell, J. (2006) How suite it isn't: a dearth of female bosses. *New York Times*, December 17. Retrieved from www.nytimes.com/2006/12/17/business/yourmoney/17csuite.html?ex=1167800400&en=b00eeabd820d99dc&ei=5070
23. Jackman, M. R. (1996) *The Velvet Glove: Paternalism and Conflict in Gender, Class, and Race Relations*. Berkeley, CA: University of California Press.
24. Mayer, J. D., Salovey, P., and Caruso, D. (2002) *The Mayer-Salovey-Caruso Emotional Intelligence Test (MSCEIT)*. Toronto: Multi-Health Systems.
25. Mayer, J. D., Salovey, P., and Caruso, D. (2004) Emotional intelligence: theory, findings, and implications, *Psychological Inquiry*, 60, 197–215.

26. Eagly, A. H. (2005) Achieving relational authenticity in leadership: Does gender matter? *The Leadership Quarterly*, 16, 459–74.

27. Eagly A. H. and Karau, S. J. (2002) Role congruity theory of prejudice toward female leaders, *Psychological Review*, 109, 573–98.

28. Fairclough, N. (1989) *Language and Power*. New York: Longman.

29. Bar-On, R., Brown, J. M., Kirkcaldy, B. D., and Thomé, E. P. (2000) Emotional expression and implications for occupational stress: An application of the Emotional Quotient Inventory (EQ-i), *Personality and Individual Differences*, 28, 1107–18.

30. Bar-On, R. (2001) Emotional and social intelligence: insights from the Emotional Quotient Inventory. In Bar-On, R. and Parker, J. D. A. (eds) (2000) *The Handbook of Emotional Intelligence*. San Francisco: Jossey-Bass, 363–88.

31. Shields, S. A. and Steinke, P. (2003) Does self-report make sense as an investigative method in evolutionary psychology? In Travis, C. B. (ed.) *Evolution, Violence, and Gender*. Cambridge, MA: MIT Press, 87–104.

32. Robinson, M. D., Johnson, J. T., and Shields, S. A. (1998) The gender heuristic and the data base: Factors affecting the perception of gender-related differences in the experience and display of emotions, *Basic and Applied Social Psychology*, 20, 206–19.

33. Dawda, D. and Hart, S. D. (2000) Assessing emotional intelligence: reliability and validity of the Bar-On Emotional Quotient Inventory (EQ-i) in university students, *Personality and Individual Differences*, 28, 797–812.

34. Bradberry, T. and Su, L. D. (2006) Women feel smarter, *TalentSmart* "whitepaper." www.talentsmart.com/media/uploads/pdfs/Women_Feel_Smarter.pdf.

35. Mandell, B. and Perwani, S. (2003) Relationship between emotional intelligence and transformational leadership style: a gender comparison, *Journal of Business and Psychology*, 17, 387–404.

36. Eisenberg, N. and Lennon, R. (1983) Sex differences in empathy and related capacities, *Psychological Bulletin*, 94, 100–31.

37. Archer J. (2004) Sex differences in aggression in real-world settings: a meta-analytic review, *Review of General Psychology*, 8, 291–322.

38. Hare-Mustin, R. T. and Marecek, J. (1994) Asking the right questions: Feminist psychology and sex differences, *Feminism & Psychology*, 4, 531–7.

39. Fletcher, J. K (1999) *Disappearing Acts: Gender, Power, and Relational Practice at Work*. Cambridge, MA: MIT Press.

40. Vescio, T. K., Gervais, S. J., Snyder, M., and Hoover, A. (2005) Power and the creation of patronizing environments: The stereotype-based behaviors of the powerful and their effects on female performance in masculine domains, *Journal of Personality and Social Psychology*, 88, 658–72.

41. Scheman, N. (1993) *Engenderings: Constructions of Knowledge, Authority, and Privilege*. New York: Routledge.

42. Shields, S. A. (2005) The politics of emotion in everyday life: "Appropriate" emotion and claims on identity, *Review of General Psychology*, 9, 3–15.

43. Fischer, A. H. (1993) Sex differences in emotionality: fact or stereotype? *Feminism & Psychology*, 3, 303–18.

44. Zammuner, V. L. (2000) Men's and women's lay theory of emotion. In Fischer, A. H. (ed.) *Gender and Emotion: Social Psychological Perspectives*. London: Cambridge University Press, 48–70.

45. Ridgeway, C. L. and Bourg, C. (2004) Gender as status: An expectation states theory approach. In Eagly, A. H., Beall, A. E., and Sternberg, R. J. (eds) *The Psychology of Gender*. New York: Guildford, 217–41.

46. Timmers, M., Fischer, A. H., and Manstead, A. S. R. (2003) Ability versus vulnerability: Beliefs about men's and women's emotional behaviour, *Cognition & Emotion*, 17, 41–63.

47. Fabes, R. A. and Martin, C. L. (1991) Gender and age stereotypes of emotionality, *Personality and Social Psychology Bulletin*, 17, 532–40.

48. Ellison, K. (2005) *The Mommy Brain: How Motherhood Makes Us Smarter*. New York: Basic Books.

49. Warner, L. R. and Shields, S. A. (2006) The perception of crying in women and men: Angry tears, sad tears, and the "right way" to weep. In Hess, U. and Phillipot, P. (eds) *Emotion Recognition Across Social Groups*. New York: Cambridge University Press.

50. Hochschild, A. R. (1983) *The Managed Heart*. Berkeley, CA: University of California Press.
51. Einarsen, S., Hoel, H., Zapf, D., and Cooper, C. L. (eds) (2003) *Bullying and Emotional Abuse in the Workplace: International Perspectives in Research and Practice*. London: Taylor & Francis.
52. Lim, S. and Cortina, L. M. (2005) Interpersonal mistreatment in the workplace: The interface and impact of general incivility and sexual harassment, *Journal of Applied Psychology*, 90, 483–96.
53. Valian, V. (1998) *Why So Slow? The Advancement of Women*. Cambridge, MA: MIT Press.
54. Chin, J. L. (ed.) (2004) *The Psychology of Prejudice and Discrimination*, Vol. 3, *Bias Based on Gender and Sexual Orientation*. Westport, CN: Praeger.
55. Swim, J. K., Hayes, L. L., Cohen, L. L., and Ferguson, M. J. (2001) Everyday sexism: Evidence for its incidence, nature, and psychological impact from three daily diary studies, *Journal of Social Issues*, 57, 31–53.
56. Jones, C. (2006) Drawing boundaries: Exploring the relationship between sexual harassment, gender and bullying, *Women's Studies International Forum*, 29, 147–58.

CHAPTER 13

Feeling Out of Place? Towards the Transnationalizations of Emotions

Jeff Hearn

Emotions are social. The expansion of interest in emotions, especially emotions in and around organizations, that has taken place over the past 20 years or more has demonstrated that emotions are not fixed or given, personal or private, or purely and simply biological or psychological phenomena that are "held" within or inside the body. They are intensely social in form, content, experience. Emotions, like other supposedly personal matters, are becoming public; all "privacy," emotional or otherwise, is now potentially public.[1]

Emotions are also characteristically gendered in many and uneven ways, and circulate in gendered, often male-dominated organizational and other contexts and environments. With the "private" becoming more public, they are increasingly subject to constructions through and within male-dominated organizations and other similar institutional contexts in various forms of public domain. Meanwhile organizations, institutions, and public domains are becoming increasingly transnational. Thus emotions are likely to become more transnationalized in form and content.

So, what are emotions? This is not the time and place to discuss the many possible meanings, interpretations, and explanations of emotions. Suffice to say, at this point, that emotions can be understood as material-discursive processes that contextualize and construct heightened embodied experience. In this processual view, emotions tend to occur and circulate when hopes or expectations, on one hand, and realities experienced, on the other, coincide or conflict, or are experienced as such. Hopes, expectations, realities, and experiences thereof, are socially constructed, rather than individual or psychological given states.[2]

Emotions in and around organizations are affected, though not determined, by the complexities of organizational context, structure, process, and realities.[3-6] However, even within such strongly social accounts, it has been usual for the principal model and mode of analysis of emotions in/and organizations to be limited in two profound and interrelated ways. First, the organization has been generally considered as singular, so that it is *the specific* organization that is the site and context of emotions. Instead, emotions increasingly operate and are contextualized *across and between* organizations, in multiple organizations, networks, and interorganizational relations. Second, the organization, and occasionally organizations, are usually considered and placed within a single country context, rather than seen in terms of processes of globalization, glocalization (simultaneous occurrence of globalization and localization[7]) or, as I would prefer, transnationalization.

Emotions operate through circulations[i] of many different kinds, rather than static "expressions"; this is especially important in relation to transnational contexts and transnationalizations. Non-located "out of place" circulations may themselves contribute to various intensifications and materializations of emotions. Importantly for present purposes, these circulations are increasingly transnational in form and content, involving transnational organizational technologies, media, and processes. Transnational emotions tend to have certain characteristics: operating at a distance, across countries and nationalities, involving those not known or not well-known to each other; with linguistic and other differences, and multiple and contradictory relations, loyalties, and antagonisms. The study of emotions in and around organizations needs to address the realities of transnational processes today.

Organization studies, like much of the social sciences, have often been less comfortable with the spatial/temporal features of social reality than the social features of spatial/temporal reality. The principal way of talking about variations across place and space, and thus what is "out of place," in the social sciences has gone under the broad title of "culture" and the equation of culture with a "people" (as if cultures are like islands in an archipelago) and the cross-cultural paradigm. Much cross-cultural research on organizations has not considered issues of gender, sexuality, violence/violation, and emotions. When gender has been analyzed, it has often been by comparing cultural *values* in national cultural environments.[9] Gendered culture is reduced to values rather than contested material discourses, practices, processes, and emotions. Cross-cultural framing remains very powerful; it tends to reduce place and space to the non-spatial social set *within* particular places and spaces, rather than seeing culture as a political process of contestation over power to define concepts, including that of culture itself.[10] Addressing transnationalizations of emotions involves more than resort to cross-cultural analysis, even if that analysis is made more sophisticated through critical theory, poststructuralism, and postcolonialism.

In this chapter, in contrast to most cultural traditions, I address moves towards transnationalizations of emotions. I first examine some understandings of globalization, glocalization, and transnationalization before turning to how transnationalizations of emotions operate within five social and organizational arenas. These arenas, though very different in form, are all heavily gendered with clear domination by men of their organizations and top management. The chapter concludes with analysis of transnational emotional processes.

From Globalization to Transnationalization

Contemporary debates on and interest in globalization, and global economic, political, and cultural processes, are huge. However, it is also clear that globalization is not new:

it has been part of the world story since the beginnings of exploration. The historical intensity of global developments increased greatly with the growth of more organized conquest, mercantilism, colonialism, imperialism, long-distance capitalist trading, and integrated production. Such historical global moves construct emotions powerfully and deeply.[11] The theme of globalization is also central to the dominant problematic of modern social sciences from, among others, Marx, Durkheim, and Weber.[12] These can be seen as attempts to understand the complex effects of globalization on emotions. The contemporary era has brought global intensification, with advancement of technologies of transport, communication, refrigeration, production, information, and media. Through these socio-technical processes, place, and space have new meanings.

Within the massive growth of literature on globalization, there is much variation in analysis of contemporary economic, political, and cultural change; even so, some key themes can be discerned. Many commentators emphasize transnational economic units. Robertson[7] asserts the importance of greater material interdependence and unity, but not greater integration, of the world; greater world consciousness; the promotion or "invention" of difference and variety in globalization; and, indeed, "clashes, conflicts, tensions and so on constitute a pivotal feature of globalization."[13] Giddens[14] highlights the nation-state, modernity (capitalism, surveillance, military order, industrialism), time-space distanciation, and reflexivity. Lash and Urry[15] emphasize transcendence of the nation-state, and increasing importance of signs, symbols, and transnational cultures. In reviewing such theories, Waters argues that globalization affects movements of people, goods, services, and information, through material, political, and symbolic exchanges. He could have added emotions. He defines globalization as: "[a] social process in which the constraints of geography on social and cultural arrangements recede and in which people become increasingly aware that they are receding."[12:3] Reduction of the "constraints of geography" also applies to emotions.

Rather few theories and theorists have explicitly linked globalization to gender, sexuality, violence/violation, and emotions.[16–18] Moreover, the terms, globalization and glocalization remain unclear, with multiple meanings, often used with strong positive or negative connotations. Very few social phenomena can be characterized as fully global, operating across the whole globe. In contrast, the concepts of the transnational and transnationalization are more specific – less encumbered by the above confusions. More simply, they depend on two fundamental elements: the nation or national boundaries; and "trans" (across) relations, as opposed to "inter" or "intra" relations. Differences can be noted between transnational relations and international relations, in which the nation might be less problematized. Portes[19] distinguishes "international" in relation to activities and programs of nation-states, "multinational" to large-scale institutions, such as corporations, and "transnational" to activities initiated and sustained by noninstitutional actors, networks, or groups across borders.

Transnational processes facilitate, produce, and contextualize emotions. Thus one can talk of various transnationalizations of emotions in and around organizations. For example, those working in and around transnational organizations may become involved in intense emotional experiences and circulations with individual colleagues or groups of colleagues from the same or other, perhaps competing, organizations in other countries, or even more abstract parts or aspects of such organizations that may frustrate or facilitate their work. Transnationalizations bring not only complex, often novel, organizational and emotional situations and challenges, but also intersections with geography, place and space, and various forms of citizenship, culture, ethnicity, identity, language, locality, nationality, racialization, region, and religion. Even so, speaking of transnational relations raises a paradox: that they refer to the nation and nationality at the same time as they refer to relations across nations and between nationalities. The nation is simultaneously affirmed and deconstructed. This is partly a question of what is meant by "trans." In short, the "trans" in transnational refers to two basically different notions, as well as several more subtle distinctions:

- *moving across* something or *between* two or more somethings – in this case, across national boundaries or between nations;
- *metamorphosing*, problematizing, blurring, transgressing, breaking down, even dissolving something(s) – in this case, nations or national boundaries; in the most extreme case, leading to the demise of the nation or national boundaries.

These two approaches are represented in various ways in understanding different transnational organizational sites and arenas, and it is to these I now turn. I begin with science and academia, specifically a personal interpretation and positioning, before considering the two most extensively researched aspects of transnationalization: migration and multinational corporations, and their implications for emotions. This is followed by focus on two especially emotional areas of life – violence and sexuality – discussed in relation to the military, and information and communication technologies respectively. All these arenas are male-dominated, with representation of women at top organizational levels ranging from negligible (with the military) to 25 percent (for the highest international figures for women occupying professorships). Generally, women's representation at the highest levels is between 2 and 10 percent. Though these are all key aspects of transnationalization, this range is far from comprehensive; other major arenas include international finance, transnational governmental politics, NGOs, media, energy, and environment. Transnationalizing processes provide many possibilities to extend gendered powers – to further transnational patriarchies (or transpatriarchies) and the associated emotions.

Some Transnational Organizational Arenas

Science and academia: a personal interpretation, and the question of time

Science and academia more generally are transnational arenas that are, for obvious reasons, of special interest to me. Thus I begin with brief descriptions of how transnationalizations of emotions have shifted for me. This is to attempt to position myself, to give examples of how emotions mix with various transnationalizations, and to show my own contradictory privileging together with experiences latterly of being *othered*, treated as an "outsider," "not one of us." In these transnational moves I have experienced many contradictory emotions, overlain by such differences as nationality, language, and geography. Emotions change both in relation to place and over time.

I can easily discern some wildly different phases, and three main ones, in my own relations to the transnationalization of emotions. They all relate to "science and academia," albeit in very different ways. First, an early "childhood" phase was centered on family, schooling, and education. In this, I lived in working-class London, between Charlton Football Ground (then with the largest capacity outside Wembley) and the Greenwich Meridian (the line on the ground you can stand astride, Colossus-like), and became very keen on mapping my own geographical relations (to the world) to the extent of going on to study Geography at Oxford University. I felt I was on some fortunate imaginary ley line combining geography and education, whereby I was connected to the world, through being at its (mythological, imperial) center. Emotions were not transnational in the sense of physically moving across countries; rather, my emotional engagement with the transnational was through intellectual and political spatial dispersion, though set locally in London and Oxford. My major academic and political interests developed around two areas: urban social geography and political geography, especially of the territories of the former British Empire and Commonwealth (what might now be called postcolonialism). I can now see such transnational interests as both an intellectual and emotional translation of my politics: by this time Christianity was superseded and from the experience of the London–Oxford contrast I was a closet marxist. After doing my finals in May 1968, I made a major social move, turning down the chance to do a doctorate at the privileged University, and instead studying the "more useful" urban planning and sociology up the hill in the Polytechnic, now Oxford Brookes University.

That shift, perhaps risk, merged into the second "younger adult" phase in which I was married (at just 22), became a young professional, and moved first to Hertfordshire, then Northampton (to work in the "New Town"), and then, just before becoming a father, shifted again to (take the risk to) leave the relatively well-paid job and return to study, this time Organization Studies at Leeds University. At the end of that course I looked forward to some time at home, but immediately got a job as a lecturer at nearby Bradford University. There I stayed working and married, with three children, for 21 years. Emotions were predominantly local, at home, at work, in my "political" and other time. For most of that time I didn't travel much at all, limited to one main conference away each year.

In the middle of this second period I remember vividly a rare overseas conference – the 1985 US Academy of Management in San Diego – where five of us presented a symposium on sexuality in organizations. I think we were somewhat apprehensive beforehand as the Academy was and is dominated by mainstream malestream research. However, the event went well, probably very well. Afterwards four of us from Canada and the UK literally skipped together in glee, hand-in-hand and arm-in-arm, across the conference campus: a memorable transnational emotional moment.

Increasingly I was being moved into international contacts through various research and writing, especially through Organization Studies and various studies on gender, men, and masculinities (Critical Studies on Men). Living all this time in Bradford was an educational experience, as it became the UK city with the highest proportion of Moslem people and people from Pakistan. In this way, there were many links and also major disjunctions in the transnational life of the city,[20,21] ranging from political impacts on the city from Pakistan politics, new friends (especially for our children) and neighbors, and sometimes incongruous juxtapositions of different ethnic and religious practices. I remember the first time I saw veiled Pakistani women walk by white prostitute women. Postcolonialism was on the doorstep: the emotional terrain was uncertain; new emotional practices had to be invented.

More recently, over the last ten years or more, a third "older adult" phase has followed. In 1995, I changed jobs, moving to Manchester University to take up a research professorship ("the perfect job"), and then very shortly after, during a visit to Helsinki, and to my surprise, met my Finnish partner. We effectively got to know each other virtually, and decided to change our lives having had minimal face-to-face contact. This ushered in a much more transnational life. In 1997, I effectively moved to Finland. Over the past ten years or so I have learnt what it means to be *othered* and to be marginalized, while having had welcomes at Åbo Akademi University and the Swedish School of Economics, Helsinki (both Swedish language universities in Finland). This has not only involved a lot of traveling back and forth to the UK, but also many transnational research contacts and projects. These latter developments have mainly been in the Nordic region, and within European (that is, EU) projects, including much contact with Central and Eastern European scholars. The Europeanization of science has offered both joys and sorrows. I have witnessed both wonderful cooperation and abuses that have made me despair, both complicated by national and other differences. The other obvious change has been the growth of the internet and information and communication technologies more generally. Emotions now are routinely transnational: my current relationship was initially, and in some ways remains, transnational; most of my research work is also transnational in some sense; emotions have been transnationalized. Most recently, I have also taken up a post in Sweden part-time, in what seems in some ways another dream job. Emotions are now frequently transnational in multiple ways; my emotional life operates routinely and by the minute between Finland, Sweden, the UK, and other countries (with adult children at different times in Hong Kong, Japan, and Spain), in terms of people, organizations, and institutions.

In the third period there have been both joyful experiences of very productive transnational cooperation, and some dire and dismal experiences of transnationalizations. While Finland may stand at the top of the international league table for low financial corruption, xenophobia appears to remain rather common, even from my white male experience. There are many examples I could give, but I select three. One concerns a long-running saga over three years (1998–2001) when I applied, naively, for a chair in sociology at University of Helsinki. This led to, from my point of view, an unbelievable series of discriminations, unequal treatment, misrepresentations, and procedural irregularities. All this could be analysed, as Finland operates a rather efficient system of open documentation so that at least all formal minutes of meetings, "expert" references and statements, and other memoranda are in theory available.[22,23]

Other examples come from dealing with academic journals. Over my academic career I have had about 90 articles published in international, refereed journals. Over the years I have also had a few articles rejected and, before coming to Finland, only two examples of what I would call a bad, unprofessional experience from international, refereed journals. In contrast, in three of my first five experiences with journals with Finnish editors and reviewers, I had severely emotionally negative experiences from what I would call the unprofessional tone and manner of the exchanges. One editor tried to bargain with me over whether to look at my article more closely (after receiving one extremely positive review, and one very hostile review), on condition I reviewed another article for "his journal" first. In one of the three cases the article was published; in the other two I/we decided not to waste time on the process.

And recently, in a "league table" of most cited professors in Finnish business schools, I was not listed at all,[24,25] despite having one of the highest citation rates. While it later came to light that some others were also excluded, I find it hard to avoid clear, strong repeated feelings that (though welcomed by some, especially my immediate, colleagues), my presence is either not wanted or made invisible by many academics here in Finland. Although, on paper, much formal academic policy favors "internationalization," in practice it is widely resisted, as it threatens local, often patriarchal, power centers and relations, and seems to engender envy from some.

Some of these memories attest to the rather peculiar characteristics of much academic life: individualism, competitiveness, intellectualism, achievement-orientation, hierarchy, and evaluativeness. One does not have to be psychoanalytically inclined to see how ideologies of gender – and other forms of neutrality, objectivity, and value-freeness – can mask the vast potential for all manner of high emotions, anxieties, defences, denials, deceptions and self-deceptions, rivalries, insecurities, threats, vulnerabilities, intimacies, and so on. These can make for a heady mixture. Science and academia are also sets of places that are becoming increasingly non-local, post-local, transnational; the intense interpersonal and institutional relations, and strong personal identifications with particular ideas and people, are also becoming transnationalized. This can apply in both the individual scholarly research and in the increasing power of research teams and "centers of excellence."

There are many well-known examples of intense cooperation and conflict in science and academia showing how pervasive emotions are, and standing in uneasy positioning with the supposed neutralities and objectivities. Some of these are well documented, such as the Popper–Wittgenstein fracas[26] in Cambridge in 1946, and the race to complete the human genome project[27]. These examples of the emotional, conflictual processes are themselves transnational. It is likely that the increasing transnationalization of science and academia, through transnational research projects, teams, evaluations, information exchange, and so on, will increase the transnationalization of emotion there, in the form of positive, negative, and ambivalent feelings across countries, sometimes towards those hardly or not known.

Transnational migration: movements and emotions

Migrants are of many and various kinds and combination. Transnational migration may refer simply to the movement of people across national boundaries, without or with little problematization of nations or boundaries, as in some migration statistics. Transnational migration can also be seen in terms of the creation of transnational communities, social locations, and identities that *problematize* nations and national boundaries. Many transnational studies recognize transnational social spaces and flows and various forms of deterritorialization, translocality, and transnationality[28-30] in which space, social space, is not strictly or primarily experienced or understood in terms of physical, geographical space of the nationally located place occupied. In these situations emotions are also likely to be transnationalized.

Transnational social space provides the shifting ground for complex processes of hybrid, deterritorialized identities, subjectivities, and emotions. Some migrants stay in their adopted country; others travel continually back and forth between two or more countries. This may involve complex financial transaction and investments: for example, many factories in the Dominican Republic are owned and operated by individuals who have returned after migrating to the US, while other businesses are supported by migrant investors who have remained in the US. Unlike traditional transnational migrants, these migrants make this difficult journey often seeking to bolster both economies.[31] Basch et al.[32] give a clear reformulation of nation and national boundaries in transnational migration in their definition of "transnationalism" as:

> . . . the process by which immigrants forge and sustain multistranded social relations that link together their societies of origin and settlement. We call these processes transnationalism to emphasize that many immigrants today build social fields that cross geographic, cultural and political borders.

Such "multistrandedness" operates in economic, political, symbolic, and emotional realms, personified in the female Caribbean higgler, who lives and manages by complex patterns of traveling, trading, and exchanging goods and services across and between different islands.[33]

The emotions found in transnational communities may be both deeply interconnected across national boundaries, sometimes as if making a single community, and yet diverse and fragmented. Place is necessarily not one place; place may be transnational, shifting across time, aging, and generation; place and the emotions engendered are frequently out of place. Unsurprisingly, ambivalence can be one of the main emotions for migrants: sometimes, financial gains but emotional pains[34]; emotional relief with emotional anxiety; economic, political, or personal liberation together with experiences of racism, oppression, and marginalization. Grzywacz et al.'s study of 60 Mexican migrant farmworker men in North Carolina found 75 percent reported ambivalence about leaving wives and children, and two-thirds were torn about leaving their parents.[35] Each type of ambivalence was associated with more symptoms of anxiety and poorer mental health. The consequences of poor mental health can be especially serious with farm or other hazardous work if safety precautions to prevent occupational injuries are not taken.

Transnational migration also provides a means for the global distribution and dispersion of emotions unevenly across the regions of the world. With the so-called "nanny chain,"[36,37] expatriate movements of more privileged people from richer countries can in turn prompt further transnational movements, especially of women, to care for them and their children, as nannies and other domestic and servicing workers. Such movements and migrations in part construct an uneven and unequal transnational geopolitics of emotions, involving those who are cared for and who provide paid care and unpaid care. Emotions are transnationalized in complex ways, including through intimate support and work on others' bodies, exploitation, dependence, love, and violence, as well as intersections with languages, nationalities, ethnicities, and religions. Meanwhile those who migrate to care, to do emotions for others, often have to arrange for the care and emotions for their own children, from other, usually female, relatives, friends, neighbors, and workers. This can be intensely emotionally distressing. These movements transnationalize racialized processes of care and emotion from specific slave, colonial, and apartheid societies to post-slavery, postcolonial and post-apartheid transsocieties.

Debates on relations of emotions, ethnicity, and racialization are likely to increase, not least through widespread contemporary turns to notions of "authentic" nation, religion, or ethnicity, often with heavily emotionalized migrations, memories, and "traditions." Some migrants retain an overly nostalgic and even very "old-fashioned" view or version of the communities from where they have migrated. Memory and tradition themselves can be heavily emotional, as well as providing resources for the constructions of new, complex, hybrid emotions.

Transnational corporations: organizations and emotions

The terms transnational corporations (TNCs) and multinational corporations (MNCs) are both used in various ways: they can signify those corporations operating across more than one nation, across national boundaries, or they can reference corporations as collective actors that are relatively independent from nations. In the latter sense, they constitute socio-economic actors that may transcend the nation, being in some cases larger than individual nations. Of the 100 most important economic units in the world, half are nation-states and half are MNCs or TNCs that transcend nations and national boundaries. There are about 180 recognized states in the UN, so that means that 130 of these have smaller economies than the largest 50 MNCs and TNCs.[38] Korten[39] has reviewed the situation:

> The world's 500 largest industrial corporations, which employ only five hundredths of 1% of the world's population, control 25% of the world's economic output. The top 300 transnationals, excluding financial institutions, own some 25% of the world's productive assets. Of the world's one hundred largest economies, fifty are now corporations – not including banking and financial institutions. The combined assets of the world's 50 largest commercial banks and diversified financial companies amount to nearly 60% of The Economist's estimate of a $20 trillion global stock of productive capital.

Concentrations of capital are increasing:[40] ". . . in the consumer durables, automotive, airline, aerospace, electronic components, electrical and electronics, and steel industries, the top five firms control more than 50% of the global market . . ."[39]

Some commentators restrict transnational corporations to those where management and ownership are divided equally between two or more nations.[41] The nation is not problematized; there are simply combinations of ownership and capital between them. Others approach the transnational corporation as that which:

> ... builds and legitimizes multiple diverse internal perspectives able to sense the complex environmental demands and opportunities; its physical assets and management capabilities are distributed internationally but are interdependent; and it has developed a robust and flexible internal integrative process.[42]

This means a corporate form combining global integration and local responsiveness – that is thus multidomestic. Transfers of knowledge, components, and money may proceed between markets in which subsidiaries operate, with benefits from local companies along with competitive advantages of integration. Emotions of those within and outside are constructed through such complex multidomestic, transnational organizational frames, where there is not *one* given organizational context, but a number of overlapping organizational contexts, operating in and across different countries, ethnicities, and languages.

Redrawings of nations by organizations bring transnationalizations of emotions. Interestingly, the focus on transnational migration and that on transnational organizations are often not put together,[43,44] even though these arenas link in internationalization of capital and labor. Transnational organizations are involved in organizing migrations, be they transnational recruitment, policing, or trafficking. Transnational organizations function partly by transnational movements in the relocation, expatriation, and repatriation of managers and workers, with major complicating implications for their domestic and emotional lives, such as complex time and travel demands, arrangements for spouses, schooling, and childcare.[45–47] They also have huge power in controlling the livelihoods and emotions of employees, potential employees, and their families and communities. There is great scope for greater attention to emotions, often intense emotions, in gendering international business-to-business activity, alliances, mergers and acquisitions, supply chains, financial dependencies, and intercorporate relations – formal or informal, and often involving mainly men competing and cooperating at the high levels.[46] Transnational corporations also enter into complex transnationalizations of consumption of objects made in one place, and with very different emotional meanings of products in other local places, such as trainers as sports wear or high fashion[48] and cola as youth drink or religious drink.

The military and militarism: the case of violence

Transnational organizations are also means to violence and violation; violence and violation are among the most emotional of actions in their effects and sometimes in their enactment. The militaries and various militarisms, both state and non-state, are major sources of actual and potential destruction, and thus negative emotions of grief, sadness, and desperation. It is very difficult to appreciate the global scale of violence and men's violence. Estimates of death in the twentieth century *caused by humans* (that is, mainly men) are between about 188 and 262 million (i.e. roughly 5 percent of total deaths).[49,50] The World Health Organization estimated that 520,000 people died from homicide and 310,000 from war-related acts in 2000.[51] Global military spending is about US$1,000 billion per year, 20 times the development aid from the rich countries to relieve poverty in the poor countries.[52] In 2002, the *increase* in US military spending was about the same as *total* of poverty aid from rich to poor countries.

The military and militarism themselves house many contradictory emotions: strict hierarchical remoteness and close camaraderie; solidarity and psychological "escape"; bravery, self-sacrifice, and cowardice; hate and love. They depend for their continuation on a complex mix of positive emotionalization of comrades (by country, "blood," religion), de-emotionalization (often through various kinds of order and orders), and negative emotionalization of others.

A central issue, indeed difficulty, for military, paramilitary, and similar organizations is maintaining the potential for physical violence to others outside the organization while minimizing, or reducing, that violence to each other and the self within it. This dilemma for armies is the subject of Dixon's[53] analysis of "the psychology of military incompetence." He argues that the primary anxiety is redirected by and controlled through organizational devices such as rules and procedures.

Organizational processes in military organizations produce and reproduce violation, damage, pain, and grief, typically transnationally. Those likely to receive violence can be constructed without emotion, *as less than human*, as numbers, as not people at all, as when bomber crews adopt trivializing, casual, ironic, and supposedly humorous psychological and linguistic methods – such as "There goes the cookie" – in doing their bombing without much thought for their bombs' impact.[54,55] Meanwhile, colleagues and comrades in arms may be reduced to "casualties" and "body counts" through "collateral damage" and "friendly fire."

Information and communication technologies: the case of sexuality

When Jane Rolan, 42, went to the internet to look up an old [unnamed] friend, she ended up having a torrid [non-contact] e-mail affair with a man she had met briefly 20 years earlier. "In three months we exchanged about 2,000 e-mails. . . . Every evening I would lock myself away with the computer for six or seven hours. . . . I was exhausted from night after night of frantic e-mailing."[56]

Information and communication technologies (ICTs) involve the use of multiple complex technologies and have several characteristic features, including: time/space compression, instantaneousness, asynchronicity, reproducibility of image production, the creation of virtual bodies, and the blurring of the "real" and the "representational."[17] Wellman[57] describes the "social affordances of computerized communication networks" as: broader bandwidth (greater effectiveness); wireless portability; globalized connectivity; and personalization. Interplays of virtualities and surveillances bring complex transnational restructurings of emotions; emotions become transnational.

Sexuality has long been subject to increased publicization,[1,17,58] a process extended through ICTs. Sexuality is a very emotional and emotionalized arena, subject to major impacts from ICTs. These include specific changes around cybersexualities at a distance, often a transnational distance, and nondirect contact mediated by "new" technologies. They constitute major historical changes, bringing new transnationalizations, imperialisms, and neocolonialisms to intensely emotional experiences.[59–61]

ICTs have been hugely successful in promoting global trafficking and transnational sexual exploitation of women through supplying encyclopedic information on prostitution and the reconstitution and delivery of the sex trade.[17,62] Live videoconferencing is among the most advanced technology currently on the web: live audio and video communication is transmitted over the internet from video recorder to computer, and back again. This involves buying live sex shows, in which the man can sometimes direct the show, with real-time global communication possible. Pornographers are also leaders in developing internet privacy and secure payment services. DVDs provide more possibilities for making videos with scenes shot from multiple angles, so viewers can choose what they prefer. Viewers can interact with DVD movies similarly to video games, giving the man a "more active" role. The "real" and the "representational" converge; and sexual commodification and emotional desensitization can proceed apace.

ICTs create opportunities to organize sexuality differently, and for the practice and experience of new forms of sexuality: techno-sex, high-tech sex, non-connection sex, mobile phone sex, internet dating, email sex, cybersex, cyberaffairs, virtual sex, multimedia interactive sex, as well as virtual harassment, and so-called "net sleazing" and "trolling for babes." Virtual communities of interest, around, for, or against particular sexualities, may appear to offer safe trustworthy places of support. Yet the web's emotional familiarity can be deceptive; comparison may be made with engineered "familial" corporate cultures[63] developed along with disembodiment of global corporate institutions. ICTs and the WWW increasingly offer an apparent "home" for sexual communities, but are also sites for the extension and diffusion of disembodied sexual-emotional capitalism, consumer cultures, and pleasures.[64] MySpace.com, the networking and blog community, reportedly with 92 million registered users and widely used by young people to meet virtually, was recently bought from Intermix Media by Rupert Murdoch's NewsCorp. What may initially be self-help social-sexual interest communities can become pay-to-use capitalist enterprises; emotions become commodified.

ICTs are not merely media for emotions and sexualities but can reconstitute them. Sex is increasingly constructed in the context of disembodied social institutions, the state, and large corporations, and laws, controls, and ideologies engendered. However, "private" sex can be recorded, written about, photographed, videoed, televised, placed on the web, with various access rights, retrieved from ICT interfaces, with or without participants' permission or knowledge, and transferred to other technologies and multimedia. Sexual practices can be enacted forcibly or non-forcibly, with or without payment.

As modes of exchange, production, and communication become more disembodied, possibilities for reproduction of sexual texts increase, accessible on millions of PC screens worldwide through photo- and video-sharing. Uses of ICTs for sexualities and sexually violent purposes can blur into each other; representation is pornographized globally; pornography is liable to virtualization, as images stored electronically can be reproduced and manipulated – "the woman," and perhaps "the man," become dispensable. ICTs facilitate global/local sexualized cultures and pornographizing of sex. With sexuality and sexual violence, information or advertising of sexuality and sexualized violence can themselves comprise the sexual(ized) offer and experience, with, for some, little separation of sexual information, sexual advertising, production of sexual material, and sexual experience.

There are greater possibilities for cyborg sexualities and cyborg emotionalities. These can take rather mundane forms, such as possibilities of greater sexual exertion following medical interventions. Farther-reaching innovations might be sexually coded "implants" allowing people to seek others with similarly or presumed compatibly coded sexualities.[65] Such technologizations can be either external to the body skin, in a "BlackBerry" or mobile-type device, or physically implanted within. ICTs provide possibilities for various forms of sexual experience, such as places for meeting by mutual agreement potential romantic/sexual partners (sometimes with less emphasis on physical appearance) or "safer" sexual experimentation and identity exploration. There are increasing technical possibilities for many-to-many "social software" and "new sexual affordances" for mutual identification, as with the Yenta matchmaker system that combines virtual community, collaborative filtering, and web-to-cell-phone technology, so people can know who is in their physical vicinity at that moment and who shares certain affinities and willingness to be contacted.[57,66]

ICTs also bring greater, often transnational, sexual surveillance. Google and similar organizations hold masses of information on people's personal preferences, shown through their virtual inquiries and searches.

> Amazon is hoping to patent ways of interrogating a database that would record not just what its 59 million customers have bought – which it already knows – or what they would like to buy (which, with their wish lists, they tell the world) but [also] their income, sexual orientation, religion and ethnicity.[67]

Compilations of information and surveillances, sexual or otherwise, promoted in trends to combinations of technologies and systems integrated into larger wholes, are part of "surveillant assemblages." These are producing, and are likely to further produce, new commodifications of the body and self, where flesh, sexualities, and emotions are partly reduced to transnationally mobile "data doubles."[68] ICTs offer possibilities for new forms of emotions and sexualities whereby people, individually or in groups, display their sexualities, even the "whole" of their lives. Webcams, mobile phones, and television reality shows offer new possibilities for practice, identity, and image-making through "revealing" rather than hiding from surveillance[69] and thus new possible forms of sexuality with the decreasing possibilities of remaining unsurveilled, the so-called "the disappearance of disappearance."[68]

Other recently recognized emotional possibilities include: egosurfing (narcissistic observation of one's own name or reputation on the web), blog streakers (revealing secrets or inappropriate personal information online), google-stalking (snooping and seeking information about old friends, ex-lovers, etc.), photolurkers (obsession with images of unknown people), infornography (obsessive search and distribution of internet information), and crackberry (being unable to stop checking one's Black-Berry, even at the most inappropriate times).[70] These are all well-suited to facilitating transnational contacts and emotions.

Analyzing Transnational Emotional Processes

In this chapter I have considered some movements towards transnationalizations of emotions. In this, I do not suggest that emotions are being transferred wholesale into a global field. Many emotions continue to be experienced in immediate, localized ways: for example, in relation to those loved or hated, lived or worked with, seen every day or once in a lifetime. Rather, various forms of transnationalization appear to be constructing the content and process of emotions in complex, more transnational ways. Transnational processes are also providing the potential for the extension of dominant forms of power – that is, largely the power of certain men, through corporations, militarism, ICTs, and to some extent migration.

Globalization, glocalization, and transnationalization are shorthands for contemporary and substantial historical, social, and emotional change; they are attempts, however flawed, to talk about those changes. They are matters of value, capital, exploitation, accumulation; and they are intensely gendered, sexualed, violenced,[17] constructed through and constitutive of age, class, disability, ethnicity, racialization, and, crucially, emotions. While a global approach to emotions is necessary, this should not be equated with mainstream political economy. Globalization and global political economy provide broad contours of emotions, with uneven emotional distributions. Just as there are international sexual divisions of labor, so too there are international emotional divisions of labor, most obviously in "nanny chains" and the realm of care.

The concepts of globalization, glocalization, and transnationalization may assist understanding how contemporary changes have an impact on organizations, emotions, and their locations in time and space. TNCs and ICTs are difficult to control and police, and take new, extended, socially pervasive forms. Transformations of clear organizational boundaries create many possibilities for expansions and elaborations of emotions. Organizations are becoming in some ways more permeable and in others more closed, so that hopes, expectations, and realities diverge and sometimes converge in new combinations. Changing social divisions around nationality, citizenship, migration, and regional geopolitical developments, such as EU expansion, interact with changes in organizational boundaries, and such intersections may grow in importance in constructing organizational emotions.

In this analysis I have sought to avoid and move beyond both a transmission model of the communication of emotions[71] and a deterministic economistic political economy of emotions.[72] Instead I see emotions are material-discursive processes. Just as sexuality is not a fixed thing or simply a set of acts, but a process of desiring, and violation is not only specific violent incidents but a process of damaging, so emotions refer to processes of emotionalizing and the emotionalized, or more precisely emoting and the emoted, rather than fixed states of being. These emotional processes are embodied, material, and discursive, comprising emoting/emoted events and circulations, and responses to them.

Emotions are increasingly done by actors acting within transnational organizations and transnational contexts, even though emotions often appear to lie within individuals. Emotions are not simply fixed inside bodies, selves, and persons. Rather, emotions involve, and invoke, both subjects and objects, but do so without residing positively within them. In turn, emotions are directed from subjects towards objects – other actors, human or non-human, in other parts of the same or different transnational organizations or other objects – or objects exist in relation to emotions experienced. Subject and object are relationally constructed, sometimes reciprocally, as in processes of reciprocal love or reciprocal rivalry between transnational actors.

Moreover, emotions restrict some bodies by movement or expansion of others, and possessions and flows associated with them.[8] For example, Ahmed, in discussing the "emotional topics" of asylum seekers and international terrorism, notes:

> . . . how the mobility of bodies of subjects in the West, while presented as threatened, is also defended, along with the implicit defense of the mobility of capital in the global economy (whereby capital is constructed as "clean money" and defined against the "dirty money" of terrorism, which must be frozen or blocked).[8:128]

Perhaps most challenging of all, in terms of understanding and practice, these circulations and emotions can involve complex, multiple actors, interorganization relations, or "trans-actors," themselves formed transnationally. These moves through such collective actors to transnationalizations facilitate new extended relations of power, characteristically gendered, that shift societies not just towards public patriarchies but to transnational patriarchies. In these transpatriarchies, emotions are simultaneously patriarchal and transnational.

Acknowledgment

With thanks to Stephen Fineman for his patience and comments on an earlier draft.

Note

i.   Ahmed[8] has written how emotions ". . . play a crucial role in the 'surfacing' of individual and collective bodies through the way emotions circulate between bodies and signs" (p. 117). She continues: "(a)ffect does not reside in an object or a sign, but is an affect (sic.) of the circulation between objects and signs . . ." (p. 120); and concludes that "*(i)t is the very failure of affect to be located in a subject or object that allows it to generate the surfaces of collective bodies*" (p. 128) (emphasis in original). She also discusses how the process of "passing by" of "threatening" objects may engender emotions; this would seem especially important in transnational contexts, in that such "threatening" objects may characteristically not be well-known to the subjects concerned.

References

1. Hearn, J. (1992) *Men in the Public Eye: The Construction and Deconstruction of Public Men and Public Patriarchies.* London and New York: Routledge.
2. Hearn, J. (1993) Emotive subjects: Organizational men, organizational masculinities and the (de)construction of "emotions." In Fineman, S. (ed.) *Emotion in Organizations.* London and Newbury Park, CA: Sage, 148–66.
3. Hochschild, A. (1983) *The Managed Heart.* Berkeley, CA: University of California Press.
4. Fineman, S. (ed.) (1993) *Emotion in Organizations.* London and Newbury Park, CA: Sage.
5. Fineman, S. (ed.) (2000) *Emotion in Organizations,* 2nd edn. London and Thousand Oaks, CA: Sage.
6. Fineman, S. (2003) *Understanding Emotion at Work.* London: Sage.
7. Robertson, R. (1995) Glocalization: Time-space and homogeneity-heterogeneity. In Featherstone, M., Lash, S., and Robertson, R. (eds) *Global Modernities.* London: Sage, 25–44.
8. Ahmed, S. (2004) Affective economies, *Social Text,* 22 (2), 117–39.
9. Hofstede, G. (1991) *Cultures and Organizations: Software of the Mind.* London: McGraw-Hill.
10. Wright, S. (1998) The politicization of "culture," *Anthropology Today,* 14 (1), 7–15.
11. Fanon, F. (1967) *Black Skin, White Masks.* New York: Grove.
12. Waters, M. (1995) *Globalization.* London: Routledge, 5–7.
13. Robertson, R. and Khondker, H. H. (1998) Discourses of globalization: Preliminary considerations, *International Sociology,* 13 (1), 25–40.
14. Giddens, A. (1990) *The Consequences of Modernity.* Cambridge: Polity.
15. Lash, S. and Urry, J. (1993) *Economies of Signs and Space.* London: Sage.
16. Hearn, J. (2004) Tracking "the transnational": studying transnational organizations and managements, and the management of cohesion, *Culture and Organization,* 10 (4), 273–90.
17. Hearn, J. and Parkin, W. (2001) *Gender, Sexuality and Violence in Organizations: the Unspoken Forces of Organization Violations.* London: Sage.
18. Hearn, J. and Parkin, W. (2007) The emotionality of organization violations: gender relations in practice. In Simpson, R. and Lewis, P. (eds) *Gender and Emotions.* Houndmills and New York: Palgrave Macmillan.
19. Portes, A. (2001) Introduction: the debates and significance of immigrant transnationalism, *Global Networks,* 1 (3), 181–93.
20. Hearn, J. (1996) Deconstructing the dominant: making the one(s) the other(s)', *Organization,* 3 (4), 611–26.
21. Hearn, J. (2005) Autobiography, nation, postcolonialism and gender: reflecting on men in England, Finland and Ireland, *Irish Journal of Sociology,* 14 (2), 66–93.
22. Hearn, J. (2004) Organization violations in practice: a case study in a university setting, *Culture and Organization,* 9 (4), 253–73.
23. Hearn, J. (2004) Personal resistance through persistence to organizational resistance through distance. In Thomas, R., Mills, A. J., and Helms Mills, J. (eds) *Identity Politics at Work: Resisting Gender, Gendering Resistance.* London: Routledge, 40–63.
24. Puutonen, V. (2006) Suomalaisten liiketaloustieteiden professoreiden vaikuttavuus [The impact of Finnish business studies professors], *Viikkotiedote,* 21/2006, 13–16.
25. Vihma, P. (2006) Grönroos on paras bisnetproffa [Grönroos is best business professor], *Talouselämä,* 43, 93.
26. Edmonds, D. and Eidinow, J. (2001) *Wittgenstein's Poker: The Story of a Ten-Minute Argument Between Two Great Philosophers.* London: Faber and Faber.
27. Sulston, J. and Ferry, G. (2002) The Common Thread: A Story of Science, Politics, Ethics, and the Human Genome. Washington, DC: Joseph Henry Press.
28. Appadurai, A. (1996) *Modernity at Large: Cultural Dimensions of Globalization.* Minneapolis, MN: University of Minnesota Press.
29. Hannerz, U. (1996) *Transnational Connections: Culture, People, Places.* London: Routledge.

30. Ong, A. (1999) *Flexible Citizenship: The Cultural Logics of Transnationalism*. Durham, NC: Duke University Press.

31. The Latin America Website Project (n.d.). Available at: www.intl.pdx.edu/latin/economy/ trans_ec.html

32. Basch, L. G., Schilier, N. G., and Blanc-Szanton, C. (1994) *Nations Unbound: Transnational Projects, Post-colonial Predicaments, and De-territorialization of Nation-states*. Langhorne, PA: Gordon and Breach, 6.

33. Freeman, C. (2001) Is local/global as feminine/masculine? Rethinking the gender of globalization, *Signs: Journal of Women in Culture and Society*, 26 (4), 1007–37.

34. Tahmina, Q. A. (n.d.) Financial gains, emotional pains. Available at: http://ipsnews.net/migration/ stories/gains.html

35. Grzywacz, J. G., Quandt, S. A., Early, J., Tapia, J., Graham, C. N., and Arcury, T. A. (2006) Leaving family for work: Ambivalence among Mexican migrant farmworker men. *Journal of Immigrant and Minority Health*, 8 (1), 85–97. Available at: www.springerlink.com/content/ ?Author=Joseph+G.+Grzywacz

36. Hochschild, A. (2000) The nanny chain, *The American Prospect*, 11 (4), January 3. Available at: www. prospect.org/print/V11/4/hochschild-a.html

37. Ehrenreich, B. and Hochschild, A. (eds) (2003) *Global Woman: Nannies, Maids and Sex Workers in the New Economy*. New York: Metropolitan Books.

38. Cohen, R. (1998) Transnational social movements: an assessment, WPTC-98-10, 2. Available at: www.transcomm.ox.ac.uk/working%20papers/cohen.pdf

39. Korten, D. (n.d.) Taming the giants. Available at: www.resurgence.org/resurgence/articles/korten. htm

40. Banerjee, S. B. and Linstead, S. (2001) Globalization, multiculturalism and other fictions: colonialism for the new millennium? *Organization*, 8 (4), 683–722.

41. Parhizgar, K. D. (1999) Globalization of multicultural management, *Journal of Transnational Management*, 3 (4), 1–23.

42. Bartlett, C. A. and Ghoshal, S. (2000) *Transnational Management: Text, Cases and Readings in Cross-border Management*, 3rd edn. Boston: McGraw-Hill, 512.

43. Westwood, S. and Phizacklea, A. (2000) *Trans-nationalism and the Politics of Belonging*. London: Routledge.

44. Pries, L. (ed.) (2001) *New Transnational Social Spaces*. London: Routledge.

45. Welch, D. E. (2003) Globalisation of staff movements: beyond cultural adjustment, *Management International Review*, 43 (2), 149–69.

46. Hearn, J., Metcalfe, B., and Piekkari, R. In Ståhl, G. and Björkman, I. (eds) *Handbook of Research on International Human Resource Management*. Cheltenham: Edward Elgar, 502–22.

47. Hearn, J., Jyrkinen, M., Piekkari, R., and Oinonen, E. (2007) "Women home and away": Transnational managerial work and gender relations, *The Journal of Business Ethics*, 70.

48. Carty, V. (1997) Ideologies and forms of domination in the organization of the global production and consumption of goods in the emerging postmodern era: A case study of Nike Corporation and the implications for gender, *Gender, Work and Organization*, 4 (4), 189–201.

49. White, M. (2001) Historical Atlas of 20th Century. Online: http://users.erols.com/mwhite28/ 20century.htm

50. Leitenberg, M. (2006) *Deaths and Wars in the Twentieth Century*. Cornell University Peace Studies Program, Occasional Papers #29. Online: www.clingendael.nl/publications/2006/20060800_cdsp_ occ_leitenberg.pdf

51. World Health Organization (2002) *World Report on Violence and Health*. Geneva: WHO.

52. de Vylder, S. (2004) Costs of male violence. In Ferguson, H., Hearn, J., Holter, Ø. G., Jalmert, L., Kimmel, M., Lang, J., Morrell, R., and de Vylder, S. (eds) *Ending Gender-based Violence*. Stockholm: SIDA, 62–126.

53. Dixon, N. (1976) *On the Psychology of Military Incompetence*. London: Jonathan Cape.

54. Johnson, R. (1986) Institutions and the promotion of violence. In Campbell, A. and Gibbs, J. J. (eds) *Violent Transactions*. Oxford: Blackwell, 181–205.

55. Smith, J. (1993) *Misogynies*. London: Faber & Faber.

56. Gordon, J. (2002) My virtual affair, *You* (*The Mail on Sunday*), November 17, 51.

57. Wellman, B. (2001) Physical space and cyberspace: The rise of personalized networking, *International Journal of Urban and Regional Research*, 25 (2), 227–52.

58. Hearn, J. and Parkin, W. (1995) *"Sex" at "Work." The Power and Paradox of Organisation Sexuality, Revised and Updated*. Hemel Hempstead: Prentice Hall/Harvester Wheatsheaf; New York: St. Martin's Press.

59. Pyle, J. L. and Ward, K. B. (2003) Recasting our understanding of gender and work during global restructuring, *International Sociology*, 18 (3), 461–89.

60. Hearn, J. (2006) The implications of information and communication technologies for sexualities and sexualized violences: Contradictions of sexual citizenships, *Political Geography*, 25 (8), 944–63.

61. Hearn, J. (2007) Sexualities future, present, past . . . Towards transsectionalities, *Sexualities: Studies in Culture and Society*, 10.

62. Hughes, D. (2002) The use of new communication and information technologies for the sexual exploitation of women and children, *Hastings Women's Law Journal*, 13 (1), 127–46.

63. Ezzy, D. (2001) A simulacrum of workplace community: Individualism and engineered culture, *Sociology*, 35 (3), 631–50.

64. Bernstein, E. (2001) The meaning of the purchase: Desire, demand and the commerce of sex, *Ethnography*, 2 (3), 389–420.

65. Monbiot, G. (2006) When it won't need a tyranny to deprive us of our freedom, *The Guardian*, February 21, 23.

66. Rheingold, H. (2000) *The Virtual Community*. Cambridge, MA: MIT Press.

67. Brown, A. (2006) They know all about you, *The Guardian*, August 28. Available at: http://technology.guardian.co.uk/online/search/story/0,,1859785,00.html

68. Haggerty, K. D. and Ericsson, R. V. (2000) The surveillant assemblage, *British Journal of Sociology*, 51 (4), 605–22.

69. Koskela, H. (2004) Webcams, TV shows and mobile phones: Empowering exhibitionism, *Surveillance and Society*, 2 (2), 199–215. Available at: www.surveillance-and-society.org/articles2(2)/webcams.pdf

70. Fisher, R. (2006) Just can't get e-nough, *New Scientist*, 2583, December 20, 34–7.

71. Hearn, J. and Parkin, W. (2006) Gender relations, violation and communication. In Barrett, M. and Davidson, M. (eds) *Gender and Communication at Work*. Aldershot: Ashgate, 111–26.

72. Povinelli, E. A. and Chauncey, G. (1999) Thinking sexuality transnationally: an introduction, *glq: A Journal of Lesbian and Gay Studies*, 5 (4), 439–49.

CHAPTER 14

It's All Too Beautiful: Emotion and Organization in the Aesthetic Economy

Philip Hancock and Melissa Tyler

In this chapter we explore the relationship between emotions, aesthetics, and organizations. We ask whether or not when we think about organizational aesthetics, and indeed the organization of aesthetics, we also need to think about emotions. If so, how might this relationship be conceptualized? The approach that we take is a critical one insofar as one of our primary concerns is: whose interests might the management of aesthetics and emotions serve? In this sense, we are also concerned about the relationship between the management of emotions and aesthetics and the maintenance of predominantly asymmetrical relations of economic and organizational power.

We begin by addressing some of the problems associated with the nature of the relationship between aesthetics and emotions. We then consider this relationship specifically with reference to organization theory, focusing on the performance of emotional and aesthetic forms of labor. We then turn to the concept of the *aesthetic economy* as a way of making analytical sense of the changing role of emotion and aesthetics in organizational life, highlighting the increasing significance of what has been termed "staging value" – the value attributed to the capacity of a product or service to enhance the emotional and aesthetic qualities of social relations and experience – to contemporary organizations. We then consider some of the ways in which aesthetic and emotional experiences are structured by organizations, reflecting on this process with reference to a philosophy of art known as expressivism. This broadly refers to the idea that art is defined by its capacity to "move" those who are exposed to it by conveying something of the artist's own emotions. We argue that, while the products of contemporary corporate culturalism (corporate mission statements, recruitment brochures, corporate logos, and the like) cannot of course be thought of as works of art in the same way that expressivists might talk about a great painting or a poem, they are technologically comparable insofar as the former often use particular aesthetic cues or signifiers (such as colour, style, imagery, and so on) in an attempt to secure the kind of emotional intensity associated with art. In conclusion, we argue that although corporate capitalism attempts to "move" employees, customers, shareholders, or the public more generally into brand identification and consumption, this process is driven largely by an accumulation imperative designed to enhance organizational efficiency and effectiveness rather than to engender genuine spiritual, emotional, or aesthetic enhancement.

Emotion and the Aesthetic

For many of us, the idea of an aesthetic experience is one that only really makes sense in relation to, say, watching a play, viewing a painting, or witnessing a "dramatic" sunset. Under such circumstances, we are often moved to feelings such as joy, awe, or perhaps even repulsion as the impact on our senses evokes a powerful and often multifaceted emotional response. In this manner, therefore, the aesthetic and the emotional are frequently intertwined and possibly indistinguishable at the moment of their manifestation. Yet, as is so often the case, on closer examination things are perhaps not as clear-cut as we might believe.

First and foremost, aesthetic experience cannot simply be confined to the realm of that somewhat slippery category we call art. Nor can we restrict it to (or perhaps conflate it with) our apprehension of the majestic and, as Kant would have it, sublime qualities of nature. Rather aesthetic experience can pertain to any sensuous, embodied experience. It is a means by which we obtain knowledge of the world, not purely through intellectual cognition, but through the immediacy of our sensual faculties and the impression these sense perceptions leave on us. The sources of aesthetic experience are, therefore, all around us. They are in the design of everyday artifacts such as a telephone, the spatial layout of a shopping mall or office, and the smells, sounds, and other sensations of a factory floor, a café, or a ploughed field. Indeed, as these examples might suggest, aesthetic experience is also increasingly organized experience. That is to say, it is tied up with and embedded within the production, reproduction, and distribution of society's economic resources, and, as such, is a matter of concern for organization theorists.

As for the emotional content of aesthetic experience, despite what might appear to be a somewhat commonsense assertion that aesthetically efficacious artifacts or situations make us feel particular emotions, once again things are not so obvious or clear-cut. Philosophically, the relationship between the aesthetic and the emotional continues to be a vexed one. Is there, for instance, a single *aesthetic emotion*, or can aesthetic experience be associated with any range of emotional responses? Indeed, it is quite possible that while we might in part apprehend something, such as the decor of an office, in an aesthetic manner – being vaguely aware of its size, colour, ambience, or whatever – that does not necessarily mean we will experience any particular emotional response to it.

In many respects, it is probably this potential complexity and the contested nature of such questions that have discouraged much in the way of a sustained engagement with the relationship between the emotional and the aesthetic in organization studies. This is not to suggest that such a concern has been entirely absent. As we shall see in the following section, there are examples of work in which this question is addressed either directly or more indirectly. Nevertheless, during a period within which concern with both elements of organizational life appears to be on the increase, this omission is clearly noteworthy.

Emotion and Aesthetics in Organization Theory

Research into both the emotional and aesthetic dimensions of organizational life is now fairly well documented. The former, for instance, owes much to the groundbreaking work of scholars such as Hochschild[1] and her seminal study of what she described as the "commercialization of human feeling" as well as Fineman's[2] exploration of organizations as what he terms "emotional arenas." As for organizational aesthetics, while both empirically and conceptually somewhat less developed, its evolution equally owes much to the work of pioneering individuals such as Strati,[3] who has convincingly reminded us that organizations are not only profoundly aesthetic entities in that they stimulate our senses but, as such, they are also amenable to aesthetic analysis even in terms of their most mundane properties and features.

As we also noted above, however, what has been less apparent in organization studies has been any concerted attempt to explore the interrelationship between the emotional and the aesthetic at a conceptual or analytical level – that is, to critically evaluate and explain organizational practice in this respect. Indeed, there are plenty of examples one can point to within the arena of organizational life that quite evidently link the organization of aesthetics with a desired emotional outcome. Advertising and marketing imagery, company logos and brand identities, the design of corporate artifacts and spatial architecture, indeed the entire machinery of corporate relations and communications, have a well-established history of seeking to promote particular emotional responses, or forms of emotional identification, through the manipulation of aesthetics. While this commercialization of the aesthetic trades most obviously on the positive – that is, on evoking "happy" feelings – managing the aesthetic dimension of organizations can also, of course, be underpinned by the desire to evoke feelings of fear or intimidation (think of the aesthetic disposition of bouncers and other security workers, or debt collectors) or solemnity and sadness (as in the case of funeral directors, for example).

As the likes of Norman[4] and Forty[5] have argued, from the design of commodities as simple as an orange squeezer to that of an office space, the aesthetic is at its most powerful when it evokes strong (and albeit in such instances, largely positive) emotional responses. Today, perhaps this is best illustrated by the argument put forward by Roberts[6] in his book *Lovemarks*. Writing from the perspective of an experienced and highly successful advertiser, he demonstrates how the most prominent brands of our age have been those that have consistently established a deeply emotional basis for the loyalty they enjoy, both from those who work for them and those who consume them.

While such an emotional attachment can be achieved through many media, it is clear that for Roberts one important such medium is that of the aesthetic. In many of his illustrations, visual image, sound, and smell all coalesce around aesthetic categories aimed at, to use Roberts' terminology, being a "game-breaker." Even the childhood novelty of scratch and sniff has been taken to a new level in an advertising campaign for a well known anti-dandruff shampoo when, to consolidate the brand's "lovemark," the advertisers produced a poster campaign that not only featured an image of a young woman with the wind in her hair, but also the opportunity for passers-by to press a button to activate a puff of citric-scented mist. Similarly, the value of combining highly aestheticized media with strong appeals to an emotional response is something that architects have long since realized. From the imposing civic and commercial edifices of the Victorians to the awe-inspiring tower blocks of high modernism, such structures have performed a notable function in eliciting emotional attachments or, even, in some instances, feelings of repulsion, disengagement, or fear.

As we commented above, however, there has also been a level of self-conscious recognition amongst organizational scholars of both the emotional and aesthetic that one frequently (though not invariably) leads to the other. Thus for Strati,[3] while emotions do not necessarily equate to what he terms "aesthetic sentiments," they do provide a common ground on which the lived, aesthetic experience of organizational life might be glimpsed. Perhaps more easy to grasp is the proposition put forward by Wasserman, Rafaeli, and Kluger[7] that, due to the embodied, sensual nature of aesthetic experience, it will frequently generate particular emotional responses that are amenable to empirical correlation. In what is one of the very few attempts to directly relate the emotional and the aesthetic components of an organizational environment, they correlate the interior designs of a series of bars and restaurants with the emotional response these evoke in their clients. While there is no doubt that their research could be criticized for its somewhat positivistic and descriptive flavor (despite their claim that it contributes to a "theoretical understating" of the aesthetic–emotive relationship), it does produce some insights that are revealing. In particular, they suggest that interior designs that reflect differing orientations to the relationship between the natural and the cultural (i.e. in terms of the material and colours used) elicited different reactions from people. These differing reactions worked by locating the aesthetic experiences of the designs in certain learned orientations towards particular values, such as those associated with civility and/or unregulated, impulsive action.

While such observations are in themselves perhaps of little immediate relevance here, what is significant is that from this analysis the authors go on to recognize the potential that an understanding of aesthetic and emotion management, as they relate to each other, presents a way of thinking about power and control in and through organizations. That is, they recognize the technological dimension of the aesthetic–emotive complex as it pertains to the possible shaping and propagation of organizational desirable practices and identities. In other words, they highlight the aesthetic as a mechanism or a medium of exerting some degree of power and control over the emotional aspects of organizational life. One field of research that has generated a number of interesting and provocative ideas relating to organizational power and control in this respect is the study of emotional and aesthetic forms of labor, and it is to this body of work that we now turn.

Emotion, Aesthetics, and Labor

When one considers the popularity of work that has focused on the organization, performance, and management of emotional and aesthetic forms of labor, one common element tends to unite it – namely, that it draws attention to the ways in which workers' bodies are increasingly required to function as material signifiers of a customer-orientated corporate culture. As Thrift[8:6] has observed in his recent account of "soft capitalism," characterized by what he describes as "a touchy-feely replay of Taylorism," contemporary forms of organization demand that workers' bodies are constantly attentive and attuned to the production and management of experience.

The evolution of this "touchy-feely" form of capitalism has, arguably, led to a shift in the nature and intensity of organizational intervention into the body. In doing so, it has formed the basis of what is often a "hands-on" management style. Here, management techniques have moved away from a focus on the substance of the body as the site of labor power, towards a more emotional and aesthetic concern with the sensory aspects of the body – that is, with the stylization and presentation of how the body looks and feels as a projection of corporate values and aspirations. With this in mind, Hancock and Tyler[9:117] have noted with reference to the work of flight attendants how:

> The organizational bodies of these employees were required to embody the desired esthetic of the company – to speak in the organizational "tone of voice" and to adopt a flexible, organizational "personality," of which their embodiment became a material artefact.

The expansion of soft capitalism has also increased the demand for workers to act as what have been termed "branded bodies,"[10,11] literally embodying the look and feel of their employer's corporate identity, or the quality of the product or service on offer. As Hurley-Hanson and Giannantonio[12:450] have recently noted, however, such a requirement can have particularly disturbing consequences when image norms that shape recruitment and selection practices exert a strong influence over recruiters' evaluations of applicants; so much so that image norms can lead to a process of stigmatization whereby "applicants who are denied entry into organizations on the basis of their appearance or image, experience a subtle, yet unacceptable form of employment discrimination."

Yet, as we have noted above, the nature of the relationship between the emotional and their aesthetic, and the way in which both relate to the performance of labor, particularly within the ever-expanding service economy, remains a relatively neglected aspect of the critical analysis of organizational life. For instance, while Hochschild[1] in her pioneering studies of emotional labor emphasized that an aesthetic component was clearly essential to its successful performance and management, the aesthetic remained a relatively underdeveloped aspect of her analysis; a problem characterizing most of the work that has subsequently built upon it. Equally, those studies that have sought to address this have largely done so by attempting to supplement the concept of emotional labor with that of aesthetic or sexualized forms of labor. However, the element of exclusion that characterizes emotional labor has been largely replicated in this body of literature, with many of the empirical studies of aesthetic labor, such as those by Hancock and Tyler[9] and Thompson, Warhurst, and Callaghan,[13] sidestepping the inter-relationship between the emotional and the aesthetic and therefore reproducing the same duality that is never fully conceptually or empirically developed.

A notable exception to this lack of conceptual and empirical development can perhaps be found in recent research on sex workers, which has emphasized the emo-tional labor that such workers have to undertake in servicing clients, as well as the emotion and aesthetic work they have to perform on themselves and their co-workers to develop and maintain some self-protection mechanisms.[14–17] Sanders[17:322] in particu-lar teases out the emotional, sexual, and aesthetic aspects of prostitution, as well as the amount of "body work" required (involving breast implants, working out, or minor facial surgery, for instance), when she argues that:

> Sex workers create a manufactured identity specifically for the workplace as a self-protection mechanism to manage the stresses of selling sex as well as crafting the work image as a business strategy to attract and maintain clientele.

Similarly, Sharma and Black[18] have described how beauty therapists perform both aesthetic and emotional labor to manage the precarious balance between the sexualiza-tion and professionalization of their services and occupational identities. They argue that, on the one hand, female beauty therapists must conform to hegemonic norms of femininity in the way in which they perform and present their own bodies, through the use of certain emotional and aesthetic cues such as hairstyling and makeup, for instance. Yet at the same time, they must use certain (often conflicting) artifacts to minimize the sexual connotations of their work, and to maintain a professional image that distances them from residual associations with prostitution. This latter aspect of their self-presentation often involves, for example, the use of a white color scheme (say, in their clothing and interior decor), and what is often quite a clinical aesthetic that connotes a close association with the medical and caring professions.

Highlighting similar issues relating to the performance of aesthetic labor, Entwistle and Wissinger's recent analysis[19] has argued that the concept suffers from a number of "problematic absences and limitations." These stem largely, they argue, from the tendency, particularly in accounts by Witz et al.,[20] to shift away from the emotional in favor of the aesthetic as a way of foregrounding embodiment. So, for instance, in Witz et al.'s research into aesthetic labor in wine bars and hotels, they maintain that the concept of emotional labor "is impeded by the way in which the corporeal aspects are retired," as it "foregrounds the worker as mindful, feelingful self."[21:35–6] In contrast, aesthetic labor, they argue, allows for a conceptual recuperation of the embodied character of service work.

However, as Entwistle and Wissinger have put it, Witz et al.'s account effectively reproduces the traditional Cartesian dualism (between mind and body) that they expressly want to overthrow, most obviously in equating emotion with the mind, and aesthetics with the body. Rather than thinking through the relationship between the aesthetic and the emotional, or even of sliding between the two, they merely reduce them to separate domains and, hence, leave the connections between aesthetic and emotional forms of labor unaddressed.

With this limitation in mind, Entwistle and Wissinger have attempted, through their study of labor in the fashion industry, to extend the conceptual and analytical range of aesthetic labor, both in terms of the settings and occupations it can be applied to (i.e. not just interactive service workers), as well as its capacity to move beyond what they describe as "superficial appearances at work and within organizations."[19:774] In essence, this extension rests on their contention that as freelance workers, fashion models are an example of an occupational group that have to adapt to fluctuating aesthetic trends and the expectations of different clients. In doing so, they have to become skilled in managing their own presentation and performance of self accordingly, "in the absence of a corporate esthetic." This imperative is heightened by the emphasis placed on social networking in the industry, and in freelance labor more generally, which requires workers to be "always on." As they note, the freelance laborer cannot walk away from his/her product, which is their entire embodied self.

Linking the self-management of aesthetic labor to the discourse of the enterprising self, they go on to argue that those fashion models who are most successful tend to be the ones who are most adept at managing themselves as aesthetic projects, and who are able to work on and with their bodies as tools of their trade. Hence, in their conceptual expansion of aesthetic labor, they also contend that its performance and (self) management involves not merely a concern with the surface of the body, but rather the entire embodied self – what phenomenologists call the lived body. Crucially for us, however, they suggest that the effort of "keeping up appearances" within a highly aestheticized labor market, while largely physical, also has a significant emotional component (involving the need to "stay positive" in the face of frequent rejection, for instance).

What is particularly useful about the way in which they develop an alternative to the Witz et al. mind–emotion/body–aesthetic dualism is the emphasis that Entwistle and Wissinger place on the emotional aspects of aesthetic labor, as well as the aesthetic effort or "body work" in everyday life that underpins it (see also Hancock and Tyler[9]), and particularly on the entwining of emotion and aesthetics in the embodied nature of this work. Referring for instance to models' feelings about constant rejection within a highly competitive and judgmental industry, Entwistle and Wissinger[19:785] note that "the emotions generated when one is judged by appearances, and rejected if one does not measure up, have to be managed."

It has to be said, however, that their account is primarily concerned with what they describe as the emotional fall-out of aesthetic labor, drawing attention particularly to the emotional consequences of the effort required to keep up appearances at work. It does not appear, therefore, to reflect on the broader political economy of the emotional and the aesthetic. As such, while they comment briefly on the qualities of fashion models that make some more successful than others (largely, they argue, an entrepreneurial ability to self-manage the body in accordance with the demands of clients, and to network effectively), Entwistle and Wissinger neglect the differential levels of value and hence the remuneration that is accorded to different types of aesthetic and emotional labor in various settings and sectors of the economy. In other words, while they expand the concept of aesthetic labor, they still cannot account for why some forms are accorded minimal value, while others are exalted to the highest levels of the economy (a point we return to below in our discussion of the aesthetic economy). Neither does their account, at a more philosophical level, address the role of aesthetic labor in the evocation of a desired emotional response in others (in clients, customers, or colleagues, for instance).

Not that such issues have been entirely neglected elsewhere, however, with a number of macrolevel accounts having emerged which have attempted, for instance, to link the demand for both aesthetic and emotional labor to the emergence of consumer-orientated, service economies. Hardt and Negri,[21:53] for example, have documented the rise of what they term "immaterial labor" – labor that involves "communication, cooperation, and the production and reproduction of affects." While multifaceted, a significant dimension of such labor, they argue, is the requirement for service workers – who, as with other immaterial laborers, are no longer primarily concerned with the production of material goods – to generate an aesthetic and emotional effect in others. This emotional aspect of immaterial labor, what they call "labor in the bodily mode,"[21:293] primarily involves the production of particular emotional responses through the self-management and regulation of the body. This can involve something as complex as the caring work involved in nursing, or as simple as smiling at a potential client at a reception desk. In their analysis, it is this type of immaterial labor that unites the instrumental imperatives and actions of the economy (that is, the pursuit of surplus value) with the more communicative, intersubjective aspects of social relations, another point we return to below in our discussion of the aesthetic economy.

In a similar vein, Bryman argues that central to what he terms "the Disneyization of society" is the spread of a service model of industry that relies, in large part, on the emergence of a model of "performative labor." Characterized by a labor process akin to a theatrical performance, performative labor witnesses, in Bryman's view, a combination of the aesthetic and emotional into a single mode of delivery directed at the generation of brand differentiation and espoused customer "care." This theatrical analogy notwithstanding, Bryman's[22:2] concept of performative labor effectively remains very close to Hochschild's earlier work on emotional labor as the commercialization of human feeling within the labor process. He claims, for instance, that performance labor involves "the deliberate display of a certain mood . . . as part of the labor involved in service work." Aesthetic labor, he maintains, occurs as part of performative labor, alongside its more emotional dimension, when the worker's appearance forms part of the process of managing and displaying mood.

As these authors recognize, therefore, the intensification in the demand for such patterns of labor, and increasingly sophisticated and intrusive ways of managing them, can perhaps be attributed most convincingly to the so-called "shift to service" in contemporary market societies. Over the past 25 years or so, there has been a significant decline in (but by no means eradication of) the importance of traditional manufacturing-based industries in favor of the expansion of more service-orientated sectors of the economy. Indeed, in most market societies, by far the majority of people who engage in paid labor work in some form of service or service-related sector.

One of the main consequences of this shift, which we attempt to think through in more depth below, is that it has contributed to the emergence of an increasingly educated and culturally literate populous, one that has greater access to cultural and economic resources, and to ever-more sophisticated information and communication technologies. This in turn has been accompanied by a "shop 'til you drop" culture that has become less willing to accept the Fordist standardization of consumer products, and more aware of, and seemingly enchanted by, the (albeit illusory) cult of consumer sovereignty. Similarly, the expansion and deregulation of global markets in financial and knowledge-based services, as well as in retail, leisure, and telecommunications, means that the drive to maintain competitive advantage largely through the delivery of quality customer service has increased employer demand for the performance of emotional and aesthetic forms of labor. All of this has contributed to the emergence of a form of economic relations that not only requires, but indeed depends on, the co-option of the emotional and aesthetic dimensions of everyday life; an idea we develop next.

Towards an Aesthetic Economy

As we have already suggested, while the organizational preoccupation with emotions and aesthetics is not entirely new, there is good reason to argue that this preoccupation has become both more sophisticated and more intense in recent years, particularly given the "shift to service" discussed above. Schultz, Hatch, and Larsen,[23] for instance, have referred to the present era as an age of the *expressive organization*, one in which the perceived need to ensure one's organization appears, sounds, or even smells good has become commonplace, while the likes of Carr and Hancock[24] have similarly pointed towards an expansion of aesthetic concerns among both organizational theorists and management practitioners, as well as across the social environment more generally.

In some respects, however, the proposition that we live in a world more widely impregnated by the emotional and aesthetic priorities of organizations is a difficult one to demonstrate. This is in part due to the fact that what sociologists have referred to as the "aestheticization of everyday life" has become so integral to our everyday experiences that we perhaps barely notice it anymore. We have grown so accustomed to the ever-present face of corporate beauty and professed care, and have come to expect the (albeit transient) feel-good factor that accompanies the delivery of so many of the goods and services that we insatiably consume, that we simply see this as the natural, normal, even inevitable way of things. Indeed, it is this possible aesthetic and emotional desensitization that particularly concerns sociologists and cultural theorists such as Welsch[25] and Meštrović.[26]

Both writers draw attention to the idea that, as a result of sensory overload, we have become emotionally numb; we have become immune to genuine pleasures, but also quietly accustomed to images or reports of extreme suffering. For Welsch, this aesthetic desensitization is largely a result of the overwhelming array of aesthetic stimuli that we face in the course of our everyday lives, the vast majority of which are underpinned by corporate efforts to seduce us into brand identification and the consumption of ever-more goods and services. For Meštrović, the rise of what he terms the "authenticity industry" – those sectors of the economy that focus primarily on the commodification of emotion and aesthetics in the provision of "authentic" consumer experiences – has led to a deluge of emotional imperatives. These compel us to display what he argues are ultimately, "indolent, mindless, and kitsch emotional reactions,"[26: xvi] so much so that we have grown so used to expressing or being on the receiving end of "fake" emotions that we no longer care to pursue the genuine article.

To our mind, an interesting way of making sense of the relationship between this aestheticization of society and the increasing demand for the performance of aesthetic and emotional forms of labor discussed above is Böhme's[27] concept of the *aesthetic economy*. Building on earlier accounts of the culture industry, Böhme has described what he terms an emergent aesthetic economy as a defining characteristic of contemporary capitalism and those exchange relations that characterize it.

Central to Böhme's account is the steady emergence, from the 1950s onwards, of a new value category, which he terms "staging value." This is generated when capitalism moves from exploiting people's needs (for example, for food, shelter, clothing, transport and so on) to commodifying their desires (for pleasure, excitement, comfort, etc.). His analysis re-evaluates successive theories on the relationship between aesthetics and the economy in light of these changes, and argues that this transition to a new phase of consumer capitalism means that the economies of contemporary market societies are no longer simply dominated by the production and distribution of material commodities. Rather, they are also driven by the aesthetic values embedded within the generation and temporary satisfaction of desires; for instance, for the novelty and sensuality associated with the latest design of mobile phone.

Such an analysis can, in part at least, provide a way of thinking about, if not the nature of the internal relationship between the aesthetic and the emotional, then why they might be seen as increasingly integral to contemporary organizational practices; that is, as objects of production and exchange designed and produced to circulate within such an economic environment. For Böhme, staging value refers to a commodity's or service's *ascribed value* – that which is greater than that to be derived simply from their use or exchange, but instead is derived by virtue of "their attractiveness, their aura, their atmosphere."[27:72] It is this form of value that now dominates the minds and exertions of contemporary economic and organizational management; for instance, through manipulating the smells circulating within a retail environment such as a supermarket.

This argument only has meaning, of course, in an environment within which economic scarcity has largely been eradicated and the primary drive to consume is no longer *need* or *use*, but rather, as Böhme suggests, *desire*. As Campbell[28] has noted, the latter provides an unlimited source of economic activity because of its relative inexhaustibility. Desire, by its very nature, can only be satisfied temporarily and, as Campbell proposes, its temporary satisfaction tends to intensify rather than subdue it. With the right marketing and "steering," then, desire can produce a self-perpetuating drive to consume and, for organizations, the need to compete not simply on the substance of their products or services, but rather on their style; not on what a product or service *is* but on *how* that product or service is delivered.

To summarize: to raise the exchange value of a commodity or service in an aesthetic economy they "are treated in a special way: they are given an appearance, they are estheticized and *staged* in the sphere of exchange."[27:72] These aesthetic qualities of the commodity then develop into an autonomous value because they play a role for the consumer, not just in the context of exchange, but also in their use beyond the immediate sphere of consumption – that is, "they serve to stage, costume, and intensify life."[27:2] The notion of an aesthetic economy constitutes, we would argue, therefore, a way of conceptualizing the relationship between the aesthetic and the emotional insofar as both have become organizational resources geared specifically towards the generation of staging value.

Through a combination of aesthetically refined presentation and affectively charged emotional responses, organizations in the aesthetic economy make increasingly intensive attempts to appeal directly to the immediacy of the senses, and hence the desires of consumers (and here we refer to consumers *of organizations*: that is, consumers of an organization's products and services as well as those who consume its corporate identity and culture, such as employees or shareholders, for instance).

The concept of the aesthetic economy also allows us, therefore, to direct our critical attention not only toward the ways in which staging value is generated and consumed, but also more directly toward the interface between the organization and the economy. It helps us understand the ways in which a range of activities are underpinned by a connected set of accumulation imperatives and are governed by the same economic logic. This logic points to an organizationally desired emotional identification between subject and object, one engineered primarily through the purposeful organization of the aesthetic dimension of everyday experience.

Structures of Feeling and Expressivism

So far, we have argued that the emotional and aesthetic dimensions of contemporary organizational life are neither distinct nor conflated, but are integral elements of an increasingly pervasive logic of economic accumulation that is peculiar to the emergence of an aesthetic economy – that is, one ultimately grounded in the manipulation of the desire for identification between the (working and consuming) subject and the objective realm of the organization and its products and services. In these terms, therefore, all elements, from the design and carefully managed aroma of, say, a cup of coffee, through the stylization and atmosphere of the coffee shop and presentation and emotional performance of the person serving it, to the emotional response and identification of the consumer (and of course, the employee), are interconnected and important aspects of the production, management, and consumption of staging value.

One might ask, of course, where does this leave us? How does this advance our understanding of the relationship between the emotional and the aesthetic within such a framework and, perhaps more importantly, what might this say about the conceptual relationship between emotions and aesthetics more generally? To address these questions, we need to return to the problematic issue of the relationship between emotional and aesthetic experience. And, while we cannot expect here to offer direct and universal solutions to the problems and questions this relationship raises, what we might be able to do is at least consider it in relation to the value imperative of capitalism.

While, as sociologists have noted, emotions are "moving and slippery" targets,[29:12] there are perhaps some things we can say about them. Not only are emotions inter-subjective, they are also culturally and historically variable. Elias[30] has claimed that emotions represent an important juncture between highly personal and more social aspects of our being. And we might add, between our deeply held values, beliefs, and feelings, the ways in which we make sense of these, and the myriad ways in which we express, experience, and communicate these feelings. Similar claims can also be made for aesthetic experiences, of course. Neither emotions nor aesthetic feelings are natural and immutable; they are responses that are, by and large, learned over many genera-tions and through differing cultures and other experiential frameworks.

A further possible way of developing this line of thought is to try to understand such expressive practices as both a means and an outcome of what Williams[31] has referred to as "structures of feeling." For Williams, structures of feeling are meanings and values that shape what is actively felt in any given social context. They are, broadly speaking, the cultural mechanisms through which we link formally held beliefs to more nuanced and complex forms of interaction between selected and interpreted beliefs, feelings, and actions. Structures of feeling effectively constitute a realm of social experi-ence within which the specifically emotional elements of consciousness and social relations are configured. They shape the ways in which we sense and experience social relations; they are pre-cognitive, pre-rational, and, essentially, both affective and aes-thetic insofar as they constitute mechanisms through which we make sense of our feelings in relation to how those feelings are expressed or experienced.

Referring back to Hochschild,[1] the "feeling rules" she describes might be under-stood as embedded within structures of feeling in this respect, insofar as they operate as social guidelines that shape our expectations of what it is reasonable to expect in any given context – for instance, in terms of the emotional demeanor we come to expect of someone working in a service capacity. To put it simply, feeling rules are the term Hochschild uses to describe the ideological aspects of emotion; they are the norms and values that shape the social governance of the relationship between what is felt, and how that feeling is experienced and expressed; a process she describes as emotion management. Feeling rules, then, are part of the broader "structures of feeling" that Williams describes, in the sense that they operate as mechanisms through which beliefs and actions are linked. Perhaps an obvious example of this is the prolif-eration of what we might describe in short-hand terms as the "have a nice day culture," a structure of feeling linking personal feelings to social displays of emotion and aes-thetics that shapes and influences what we expect to feel, and to be felt and expressed, within the context of contemporary customer-oriented service interactions.

To establish such structures of feeling in line with various commercial imperatives, organizations appear increasingly concerned, therefore, with utilizing techniques of seduction and with carefully managing the relationship we have with them – both as employees and as consumers. In particular, or so it seems to us, organizations seek to manage meaning aesthetically (for instance through product or office design) to foster identification through and with particular corporate aspirations and ambitions. That is, they look to engender a sense of emotional resonance between the objective attributes of the organization's material presence and the subjective emotional state of the individual.

To summarize, then, the aesthetic can be regarded as a technology of organizational power by which the emotions are brought into the service of value reproduction through the seduction and regulation of both the laboring and consuming subject. That is, power is exercised, in this instance, at a pre-intellectual level in an attempt to bypass our everyday sensemaking practices and establish a strong, emotional connection between the consumer/client, the employee, and the organization and its products and services. Put simply, we are referring here to a type of power that has a direct impact on the immediacy of the senses. Now, one way in which we might conceptualize this is through the lens of what is known within philosophical aesthetics as *expressivism*. The kind of expressivism we have in mind is the notion that a work of art, such as a painting, for instance, should communicate an artist's feelings.[32] Within the tradition of expressivism, the criteria by which a work of art should be judged are, therefore, based on its capacity to *express* an artist's own emotions in such a way that by communicating these emotions the audience can not only experience them, but also identify with them.

What we are suggesting here, therefore, is that organizational activities designed to create particular structures of feeling, and engender emotional identification, rely on a similar process of expressivism as those in art. Organizational "design," for instance, is at its most effective and persuasive when it successfully expresses what is experienced as a shared emotional condition, one that brings together the subject and the object of experience in a kind of conspiracy of feeling, one that is felt as somehow personal and unique.

This is not to imply that organizational artifacts, such as recruitment posters, mission statements, or even the landscaped bodies of their employees, can be thought of as works of art. Nevertheless, the techniques involved are comparable. What organizational expressivism involves is a technologically similar attempt to evoke desire and recognition. Yet it is driven, not by the desire for artistic elevation, but by a performance-orientated concern to align the emotionally configured hopes and aspirations of the consumer, client, or potential employee with the organization's economic and political ambitions. Clearly, such endeavors are never fully realized. However, when they are even partially successful – say, in one of the most obvious examples today, the brand identity associated with Apple Macintosh computers and music equipment – the result can be spectacular, engendering as it does an almost fanatical loyalty that transcends rational calculations of utility or even notions of elevated cultural status.

We might, then, think of the management of corporate aesthetics, and their inscription on the performance of, say, aesthetic labor, as an attempt to actively manage structures of feeling – that is, as an attempt to appeal to the immediacy of the senses in order to frame or structure a series of emotional responses and, most importantly, identifications, between subject and object (such as the consumer and the company). Such an approach reflects the idea that corporate image – the way that people perceive an organization – is shaped by "their *knowledge, beliefs and feelings* about a company"[12:453] (emphasis added).

Take, as an example, the kinds of graduate recruitment brochures and posters that many of the largest employers tend to produce, and to display and circulate at university careers fairs. What we can argue here is that these kinds of artifacts, as part of the network of relations underpinning the management, performance, and consumption of a particular organizational aesthetic, ground themselves in the established cultural associations of particular images or symbols with specific sets of cultural meanings and emotional associations. So, for instance, many of the large retail-sector or supermarket employers utilize color schemes, images, and even forms of composition culturally associated with relatively abstract notions of, say, nature, vitality, and freshness. In contrast, organizations associated with what has come to be known somewhat amusingly as "extreme work" – such as that to be found in the financial, legal, and consultancy sectors – feature a far more aggressive palette of images and associated components. These include, for example, an extensive use of bold and contrasting color schemes, stop-motion photography, and performance-orientated imagery such as high-speed aircraft or athletic bodies.

Image norms, as above, are often used to differentiate people into categories according to who does and who does not belong. They derive from the belief that people must present a certain type of appearance consistent with social and cultural expectations. In the case of organizations, such norms are shaped largely by occupational, organizational, or industrial standards or the imperatives of the aesthetic economy more generally. Implicit structures of feeling suggest that once a person is classified as part of the corporate "self," or is stigmatized as "other" – that is, as someone whose face doesn't fit – then other social characteristics come to be associated with this designation. As Hancock and Tyler[33] have noted, these image norms are not only *embedded* within organizational practices such as recruitment and selection, or *enacted* in the performance of emotional or aesthetic forms of labor, they are also *encoded* in the cultural landscape of contemporary organizations within the aesthetic economy.

Concluding Thoughts

Our discussion began from the premise that a sufficiently significant intensification of organizational forms of aestheticization in recent years means that we need to re-evaluate important aspects of the study of aesthetics and emotions within organizational life, refining our understanding of emotional and aesthetic forms of labor, and broadening our analytical focus to take in other significant aspects of the generation of what Böhme calls "staging value." As such, we drew on a number of sources to relate changes in the economy to the broad range of activities and networks involved in managing aesthetics, emotions, and desires within contemporary work organizations. In doing so, we attempted to outline the basic contours of what constitutes, in Böhme's terms at least, an aesthetic economy, as well as to dwell on a number of possible implications for how we might think about, and critically engage with, dominant conceptions of aesthetic activity within organizations, and the relationship between emotion and aesthetics in organization studies as a consequence of this.

For us, this suggested that such a rethinking of the ways in which we develop our critique of organizations in the aesthetic economy also offers up an opportunity to rethink the somewhat undertheorized nature of the relationship between the aesthetic and the emotional within organization studies.

Drawing on Williams' concept of "structures of feeling" and the aesthetic philosophy of expressivism, we argued that the current bifurcation within the field between emotional and aesthetic labor in particular, and organizational emotions and aesthetics more generally, is no longer analytically tenable for any meaningful critical analysis. Rather, we must recognize that the generation of staging value requires the production and management of a (contrived) expressive identification between those relations of desire encoded into the aesthetic structuring of organizational activity, and the emotional responses of those subject to them.

Indeed, what we suggested was that, in a perversion of the artistic aspirations of expressivism (which seeks to achieve some kind of aesthetic, intersubjective communion between the artist, the work of art, and its audience), what organizations are currently presenting us with is a reified form of communion. It is a false reconciliation between corporate identity and our sense of self, achieved through the reproduction of market relations of dependency, and the apparent omnipotence of a corporate aesthetic. In the era of the aesthetic economy, our structures of feeling, the social norms governing the ways in which we experience, make sense of, and express our emotions, are increasingly shaped by the look and feel of corporate capitalism – a scenario that is expressive of little more than the relentless pursuit of staging value.

References

1. Hochschild, A. R. (1983) *The Managed Heart*. Berkeley, CA: University of California Press.
2. Fineman, S. (ed.) (1993) *Emotion in Organizations*. London: Sage.
3. Strati, A. (1999) *Organization and Aesthetics*. London: Sage.
4. Norman, D. A. (2004) *Emotional Design: Why We Love or Hate Everyday Things*. New York: Basic Books.
5. Forty, A. (1986) *Objects of Desire: Design and Society Since 1750*. London: Thames and Hudson.
6. Roberts, K. (2004) *Lovemarks: The Future Beyond Brands*. New York: Powerhouse Books.
7. Wasserman, V., Rafaeli, A., and Kluger, A. N. (2000) Aesthetic symbols as emotional clues. In Fineman, S. (ed.) *Emotion in Organization*, 2nd edn. London: Sage.
8. Thrift, N. (2005) *Knowing Capitalism*. London: Sage.
9. Hancock, P. and Tyler, M. (2000) The look of love: Gender, work and the organization of aesthetics. In Hassard, J., Holliday, R., and Willmott, H. (eds) *Body and Organization*. London: Sage.
10. Pettinger, L. (2004) Brand culture and branded workers: Service work and aesthetic labour in fashion retail, *Consumption, Markets and Culture*, 7 (2), 165–84.
11. Harquail, C. (2006) Employees as animate artefacts: Wearing the brand. In Rafaeili, A. and Pratt, M. G. (eds) *Artefacts and Organizations*. Mahwah, NJ: Lawrence Erlbaum.
12. Hurley-Hanson, A. and Giannantonio, C. (2006) Recruiters' perceptions of appearance: The stigma of image norms, *Equal Opportunities International*, 25 (6), 450–63.
13. Thompson, P., Warhurst, C., and Callaghan, G. (2000) Human capital or capitalising on humanity? Knowledge, skills and competencies in interactive service work. In Prichard, C., et al. (eds) *Managing Knowledge: Critical Investigations of Work and Learning*. Basingstoke: Macmillan Business.
14. Brewis, J. and Linstead, S. (2000) *Sex, Work and Sex Work*. London: Routledge.

15. O'Neill, M. (2001) *Prostitution and Feminism.* London: Polity.
16. Sanders, T. (2004) Controllable laughter: Managing sex work through humour, *Sociology*, 38 (2), 273–91.
17. Sanders, T. (2006) "It's just acting": Sex workers' strategies for capitalizing on sexuality, *Gender, Work and Organization*, 12 (4), 319–42.
18. Sharma, U. and Black, P. (2002) Look good, feel better: Beauty therapy as emotional labour, *Sociology*, 35 (4), 919–31.
19. Entwistle, J. and Wissinger, E. (2006) Keeping up appearances: Aesthetic labour in the fashion modelling industries of London and New York, *The Sociological Review*, 54 (4), 774–94.
20. Witz, A., Warhurst, C., and Nickson, D. (2003) The labour of aesthetics and the aesthetics of organization, *Organization*, 10 (1), 33–54.
21. Hardt, M. and Negri, A. (2000) *Empire.* Cambridge, MA: Harvard University Press.
22. Bryman, A. (2004) *The Disneyization of Society.* London: Sage.
23. Schultz, M., Hatch, M. J., and Larsen, M. H. (eds) (2000) *The Expressive Organization.* Oxford: Oxford University Press.
24. Carr, A. and Hancock, P. (eds) *Art and Aesthetics at Work.* Basingstoke: Palgrave.
25. Welsch, W. (1997) *Undoing Aesthetics.* London: Sage.
26. Meštrović, S. (1997) *Postemotional Society.* London: Sage.
27. Böhme, G. (2003) Contribution to the critique of the aesthetic economy, *Thesis Eleven*, 73, 71–82.
28. Campbell, C. (1987) *The Romantic Ethic and the Spirit of Modern Consumerism.* Oxford: Blackwell.
29. Williams, S. (2001) *Emotion and Social Theory.* London: Sage.
30. Elias, N. (1991) On human beings and their emotions: A process sociological essay. In Featherstone, M., Hepworth, M., and Turner, B. S. (eds) *The Body: Social Process and Cultural Theory.* London: Sage.
31. Williams, R. (1977) *Marxism and Literature.* Oxford: Oxford University Press.
32. Wilkinson, R. (1992) Art, emotion and expression. In Hanfling, O. (ed.) *Philosophical Aesthetics: An Introduction.* Oxford: Blackwell/Open University Press.
33. Hancock, P. and Tyler, M. (2007) Un-doing gender and the aesthetics of organizational performance. *Gender, Work and Organization*, 14 (6).

Epilogue

Stephen Fineman

It is a truism that emotions and passions matter in life. Also, in many management circles, it is a cliché to assert that "emotions shouldn't cloud your judgment." These folk wisdoms symbolize a tension, at least in Westernized circles, about where best to "place" emotion: emotion is good and bad, vital but interfering. For students of emotion it is a revealing expression of the social construction of emotion. Emotion acquires its force, credibility, and value from how we talk about it, how we share it, and how we judge others by it. Whatever emotion *is* in its biological stirrings or traits, what is most consequential is how emotion as a discourse is managed and manipulated by social actors. In this respect, emotion and emotional practices are saturated with values, partialities, and interests – even among those who claim to be objective researchers and measurers of the field. Moreover, these values, partialities, and interests are themselves not free floating; they are products of the cultural emotionologies to which we are exposed.

Critical theory and its variants are vibrant vehicles with which to explore emotion's bigger picture. The contributors to this book have demonstrated how a wide range of organizational settings, from hospitals to sports centers, prisons to call centers, are politicized emotional arenas. In other words, what individuals feel and are able to express are not just of their own making. A critical perspective brings power out the shadows: the power of collegiality and peers; of hierarchically enforced emotion rules; of well-placed humor. Criticality exposes the occupational and professional status-orders that govern who can express what feeling, where, and when. It reveals the simmer of gender, class, ethnic, and racial divisions that emotionally advantage some people, while depressing or oppressing others. It shows how societal discourses on the sovereign consumer, service-with-a-smile, female emancipation, and being a good parent seep into the construction, meanings, and politics of emotion.

Identity has been spotlighted in several chapters. Together, these begin to fill a yawning gap in current identity theorizing – the absence of emotion. Their critical examination reveals emotion's centrality in two interrelated ways:

- First, as an intrinsic feature of identity work – people strive for coherence when their identity frames are shaken by organizational, national, or transnational changes.
- Second, in terms of the emotionologies and aesthetic preferences that are current or fashionable – being emotionally intelligent is one of these, and is revealed to be Janus faced. While it holds promise of fair opportunities for women in the upper echelons of organizations, it simultaneously conspires to exclude women from the kind of emotional intelligence that, supposedly, defines success at the top – a male emotionology.

One of the delights of a critical framing is that it de-individualizes emotion, making room for insights, perspectives, and methodologies from sociology, social history, social psychology, political economy, and social philosophy – now neatly brought together in organization studies (as well as this book). In short, it places emotion within the complex of social forces that mark the continuing evolution of institutions and organizations. It contextualizes and problematizes emotion and its managers/stakeholders, while not losing sight of felt experiences and passions. And finally, it is not shy about exposing, and seeking correction for, institutional structures that trap people in emotionally impoverishing conditions of work.

Index